IN PURSUIT OF VALIS:
SELECTIONS FROM THE EXEGESIS

Philip K. Dick
408 Edick Cen
301
Santa Ana
Calif 92701
(714) 836-636 7

3/20/74
4/22/80 12-2-80

THE DIALECTIC:
God against Satan, & God's Final Victory foretold & shown

philip K. Dick

AN EXEGESIS

Apologia pro Mia vita

IN PURSUIT OF VALIS
SELECTIONS FROM THE EXEGESIS
PHILIP K. DICK
EDITED BY LAWRENCE SUTIN

UM

UNDERWOOD-MILLER
NOVATO, CALIFORNIA
LANCASTER, PENNSYLVANIA
1991

In Pursuit of Valis: Selections from the Exegesis
Clothbound: ISBN 0-88733-091-6
Softcover: ISBN 0-88733-093-2

For information about the Philip K. Dick Society, write to:
PKDS, Box 611, Glen Ellen, CA 95442.

Book design by Underwood-Miller
Softcover type designed by Daniel Will–Harris
Printed in the United States of America
All Rights Reserved
FIRST EDITION
Library of Congress Catalog Number 89-20532

CONTENTS

ON THE EXEGESIS
OF PHILIP K. DICK

The Exegesis of Philip K. Dick has too long remained a *terra incognita*. As a practical matter, that is hardly surprising: The unpublished form of the Exegesis consists of over eight thousand pages without a unifying numbered sequence, most of which are handwritten in a scrawling script, and all of which were arbitrarily sorted into ninety-one manila folders following Dick's death in 1982. Thus, while the 1980s saw the posthumous first publication of numerous Dick mainstream novels of the 1950s, the Exegesis remained out of view as an archival nightmare. But one with a curiously legendary status.

For readers of Dick's work had already encountered mention of an "exegesis" in VALIS (1981)—a brilliant novel on the impossible quest for mystical truth in the pop-trash wonderland of modern-day America. In VALIS, we are told of a journal kept by fictional character Horselover Fat, the alter ego of fictional character Phil Dick. Horselover Fat has gone through an intense mystical experience a/k/a direct encounter with higher wisdom, one that has transformed his life and caused many to question his sanity.

Horselover Fat can barely make sense of it himself, and at times he is tormented by the thought that it was a delusion—or even an outright breakdown. Hence his pressing need to keep a journal, to make a record of his theories, his doubts, his joys, and his fears. As fictional character Phil Dick explains:

> The term "journal" is mine, not Fat's. His term was "exegesis," a theological term meaning a piece of writing that explains or interprets a portion of scripture. Fat believed that the information fired at him and progressively crammed into his head in successive waves had a holy origin and hence should be regarded as a form of scripture [. . . .]

VALIS is an indispensable introduction to the world of the Exegesis; readers of the present volume would benefit greatly—and most likely derive considerable pleasure—from a prior study of it. The first eight chapters of VALIS, which are largely autobiographical, portray the central events of February-March 1974— "2-3-74" in Dick's standard shorthand form—and the year that followed. These events cannot be easily summarized, consisting as they do of a tumultuous stream of visions, hypnagogic voices, dreams, and altered states of consciousness. Readers may consult chapter ten of my biography, DIVINE INVASIONS: A LIFE OF PHILIP K. DICK (1989), in which these events are placed in an orderly chronological sequence by way of letters, interviews, and quotations from VALIS and from the Exegesis.

On March 21, 1975, Dick wrote a vivid and concise account of the visions that had enthralled him one year earlier. Its fervent tone indicates just why Horselover Fat—and the real-life Philip K. Dick—felt that the term "exegesis" was justified as a title for his journal speculations:

I speak of The Restorer of What Was Lost

The Mender of What Was Broken

March 16, 1974: It appeared—in vivid fire, with shining colors and balanced patterns— and released me from every thrall, inner and outer.

March 18, 1974: It, from inside me, looked out and saw the world did not compute, that I— and it—had been lied to. It denied the reality, and power, and authenticity of the world, saying, "This cannot exist; it cannot exist."

March 20, 1974: It seized me entirely, lifting me from the limitations of the space-time matrix; it mastered me as, at the same instant, I knew that the world around me was cardboard, a fake. Through its power I saw suddenly the universe as it was; through its power of perception I saw what really existed, and through its power of no-thought decision, I acted to *free myself*. It took on in battle, as a champion of all human spirits in thrall, every evil, every Iron Imprisoning thing.

March 20 until late July, 1974: It received signals and knew how to give ceaseless battle, to defeat the tyranny which had entered by slow degrees our free world, our pure world; it fought and destroyed tirelessly each and every one of them, and saw them all clearly, with dislike; its love was for justice and truth beyond everything else.

August 1974 on: It waned, but only as the adversary in all its forms waned and perished. When it left me, it left me as a free person, a physically and mentally healed person who had seen reality suddenly, in a flash, at the moment of greatest peril and pain and despair; it had loaned me its power and it had set right what had by degrees become wrong over God knows how long. It came just prior to the vernal equinox or at it. The Jews call it Elijah; the Christians call it the Holy Spirit. The Greeks

called it Dionysus-Zagreus. It thought, in my
dreams, mostly in Greek, referring to Elijah in
the Greek form: Elias. Gradually its fierceness
turned to a gentle quality and it seemed like
Jesus, but it was still Zagreus, still the god of
springtime. Finally it became the god of mirth
and joy and music, perhaps a mere man,
Orpheus, and after that, a punning, funning
mortal, Erasmus. But underneath, whenever it
might be necessary again, Zeus himself, Ela or
Eloim, the Creator and Advocate, is there; he
never dies: he only slumbers and listens. The
lamb of Jesus is also the tyger which Blake
described; it, which came to me and to our
republic, contains both, is both. It—he—has no
name, neither god nor force, man nor entity;
He is everywhere and everything; He is outside
us and inside us. He is, above all, the friend of
the weak and the foe of the Lie. He is the Aton,
He is The Friend.   —PKD March 21, 1975

As both VALIS and the Exegesis indicate, Dick was very
much aware that these events would inspire skepticism,
and even scorn, in many persons. Whether or not one is
prepared to grant them the authentic status of a genuine
mystical vision, or prefers instead to diagnose them as the
byproducts of psychosis or other mental abnormality
(Dick himself took both positions in the Exegesis, though
the former view clearly predominated), this much is certain: they transformed Dick's life, spurred him to eight
years of devoted labor on the Exegesis, and became the
central subject matter of his final novels: VALIS (1981), THE
DIVINE INVASION (1981), and THE TRANSMIGRATION OF
TIMOTHY ARCHER (1982), termed collectively by Dick as
the "VALIS trilogy".

The very nature of this subject matter—which probes
so incessantly at the essence of reality and the prospects
for divine intervention in the world—is singularly offputt-
ing to a good number of modern day readers. After all,
"metaphysical" has become, in common parlance, synon-
ymous with "futile" and "imponderable". For such readers, who are likely to recoil instinctively from the more

abstract portions of the Exegesis, it may be salutary to recall that a skilled metaphysician (which Dick certainly was) can provide quite exact and useful delineations of experience. As Ezra Pound observed of the scholastics of the middle ages: "a medieval theologian took care not to define a dog in terms that would have applied just as well to a dog's tooth or its hide, or the noise it makes lapping water." Dick was passionately concerned with metaphysical issues; he handled the theories and terminologies of the great philosophical systems with the same loving care as a craftsman might give to his favorite tools. As a result, Dick's analyses frequently cast light on the dilemmas of absolute knowledge and ultimate being: the light cast is the presentation of multifold possibilities where once stood only "official" reality. It would be a pity if a reader were to conclude that Dick was "crazy" because he questioned so much and so frequently. After all, Dick never pretended that he had found The Truth (or not for very long, at any rate). Readers who refuse to worry over whether or not the Exegesis persuades them on any particular points may find that it illuminates any number of prospective paths for further exploration.

It is my hope that the selections included in this volume will establish that the Exegesis deserves recognition as a major work in the Dick canon. But it must also be conceded that the Exegesis is a sprawling, disconnected journal—part philosophical analysis, part personal diary, part work-in-progress notebook for the final novels—that was produced in the course of lengthy nighttime writing sessions over a period of eight years. There is no evidence that Dick ever intended it for publication either in his lifetime or on a posthumous basis. The very fact that the bulk of the entries were handwritten rather than typed indicates the "workshop" nature of the Exegesis, for Dick was a gifted high-speed typist who composed his novels and stories directly on the typewriter. The *Tractates Cryptica Scriptura* that forms the closing "Appendix" of VALIS, and is described therein as excerpts from the "exegesis" of Horselover Fat, was written by Dick especially for

VALIS. While the *Tractates* does recapitulate a number of prominent theories posed in the real-life Exegesis, it is a separate work—polished distillations intended to fit within the framework of the novel—and not a genuine selection of quotations from the Exegesis itself.

It is instructive to note certain key distinctions between the Exegesis and Dick's published fictional works. Dick himself stated that his fiction addressed two major questions—What is real? and, What is human? The former question is clearly the guiding enigma of the Exegesis. That is not to say that the latter question was not equally important to Dick, but rather that it did not puzzle him nearly so greatly. As Dick wrote of his story "Human Is" (1955), in his "Afterthoughts by the Author" to THE BEST OF PHILIP K. DICK (1977) story collection, "I have not really changed my view since I wrote this story, back in the fifties. It's not what you look like, or what planet you were born on. It's how kind you are." As to what was real, Dick changed his mind far more frequently, as the Exegesis amply testifies.

Further, the Exegesis shows little of the wild, dark humor that is a hallmark of Dick's novels and stories. In VALIS, the spiritual peregrinations and frustrations of Horselover Fat are presented in the artful pratfall tradition of the picaresque; but the Exegesis seeks not laughable ironies but rather ultimate truth. The selections in this volume confirm that Dick genuinely believed that, by sufficient pondering and analysis, the truth of 2-3-74, and of reality itself, might just be revealed to him. Despite the vivid experiential nature of 2-3-74, Dick kept faith in intellectual analysis—and not in further experience *a la* meditation or an attempted recreation of the factors that led to 2-3-74—as the key to truth. This analytical mode of writing seldom cracked a smile, although its sheer frankness and sense of wonder often makes for fascinating reading.

Happily, the Exegesis is well served by judicious selection and excerpting. The reader is enabled to follow of Dick's speculative flights on 2-3-74, the ongoing events of his life, and the nature and meaning of his own fictional works, while being spared the repetitions and digressions that naturally accompanied a journal labor of such duration. It should be reemphasized that Dick worked on the Exegesis primarily in the dead of the night. This was his preferred time for all of his writing activity, but in the case of the Exegesis he was not writing for editors and readers, and hence he drove himself to the end limits of all of his speculations without even a wayward Phildickian science-fiction plot to confine him. Certain of the Exegesis entries were written under the influence of marijuana, but for the most part Dick was "straight" during the 1974-82 period in which the Exegesis was written.

The basic principle that guided me in making the selections for this volume was to seek out the most intriguing and stimulating portions of the Exegesis. I did not seek to provide a representative sampling of all topics discussed therein, for the simple reason that certain topics—for example, the meaning of the March 20, 1974 "Xerox missive"—inspired, in my view, much heat but rather little light. Speculations on the "Xerox missive"—a xeroxed letter addressed to Dick that he felt might be a test of his political sympathies posed by U.S. or Soviet authorities—take up quite a number of pages in the Exegesis. The subject is discussed at some length in my biography of Dick, for the simple reason that it has biographical significance. But the aim of the present volume is to present writings of literary, philosophical, and spiritual significance. Nonetheless, it may be safely said that the principle theories and ideas of the Exegesis are well represented herein.

Another factor that entered into the selection process was the ongoing commitment by the publisher, Underwood-Miller, to produce a multi-volume set of Dick's collected letters. Dick included, within his Exegesis papers, copies of a number of his letters that discussed in some detail the events of 2-3-74 and after. As these letters will be published separately, they are not included in the present volume.

Let me conclude with some brief remarks on the

individual chapters. I recognize that the eight chapters constitute something of a rough and ready division of subject matter, and that a given excerpt might arguably fit in more than one chapter. What I regarded as the central topic of the excerpt governed my choice of chapter placement.

Chapter One is devoted to experiential accounts. Readers will note that, for Dick, the line between recollection of experience and analysis of its ultimate meaning is, most often, very thin.

Chapter Two contains theoretical explanations largely of a philosophical or theological nature. Readers may be interested to learn that the philosophical and theological aspects of Dick's writing—as evidenced particularly in VALIS—have already begun to earn serious attention in both scholarly and esoteric circles. See, for example, the discussion of VALIS and THE DIVINE INVASION in "Afterword: The Modern Relevance of Gnosticism," in THE NAG HAMMADI LIBRARY IN ENGLISH, ed. James M. Robinson (Harper & Row, San Francisco) (1988) (ironically, Dick quoted from the 1977 edition of this work in VALIS), and the entries for "Homoplasmate," "Plasmate," and "VALIS" in E. E. Rehmus, THE MAGICIAN'S DICTIONARY (Feral House, San Francisco) (1990).

Chapter Three will be of especial interest to readers of Dick's fiction, as it contains quite luminous accounts of his writing methods and preoccupations.

Chapter Four focuses on Dick's interpretations of his own fictional works. Note that the mainstream novels of the 1950s and early 1960s (with the exception of CONFESSIONS OF A CRAP ARTIST, written in 1959) receive virtually no attention in the Exegesis. As for his science-fiction works, Dick turned to them in the hopes of seeing some relation between their content and that of the events of 2-3-74 and after. It is striking that Dick was capable of reading his works—and being surprised by them—quite as if they had been written by someone else.

Chapter Five consists of plot notes and outlines for novelistic works-in-progress during the period 1974-81. It will be obvious to readers of the ultimate published works that the notes and outlines were highly provisional viewpoints on the plots and characters to come.

Chapter Six casts light on Dick's political and ecological concerns, as influenced by the events of 2-3-74 and after.

Chapter Seven consists of two self-examinations, one rather intensive, one rather brief. The former demonstrates (as does the novel VALIS) that Dick could be as critical of his own beliefs and preoccupations as the most skeptical reader. The latter is intended to underscore what should be evident from the whole of this volume: there is no fixed dogma or belief system set forth in the Exegesis.

Chapter Eight closes with three rather lovely parables.

Datings of the excerpts are by myself, based on internal textual evidence. All editorial emendations and interpolations of the text are bracketed and in italics. While obvious spelling errors have been corrected without indication, Dick's occasional stylistic inconsistencies as to capitalization and the like have been preserved.

May the reader enjoy these writings of Philip K. Dick— brought to light at long last!

Lawrence Sutin
June 1991

WRESTLING WITH ANGELS: THE MYSTICAL DILEMMA OF PHILIP K. DICK

In February 1974, Philip K. Dick, author of over forty published books of science fiction marked by the recurring themes of paranoia and shifting reality, had an encounter with God. Things hadn't been going well for Dick. He had been struggling with writer's block for the last few years, he was worried that the IRS was going to come down on him for withholding taxes in protest against the Vietnam War, and the hand-to-mouth existence of a pulp writer he'd been living for over 20 years was hanging heavily on his mind. To make matters worse, Dick had just had two impacted wisdom teeth pulled and was in intense pain. Consequently, cosmic revelations were the last thing on Dick's mind when the door bell rang at his modest apartment in Fullerton, California. His oral surgeon had phoned in a prescription for pain medication to a nearby pharmacy, and Dick was counting the minutes until the delivery person arrived.[1] When he opened his front door he found himself face to face with a young woman wearing a gleaming gold fish necklace.

As Dick recounted it:

> For some reason I was hypnotized by the gleaming golden fish; I forgot my pain, forgot the medication, forgot why the girl was there. I just kept staring at the fish sign.
>
> "What does that mean?" I asked her.
>
> The girl touched the glimmering golden fish with her hand and said, "This is a sign worn by the early Christians." She then gave me the package of medication.
>
> In that instant, as I stared at the gleaming fish sign and heard her words, I suddenly experienced what I later learned is called *anamnesis*—a Greek word meaning, literally, "loss of forgetfulness." I remembered who I was and where I was. In an instant, in the twinkling of an eye, it all came back to me. And not only could I remember it but I could see it. The girl was a secret Christian and so was I. We lived in fear of detection by the Romans. We had to communicate in cryptic signs. She had just told me all this, and it was true.[2]

This surprising revelation, fired directly at his head, temporarily blinded him. He experienced an "invasion of my mind by a transcendentally rational mind, as if I had been insane all my life and suddenly had become sane."[3]

Like St. Paul on the road to Damascus, Dick's experience radically reshaped the rest of his life. The last three novels he wrote before his untimely death in early 1982 (VALIS, THE DIVINE INVASION, and THE TRANSMIGRATION OF TIMOTHY ARCHER) were all attempts to process this confounding experience—and predictably they leave the reader with more questions than answers.

In March 1974, following the Golden Fish episode, Dick experienced numerous other phenomena, which he interpreted as contacts with a higher wisdom. These included hypnagogic visions, auditions, tutelary dreams,

and—perhaps best known—a beam of pink light that
imparted striking effects:

> It invaded my mind and assumed control
> of my motor centers and did my acting and
> thinking for me. I was a spectator to it. It set
> about healing me physically and my four-year
> old boy, who had an undiagnosed life-threaten-
> ing birth defect that no one had been aware of.
> This mind, whose identity was totally obscure
> to me, was equipped with tremendous techni-
> cal knowledge. It had memories dating back
> over two thousand years, it spoke Greek,
> Hebrew, Sanskrit, there wasn't anything that it
> didn't seem to know.
>   It immediately set about putting my affairs
> in order. It fired my agent and my publisher. It
> remargined my typewriter.... My wife was
> impressed by the fact that, because of the tre-
> mendous pressure this mind put on people in
> my business, I made quite a lot of money very
> rapidly. We began to get checks for thousands
> of dollars—money that was owed me, which
> the mind was conscious existed in New York
> but had never been coughed up...

(And perhaps most important of all,)

> ... it also said it would stay on as my tute-
> lary spirit.[4]

This mind, which Dick came to nickname VALIS (for
Vast Active Living Intelligence System), resided in Dick's
consciousness for approximately a year before shifting to
more sporadic contact. In March, 1974, less than a month
after the initial psychic invasion, Dick was listening to his
FM radio one night when hostile messages urging him to
die began to pour from the speaker.[5] Shortly thereafter he
was treated to an eight-hour all-night vision of thousands
of colored graphics resembling "the nonobjective paint-
ings of Kandinsky and Klee"—one image after another in
rapid succession.[6] On other nights, Dick's tutelary spirit—
who sometimes seemed to be a second-century Christian
named Thomas, and at other times an ancient Greek sibyl
or the Holy Spirit itself, as well as the more impersonal

VALIS—would utter short cryptic phrases to Dick as he lay in hypnogogic revery prior to falling asleep. Once he was asleep Dick would often have vivid symbolic dreams which he would later use, along with the cryptic phrases, in developing the philosophical and theological theories that began to preoccupy his time.

Readers of Dick's fiction first became aware of these preoccupations when his novel VALIS was published in 1981. This semi-fictional novel was built around these experiences and featured a 13-page appendix titled "Tractates Cryptica Scriptura," which contained polished versions of many of Dick's epiphanies, as well as a condensed version of Dick's VALIS-inspired cosmology, presented in a numbered, scriptural vein.[7]

Dick's main compendium of his theories, epiphanies, and cosmologies was a seemingly endless private journal that he referred to as his Exegesis. After the fish-sign experience, he spent the next seven years writing nightly in this journal, which grew to over two million hand- and typewritten words. In VALIS, Dick ironically said of the journal, "I suppose that all the secrets of the universe lay in it somewhere amid the rubble."[8] Since Dick's death in 1982, the Exegesis has been understandably the object of much curiosity among his fans. The present volume, culled from the over 8000 pages that make up the Exegesis, should go a long way towards satisfying that curiosity.

The Exegesis is in many ways a marvelous work, an extended expedition through the marshy wetlands of mystical theology and philosophy guided only by the overactive imagination of one of science fiction's most gifted authors. Yet, because it was not written with publication in mind, the Exegesis dives right into the thick of things with little or no explanation or context. The following is offered in the hope of providing that context.

DICK'S MYSTICISM

Perhaps the most baffling question facing both Dick

and his readers is that of the nature of his February/March 1974 experiences. Revelations from God, or tutelary spirits for that matter, are nothing new under the sun. The Old Testament abounds with them and the New Testament closes with the apocalyptic "Revelation of St. John," a richly symbolic vision of the end of the world. In Elizabethan times, John Dee, assisted by Edward Kelley, was certain he had conjured up and received messages from angels in a strange language called Enochian. In 1904, Aleister Crowley was contacted by an invisible entity named Aiwass, who dictated to him The Book of the Law, a dramatic announcement of the arrival of a new era—the Aeon of Horus. More recently, the advent of LSD has generated further claims of contact with Higher Intelligence, including Timothy Leary's "Starseed" messages about the cosmic significance of the fizzled Comet Kohoutek, and John Lilly's acid and Ketamine-induced contacts with aliens and his stolen glimpses of a nefarious "solid-state conspiracy" operating on a trans-galactic plane.[9]

While these cases of revelation are fascinating, they fall outside the focus of this introduction. Rather, I'd like to draw attention to another twentieth-century religious vision with remarkable parallels to Dick's, the little-known *Septem Sermones ad Mortuos (Seven Sermons to the Dead)*, written down in a three-day period in 1916 by the Swiss psychologist C. G. Jung. This pamphlet-length work of scripture-like prose forced itself upon Jung during an extended period of ennui and inner searching. In Jung's case there were no sci-fi trappings such as pink laser beams, but instead a weekend of restlessness and an ominous atmosphere in his home marked by his children having anxious dreams and sighting a ghost.

As Jung recounts it in MEMORIES, DREAMS AND REFLECTIONS:

> Around five o'clock in the afternoon on
> Sunday the front door bell began ringing frantically. It was a bright summer day; the two

> maids were in the kitchen, from which the
> open square outside the front door could be
> seen. Everyone immediately looked to see who
> was there, but there was no one in sight. I was
> sitting near the doorbell, and not only heard it
> but saw it moving. We all simply stared at one
> another. The atmosphere was thick, believe
> me! Then I knew that something had to hap-
> pen. The whole house was filled as if there
> were a crowd present, crammed full of spirits.
> They were packed deep right up to the door,
> and the air was so thick it was scarcely possible
> to breathe. As for myself, I was all a-quiver
> with the question: "For God's sake, what in the
> world is this?" Then they cried out in chorus,
> "We have come back from Jerusalem where we
> found not what we sought." That is the begin-
> ning of the *Septem Sermones* ...
>
> Then it began to flow out of me, and in the
> course of three evenings the thing was written.
> As soon as I took up the pen, the whole ghostly
> assemblage evaporated. The room quieted and
> the atmosphere cleared. The haunting was
> over.[10]

When privately published by Jung, the Seven Sermons were pseudonymously credited as "written by
Basilides in Alexandria, the City where the East toucheth
the West."[11] Basilides was a Christian Gnostic of the second century, and in crediting Basilides with the booklet's
authorship Jung was underscoring the gnostic nature of
the Seven Sermons. As the reader will soon discover, Dick
also looked to the early Gnostics for guidance and inspiration in explicating his mystical experiences.

"Gnosis" is a Greek word for "knowledge," and usually refers to a spiritual knowledge or intuitive inner
knowing, in contrast to the prevalent rational, intellectual knowledge. Prior to their denunciation as heretics,
and virtual elimination by the orthodox Christians in the
third and fourth centuries, the early Christian Gnostics
represented a vital pluralistic strain in the burgeoning
young religion. In the multiplicity of influences which
various Gnostics incorporated into their own systems

(including influences from the ancient mystery schools, Hermeticism, Persian religions, and the Far East), there lay valuable spiritual and psychological insights which have been largely lost to the West. However the discovery of the cache of ancient Coptic scrolls known as the Nag Hammadi Library, in Upper Egypt in 1945, has recently changed all that with a treasure trove of direct sources of Gnostic scriptures.

Gnosticism emphasized the preeminence of an individual *experience* of the divine over mere *belief* in dogmas about the divine passed down from theologians or church authorities. The struggle for this experience (or *gnosis*), which ultimately involves a kind of "letting go," is often characterized by Gnostics as a struggle to penetrate behind the world of appearances to a greater spiritual reality underneath. Dick believed that the pink beam granted him this "loss of forgetfulness" and he spent the following eight years trying to develop a coherent exposition of the new reality in which he lived. Jung's *Seven Sermons* similarly formed the emotional and philosophical anchor for all of Jung's subsequent psychological work. Dick and Jung both came to see in the Gnostic scriptures evidence of world views similar to those brought forth in their own respective trance-visions.

PSYCHOSIS AS SHAMANIC INITIATION

However, there is another less flattering interpretation of their experiences which deserves examination, which Phil Dick himself considered, and that is the glaring fact that—especially in Dick's case—the episodes bear more than a strong resemblance to the onset of acute schizophrenia. In his book on schizophrenia and religious experience, THE EXPLORATION OF THE INNER WORLD, psychologist Anton Boisen describes the case history of a patient, Albert W., whose psychosis was marked by phenomena strikingly similar to Dick's.

Albert W.'s disturbance began with the

idea that something strange was going on. He
felt himself in possession of a power that he
did not have before and he began to have a
'flood of mental pictures as though an album
within were unfolding itself.' Then came the
dark woman in a vision, whom he took to be
supernatural . . .

The second step which we observed in the
development of Albert's psychosis was an
acute sense of peril. He thought he was going
to die. Then he saw things in a new light and
he thought the 'dawn of creation' had come.
He was living in a different world. Then it
came to him that he had lived before this present life and that he was a much more important person than he had ever dreamed. In a
previous existence he had been Jonah. He had
also been Christ. Most of the time he had been
St. Augustine. It came to him that there was a
great 'I and You contest' going on, a struggle
for supremacy on the part of certain groups,
though in relation to this struggle it was not
clear where he stood.[12]

Like Albert W., Dick sensed that he was in the middle
of a titanic battle, in this case one that could be characterized as between the Lord of Light and the Master of the
Lie. Dick researched the historical precedents for this
dualistic world view in Zoroastrian and Gnostic cosmologies, hypothesizing at one point that possibly Ahura
Mazda was dictating his revelations to him.[13] Dick was
well aware of the ironic fact that in the final stages of his
syphilitic madness, Nietzsche similarly came to believe
that Zarathustra (Zoroaster) was speaking through him,
and Dick even joked: "I had planned to call my next book,
THUS SPOKE ZOROASTER, but I guess I had better not."[14]

In his discussion of Albert W., Boisen notes the parallels between his patient and George Fox, the visionary
founder of the Quakers, and ultimately concludes that
"there is no line of demarcation between valid religious
experiences and the abnormal conditions and phenomena which to the alienist are evidences of insanity." For
Boisen, what ultimately distinguishes madness from mys-

ticism is the direction the affected individual's life takes. For the insane, the experience leads to further disintegration; for the mystic, it leads to unification and healing.[15]

Julian Silverman of the National Institute of Mental Health makes a similar observation in his discussion of the parallels between shamans and acute schizophrenics. Personal crises of damaged self-image mark the onset of both the Shaman's initiation and the schizophrenic's psychosis.

> What follows then is the eruption into the field of attention of a flood of archaic imagery ...Ideas surge through with peculiar vividness as though from an outside source. The fact that they are entirely different from anything previously experienced lends support to the assumption that they have come from the realm of the supernatural. One feels oneself to be dwelling among the mysterious and the uncanny. Ideas of world catastrophe, of cosmic importance and of mission abound. Words, thoughts and *dreams* [author's emphasis] can easily be seen to reside in external objects.[16]

Significantly, the mental and emotional changes that the shaman undergoes in answering "the call" to his profession and surviving his journey into chaos are valued by his community; nearly identical changes experienced by those deemed mad in modern civilization are considered invalid and become sources of shame.

From this perspective, Jung—part mystic, part shaman—succeeded in integrating his unusual experience into his life's work. Dick attempted the same, and ultimately succeeded but at the cost of spending several years almost entirely focused on the task. This is not unusual. The famous German mystic, Jakob Boehme, experienced a mystical revelation in 1600 through seeing sunlight reflected in a pewter dish and reportedly spent the next ten years in a concerted effort to delineate his realizations.

During his post pink beam period (from 1974 until his death eight years later) Dick—ever the science fiction author—entertained any number of explanations for his transformation at the hands of VALIS. "This rational mind was not human. It was more like an artificial intelligence. On Thursdays and Saturdays I would think it was God, on Tuesdays and Wednesdays I would think it was extraterrestrial, sometimes I would think it was the Soviet Union Academy of Sciences trying out their psychotronic microwave telepathic transmitter."[17]

In his *Exegesis,* Dick methodically explored each explanation, finding flaws in his own logic, toying with and then abandoning pet theories only to revive them later on. However, over time certain assumptions came to the fore and tended to hang on for long stretches. One such hypothesis was the theory put forth in the "Tractates Cryptica Scriptura" in his novel VALIS:

> The universe is information and we are stationary in it, not three-dimensional and not in space and time. The information fed to us we hypostatize into the phenomenal world. ...
> Real time ceased in 70 C.E. with the fall of the temple at Jerusalem. It began again in 1974 C.E. The intervening period was a perfect spurious interpolation aping the creation of the Mind. ...[18]

The "Tractates" posit "The Immortal One" (i.e. Christ, Sophia, Buddha, et al.) returning now to dismantle "The Black Iron Prison" (the evil and spurious reign of the [Roman] Empire that has held history in its grip since 70 C.E.). The Immortal One is a *plasmate*, a form of energy, of living information.

> The plasmate can crossbond with a human, creating what I call a *homoplasmate*. This annexes the mortal human permanently to the plasmate. We know this as the "birth from above" or "birth from the Spirit." It was initiated by Christ, but the Empire destroyed all the homoplasmates before they could replicate. ... In dormant seed form, the plasmate slumbered in the buried library of codices at Chenoboskion (Nag Hammadi) until 1945 C.E.[19]

With the gnostic codices unearthed and read, the plas-mate is now seeking out new human hosts to crossbond with. This is what Dick speculated might have happened to him—he was one of an increasing number of hosts for the return of the Holy Spirit.

This explanation is so utterly fantastic that one can hardly take it seriously. If one reads further, one discovers that Dick associates the end of the "Empire" with Nixon's resignation from office, surely an instance of the banal being inflated into cosmic significance. And ultimately, of course, Dick wasn't fully convinced of even *this* scenario's validity. He presented it to the world couched in an ambig-uous science-fiction novel.

It is precisely this mix of grand metaphysical specula-tion and over the top SF wackiness that makes Dick's Exegesis so unique. Leave it to Dick, in the midst of straight-faced theorizing about God, Maya, and a fallen universe, to characterize existence as a triune "ham sand-wich," or to posit that his science fiction novels preceding the onset of psychic invasions were crafted by God, with Dick's unconscious cooperation, to be profound revela-tions of the true nature of existence!

Obviously, Dick's integration of the VALIS phenom-ena was a dynamic, ongoing process, marked by a sense of humor regarding his theories of the moment. Yet underneath his jokes and wild speculations, Dick remained firm in his conviction that *something* had hap-pened to him, something with a significance reaching beyond his own psyche. It was fortuitous for Dick that his career as a science fiction author placed him in one of the few niches in Western society where wild visions of alter-nate realities are accepted and honored.

DICK'S MYTHOS

Myths need not be *literally* true to be both meaningful and useful. The legend of the Holy Grail has a symbolic value quite apart from the historical question of whether there was ever an actual Grail. Similarly, in Dick's case, despite the palpable flakeyness of many of the specific details of his scenarios, the overall thrust of his mythologizing indicates an effort on the part of his embattled psyche to balance itself.

Dick's tutelary spirit identified herself at one point as St. Sophia, a "saint" who is not an actual person, but rather the feminine personification of divine Wisdom, the subject of the Old Testament's "Song of Songs" and the Apocrypha's "Book of Wisdom," and also the primary link between the Earth and the Unknown God in various Gnostic scriptures. As predominantly patriarchal mythoi, the Jewish and Christian religions have utilized mostly masculine symbols in their characterizations of the Absolute, although feminine components such as the Shekinah (the Presence of God), Sophia, and the Blessed Virgin Mary have survived, albeit in semi-autonomous and often underground form.

It can be argued that the monotheistic religions that have shaped Western civilization have been over-balanced towards the Logos (i.e. God as Word and this Word as the structural glue of existence). Dick as a writer—and an extremely prolific writer at that—shared this Logocentrism. Small surprise then that the eruptions in his inner world triggered by the pink beam should be clothed in the garments of Sophia or Aphrodite pointing him towards wholeness. Dick's own 1978 Exegesis account of the process is instructive:

> At the center of psychosis I encountered
> her: beautiful & kind &, most of all, wise, &
> through that wisdom, accompanying & leading
> me through the underworld, through the
> *bardo thödol* journey to rebirth—she, the embod-
> iment of intelligence: Pallas Athena herself.

Needless to say, Dick was not willing to let well enough alone and his subsequently endless theorizing about this psychospiritual abreaction threatened to bury "that which cannot be described" beneath a mountain of words. Thus the Exegesis simultaneously veils as it unveils, marching resolutely towards an ever receding horizon.

Next to Kafka, Dick is arguably this century's best novelist of alienation. Long before 1974 his books were filled with the notion—mirrored in Gnosticism—that there is a fundamental error present in Creation and that this earth is a godforsaken place. This gut-level sense of estrangement, exacerbated by heavy drug use and a series of personal upheavals, made Dick the quintessential countercultural novelist in the '60s, but it also produced a tremendous inner tension within Dick which cried out for resolution.

Dick's experience of Sophia/ Pallas Athena/ Thomas/ Elijah reaching down through the darkness to offer him saving glimpses of Light parallels the Gnostic myth of Sophia's descent into the world to gather the sparks of divine light within Creation back up to their rightful place in the Pleroma (Fullness). Or, to cite another myth, Dick, as Osiris, had been dismembered; his Anima (Soul), as Isis, was gathering together his limbs to make him whole once again.

A myth has been called "a lie that tells the truth," and this may be the best way to appreciate the significance of Dick's subjective experiences rather than quibble about their objective relation to so-called reality. Besides, as Dick would be the first to ask, what *is* reality?

Whether the events or epiphanies of Dick's final eight years were ultimately indicative of "genuine" mystical encounters or of "merely" psychological origins, I'll leave for each reader to ponder. Since Dick's death, theories have multiplied over what occurred, with critics noting parallels between the February/ March 1974 inner events and the characteristics of temporal lobe epilepsy, drug side effects, and even multiple personality disorder.

Ultimately, what matters isn't the cause of his shamanic journey so much as its effect. To his credit Dick was able to turn his experiences into compelling literature. Dick viewed his final three novels as a trilogy of sorts and VALIS, THE DIVINE INVASION (originally titled VALIS

REGAINED), and THE TRANSMIGRATION OF TIMOTHY ARCHER are proof that despite his fascinating maze-like wanderings in the Exegesis, Dick was able to rise above his musings and speak to his readers from the heart. The book that you hold in your hands is an invitation for a short excursion into Dick's maze. Be forewarned, however, that exit signs are few and the Sphinx at the middle of the maze may ask you to answer a very tough riddle before you can leave.

—Jay Kinney
May, 1991

Jay Kinney is publisher of GNOSIS Magazine, and a longtime reader of Philip K. Dick's work.

Notes:

1. An alternate chronology of these events has been expressed by PKD's wife, Tessa B. Dick, in an interview by J. B. Reynolds published in The Philip K. Dick Society Newsletter, #13, February, 1987, p. 6. According to Tessa Dick, Dick had oral surgery the day before the incident in question, was "full of codeine, for the pain" and was awaiting the delivery of medication for his high blood pressure.

2. From "How to Build a Universe that Doesn't Fall Apart Two Days Later", published as an introduction to I HOPE I SHALL ARRIVE SOON, Doubleday, 1985

3. From interview in DREAM MAKERS: THE UNCOMMON PEOPLE WHO WRITE SCIENCE FICTION, Charles Platt, Ed., Berkley, 1980, page 155.

4. Ibid, p. 155-156.

5. PKD letter to Ira Einhorn, February 1978.

6. PKD letter to Peter Fitting, June 1974.

7. VALIS, Philip K. Dick, Bantam, 1981.

8. VALIS, pg. 17.

9. STARSEED, Timothy Leary, Level Press, 1973; THE SCIENTIST, John C. Lilly, Bantam, 1981.

10. MEMORIES, DREAMS AND REFLECTIONS, C. G. Jung, Vintage, 1961, pp. 190-191.

11. Jung, op. cit., p. 190. The Seven Sermons are reprinted as an appendix in the book. For an insightful discussion of the Seven Sermons, Gnosticism, and depth psychology, see THE GNOSTIC JUNG, Stephan A. Hoeller, Quest Books, 1982.

12. THE EXPLORATION OF THE INNER WORLD, Anton Boisen, Harper, 1936, pp. 30-33.

13. PKD letter to Claudia Bush, July 16, 1974.

14. Ibid.

15. Boisen, op. cit., p. 119.

16. "Shamans and Acute Schizophrenia," Julian Silverman, American Anthropologist, Vol. 69 (1967): p. 28.

17. Platt, op. cit., p. 155.

18. VALIS, pp. 216-217.

19. VALIS, pp. 217-228.

A PKD CHRONOLOGY

1928 Dec. 16th. Philip K. Dick and Jane C. Dick born at home, Chicago, Illinois.

1929 Jan. 26th. Jane Dick dies of malnutrition.

1929 Dick family to Colorado, then northern California.

1933 Parents divorced. Phil stays with mother.

1935 January. Phil and Dorothy (mother) to Washington, D.C.

1938 June. Phil and Dorothy return to California, settle in Berkeley.

1941 Starts reading science fiction.

1942 First short story published, in *Berkeley Daily Gazette*. Writes first novel.

1944 Summer. Starts working for Herb Hollis at University Radio.

1946-47 Phil's last year at Berkeley High School. Claustrophobia/agoraphobia. Weekly psychotherapy. Studies at home, with tutor.

1947 Autumn. Enters, drops out of University of California, Berkeley.

1947 December. Moves out of mother's house.

1948 Marries Jeanette Marlin. Divorced after six months.

1949 (approx) Called for the draft; rejected because of high blood pressure.

1949 Working at Art Music, Berkeley. 1950. June 14th. Marries Kleo Apostolides.

1951 November. Sells first short story, "Roog," to Anthony Boucher at *The Magazine of Fantasy & Science Fiction.*

1952 May. Becomes client of the Scott Meredith Literary Agency. First story appears in print.

1952 Quits or is fired from Art Music.

Early 1950s Phil and Kleo approached by FBI to attend Univ. of Mexico and collect information on student activities; they decline. Phil forms friendship with one FBI agent, George Scruggs.

Early 1950s Phil taking Serpasil for tachycardia, Semoxydrine (an amphetamine) for agoraphobia.

1953 Phil's mother remarries.

1953 Thirty short stories published, including seven in one month.

1954 Sells first novel, SOLAR LOTTERY.

1955 First novel published, by Ace Books; sells two more, also to Ace.

1956-57 Writing mainstream only—no science fiction.

1958 Autumn. Phil & Kleo buy house in Point Reyes Station, Marin County; leave Berkeley. Phil meets Anne Rubenstein. Phil asks Kleo for divorce.

1959 April 1. Marries Anne Williams Rubenstein, in Mexico.

1960 February 25. Laura Archer Dick born. Phil's first child, Anne's fourth.

1963   July. Scott Meredith Agency returns Phil's mainstream novels (ten or more) as unsaleable.

1963   September. Phil wins Hugo Award for Best Science Fiction Novel of the Year (THE MAN IN THE HIGH CASTLE).

1963-64   Writes ten science fiction novels in less than two years.

1963   Phil and A start attending Episcopal Church. Phil baptized.

1964   March. Phil files for divorce, moves to Berkeley/Oakland.

1964   June. Dislocates shoulder and totals his VW in auto accident.

1966   July 6. Marries Nancy Hackett; moves to San Rafael.

1966 or early '67   Visits Bishop James Pike in Santa Barbara, participates in seance to contact Pike's dead son.

1967   March 15. Isolde Freya Dick born.

1968   Sells option on film rights to DO ANDROIDS DREAM OF ELECTRIC SHEEP.

1969   August. Hospitalized for pancreatitis.

1970   August. Nancy leaves Phil, takes Isa.

1971   November 17. Break-in and burglary at PKD's house.

1972   February. Leaves San Rafael, flies to Vancouver, B.C., to be guest of honor at SF convention; decides to stay in Canada.

1972   March. Suicide attempt; enters X-Kalay, heroin rehabilitation center, Vancouver.

1972   April. Leaves Canada, flies to Fullerton, southern California.

1972   July. Meets Leslie Busby (Tessa).

1973   January. Starts writing fiction again, after two-and-a half-year hiatus.

1973   April. Marries Tessa.

1973   July 25. Christopher Kenneth Dick born.

1974   February/March. Series of mystical experiences, as described in VALIS, RADIO FREE ALBEMUTH, the Exegesis, etc. Begins writing the Exegesis.

1974   April. Hospitalized for extremely high blood pressure.

1975   May. Phil's first non-SF novel is publisheD, CONFESSIONS OF A CRAP ARTIST.

1975   FLOW MY TEARS, THE POLICEMAN SAID WINS The John W. Campbell Jr. Award for Best SF Novel of 1974.

1975   October. *Rolling Stone* profile of PKD appears.

1976   February. Tessa leaves with Christopher; Phil attempts suicide.

1976   Moves to Santa Ana.

1977   July. Sells option on film rights to short story "We Can Remember It for You Wholesale," later (1990) filmed as *Total Recall*.

1977   September. Flies to France to be Guest of Honor at the Second International Festival of Science Fiction at Metz.

1978   August. Dorothy Hudner (Phil's mother) dies.

1981   May. Completes THE TRANSMIGRATION OF TIMOTHY ARCHER, his last novel.

1981   June 29. Sees first clip from *Blade Runner*, movie based on DO ANDROIDS DREAM OF ELECTRIC SHEEP, on television. (Movie is released in May 1982.)

1982   February 18. Suffers a paralyzing stroke and is hospitalized.

1982   March 2. Dies in Santa Ana.

IN PURSUIT OF VALIS:
SELECTIONS FROM THE EXEGESIS

Phil and Tessa Dick, 1973

CHAPTER ONE

DIRECT ACCOUNTS
OF PERSONAL EXPERIENCE

The best psychiatrist I ever saw, Dr. Harry Bryan,
attached to the Hoover Pavilion Hospital,[*] once told
me that I could not be diagnosed, due to the unusual
life I had led. Since I saw him I have led an even more
unusual life and therefore I suppose diagnosis is even
more difficult now. Something strange, however,
exists in my life and seems to have for a long time;
whether it comes from my odd lifestyle or causes the
lifestyle I don't know. But there it is.

For years I've felt I didn't know what I was doing;
I had to watch my activities and deduce, like an out-
sider, what I was up to. My novels, for example. They
are said by readers to depict the same world again
and again, a recognizable world. Where is that world?

---

[*] PKD was voluntarily admitted to Hoover Pavilion, in Palo Alto,
California, on 3 May 1971 and checked himself out on 6 May 1971 with
the approval of Dr. Bryan, the examining psychiatrist.

In my head? Is it what I see in my own life and inadvertently transfer into my novels and to the reader? At least I'm consistent, since it is all one novel. I have my own special world. I guess they are in my head, in which case they are a good clue to my identity and to what is happening inside me: they are brainprints. This brings me to my frightening premise. I seem to be living in my own novels more and more. I can't figure out why. Am I losing touch with reality? Or is reality actually sliding toward a Phil Dickian type of atmosphere? And if the latter, then for god's sake why? Am I responsible? How could I be responsible? Isn't that solipsism?

It's too much for me. Like an astro-physicist who by studying a Black Hole causes it to change, I seem to alter my environment by thinking about it. Maybe by writing about it and getting other people to read my writing I change reality by their reading it and expecting it to be like my books. Someone suggested that.

I feel I have been a lot of different people. Many people have sat at this typewriter, using my fingers. Writing my books.

My books are forgeries. Nobody wrote them. The goddam typewriter wrote them; it's a magic typewriter. Or like John Denver gets his songs: I get them from the air. Like his songs, they—my books—are already there. Whatever that means.

The most ominous element from my books which I am encountering in my actual life is this. In one of my novels, UBIK, certain anomalies occur which prove to the characters that their environment is not real. Those same anomalies are now happening to me. By my own logic in the novel I must conclude that my (own) perhaps even our collective environment is only a pseudo-environment. In my novel what broke through was the presence of a man

who had died.[*] He speaks to them through several
intermediary systems and hence must still be alive;
it is they, evidently, who are dead. What has been
happening to me for over three months is that a man
I knew who died[**] has been breaking through in
ways so similar to that of Runciter in UBIK that I am
beginning to conclude that I and everyone else is
either dead and he is alive, or—well, as in the novel I
can't figure it out. It makes no sense.

Even scarier is that this man, before his death,
believed that those who are dead can "come across" to
those who are alive. He was sure his own son who had
recently died was doing this with him. Now this man
is dead and it would seem he is "coming across" to
me. I guess there is a certain logic in this. Even more
logical is that I and my then wife Nancy participated
as a sort of disinterested team observing whether Jim
Jr. was actually coming through. It was our conclusion
that he was.[***]

On the other hand, I wrote UBIK before Jim Pike
died out there on the desert, but Jim Jr. had already
died, so I guess my novel could be said to be based on
Jim Jr. coming through to his father. So my novel UBIK
was based on life and now my life is based on it but
only because it, the novel, goes back to life. I really did

[*]   The character Glen Runciter in UBIK.
[**]   Bishop James A. Pike, who died in the Judean desert in September
1969, while in quest of the truth as to the historical Jesus. PKD and Pike
had formed a friendship in the mid-1960s. Pike was the inspiration for the
title character in PKD's final novel, THE TRANSMIGRATION OF TIMOTHY
ARCHER (1982)
[***] Bishop Pike's son, Jim Jr., committed suicide in February 1966. In
Pike's book THE OTHER SIDE (1968), Pike asserted that he had made
postmortem contact with his son through séances and other psychic
means. PKD and his fourth wife Nancy Hackett, who participated in some
of these séances, were thanked by Pike for their assistance in his
"Foreword" to the book.

not make it up. I just observed it and put it into a fictional framework. After I wrote it I forgot where I got the idea. Now it has come back to, ahem, haunt me, if you'll pardon me for putting it that way.

The implication in UBIK that they were all dead is because their world devolved in strange ways, projections onto their environment of their dwindling psyches. This does not carry across to my own life, nor did it to Jim's when his son "came across." There is no reason for me to project the inference then of the novel to my own world. Jim Pike is alive and well on the Other Side, but that doesn't mean we are all dead or that our world is unreal. However, he does seem to be alive and as mentally enthusiastic and busy as ever. I should know; it's all going on inside me, and comes streaming out of me each morning as I—he—or maybe us both—as I get up and begin my day. I read all the books that he would be reading if he were here and not me. This is only one example. It'll have to do for now.

They write books about this sort of thing. Fiction books, like THE EXORCIST.* Which are later revealed to be "based on an actual incident." Maybe I should write a book about it and later on reveal that it was "based on an actual incident." I guess that's what you do. It's convenient, then, that I'm a novelist. I've got it made.

There have been more changes in me and more changes in my life due to that than in all the years before. I refer to the period starting in mid-March (it's now mid-July) [1974] when the process began. Now I am not the same person. People say I look different. I have lost weight. Also, I have made a lot more money doing

---

* THE EXORCIST (1971), novel by William Peter Blatty.

the things Jim tells me to do, more money than ever before in a short period, doing things I've never done, nor would imagine doing. More strange yet, I now drink beer every day and never any wine. I used to drink wine, never beer. I chugalug the beer. The reason I drink it is that Jim knows that wine is bad for me—the acidity, the sediment. He had me trim my beard, too. For that I had to go up and buy special barber's scissors. I didn't know there even was such a thing.

Mostly, though, what I get is a lot of information, floods of it night after night, on and on, about the religions of the Antique World—from Egypt, India, Persia, Greece and Rome. Jim never loses interest in that stuff, especially the Zoroastrian religion and the Pythagorean mystery cult and the Orphic cults and the Gnostics—on and on. I'm even being given special terms in Greek, such as *syntonic.* I'm told to be that. In harmony with, it means. And the *Logos* doctrine. All this comes to me in dreams, many dreams, hundreds of dreams, on and on, forever. As soon as I close my eyes information in the form of printed matter, visual matter such as photographs, audio stuff in the form of phonograph records—it all floods over me at a high rate of print-out.

These dreams have pretty well come to determine what I do the next day; they program me or prepare me. Last night I dreamed that I was telling people that J.S. Bach was laughing at me. I imitated J.S. Bach's laugh for them. They were not amused. Today I find myself putting on a Bach record, rather than Rock. It's been months, even years since I automatically reached for Bach. Also last night I dreamed that I took the microphone away from Ed McMahon, the announcer on Johnny Carson's show, because he was drunk. Tonight when Ed McMahon came on I automatically got to my feet and switched the TV off, my desire to watch it gone. This fitted in fine because my Bach record was playing anyhow.

I should mention that I have become completely sophisticated now, having withdrawn all my projections from the world. I am mature and am no longer lachrymose nor sentimental. My spelling is as lousy as ever.

There is no known psychological process which could account for such fundamental changes in my character, in my habits, view of the world (I perceive it totally differently, now), my daily tastes, even the way I margin my typed pages. I have been transformed, but not in any way I ever heard of. At first I thought it to be a typical religious conversion, mostly because I thought about God all the time, wore a consecrated cross and read the Bible. But that evidently is due to Jim's lifestyle. I also drive differently, much faster, reaching for an airvent on the dashboard that is not there. Evidently I'm used to another car entirely. And when I gave my phone number the last two times I gave it wrong—another number. And to me the weirdest thing of all: at night phone numbers swim up into my mind that I never heard of before. I'm afraid to call them; I don't know why. Perhaps in some other part of Orange County someone else is giving my phone number as his, drinking wine for the first time in his life and listening to Rock; I don't know. I can't figure it out. If so, I have his money. A lot of it. But I got it from my agent, or rather ex-agent, since after 23 years I fired him.* To explain the totally different tone and attitude of my letters I told my

---

* In May 1974, PKD briefly dismissed the Scott Meredith Literary Agency due primarily to his dissatisfaction with the royalty statements supplied him by publishers. The rift was formally patched within a month, and the Meredith Agency continued to represent PKD.

agent I had my father-in-law, a CPA, working with me. At the time this was to my mind a lie, but looking back I can see a thread of truth in it. Someone was and is working with me on all business matters, making my attitude tough and shrewd and suspicious. I am hard-boiled and I never regret my decisive actions. I can say No whenever I want to. Jim was that way—no sentimentality. He was the shrewdest Bishop I ever knew.

Perhaps he is collaborating in the writing of this right now.

[. . . .]

Maybe I, Phil Dick, have just abreacted to a past personality, formed up to the mid-fifties. Lost skills and heartaches that came after that.

Well then we have here a sort of time travel, rather than someone who is dead "coming across" from the Other Side. It is still me, with my old, prior tastes and skills and habits. Mercifully, the sad recent years are gone. Another form of my odd and chronic psychological ailment: amnesia, which my head learned after my dreadful auto accident in 1964.[*]

Come to think of it, it is the memories laid down since 1964 which have dimmed. I recall saying to Tessa that it seemed to me that precisely ten years of memory was gone. That would take it right back to that day in—my god, almost ten years to the day— when I rolled my VW in Oakland on a warm Spring Saturday. Perhaps what happened that day was that from the physical and mental shock an alternative personality was struck off; I did have extraordinary amnesia during the months afterward. So that might make an excellent hypothesis: the trauma of that auto acci-

---

[*]   See next paragraph. As a result of this accident, PKD suffered a broken arm and wore a body cast for two months.

dent started a secondary personality into being, and it remained until mid-March of this year, at which time for reasons unknown it faded out and my original "real" personality returned. That makes sense. More so than any other theory. Also, it was in 1964 that I first encountered Jim Pike[. . .] No wonder I have Jim interwoven with this restored personality; he was on my mind at the time it was abolished. I've just picked up where I left off in 1964.

I've explained everything but the preference for beer over wine. I never drank beer. And the business shrewdness; I never was shrewd. And the general health kick, the religious kick, the lack of sentimentality, the resolution, the ability to discern a lie, the intention and determination never to lie, the vastly higher level of effectiveness in all fields, the trimming my beard so expertly—everything is explained but those; also I still have to explain the constant written material which I see in dreams every night, including Greek and Latin and Sanskrit and god knows what else words I never knew but have to look up. This abreaction to before the auto accident explains some things, but it doesn't explain others. Could it be that I now am what I would have been had the accident not occurred? As if I've shifted over to a sort of alternate world where I grew naturally and normally to this mature and responsible character-formation, not derailed tragically by first the accident, then the involvement with Nancy et al, which of necessity followed? This, then, would be a sort of personal alternate universe. *Ananke* . . . another Greek word flashed up to me in sleep; the compulsion which determines the outcome of even the gods' lives. There is an ananke for me which decreed that I would become what I am now, and that weird, unfortunate sidetracking cannot abolish it as my destiny.

In which case I am more truly myself now than at any other time since the accident. Which may well be. I am myself—in this, the best of all possible worlds. It's heredity, so to speak, over environment. The stars and my innate character triumphed.

Which explains why I still can't spell. It is not in my nature.

Whatever all this is, I brought it on. I had been doing months of research on recent discoveries about brain function, especially the exciting news that we have two hemispheres and use only one, the left one. They say that's where procedural thoughts such as doing math and thinking inductive and deductive logical processes take place; the other hemisphere, which people in Asia use instead, does simultaneous work, such as gestalting of a picture, intuitive and even ESP functioning. What it comprehends it comprehends in a single pattern and then passes on to the next, without there being a sequential or causal relationship between the apprehended and evaluated matrices, which I guess fly by like the frame freeze pictures on TV in the Heinz 57 Variety ad. I had read that massive doses of certain water soluble vitamins improve neural firing in schizophrenics: better synchronization and so forth. It occurred to me that maybe in a normal purpose [sic; person?] with normal, which is to say average, synchronization, it might cause firing to take place so efficiently that both hemispheres of the brain might come on together. So I found a recipe in a Psychology Today article* and I did it. I took what they prescribe schizophrenics.

In terms of my own personal life what happened made history, and I'm sure—off and on, anyhow—that

---

* The likely reference here is to Harvey Ross, "Orthomolecular Psychiatry: Vitamin Pills for Schizophrenics," Psychology Today April 1974.

whatever happened then and from then on has to do with my getting what I set out to get: such improved neural firing that both hemispheres came on together, for the first time in my life. It is the contents that puzzle me, not what happened in the biochemical or physiological or even psychological sense. Even allowing for the obvious fact that since my personality must have formed in the left hemisphere alone then whatever happens in the right would be subjectively experienced as the Not-I, our [sic; or?] lying outside of my self system and therefore not me and not my thoughts, I still can't for instance understand why when I begin to fall asleep my thoughts switch from English to Greek, a language I don't know.

All my thoughts and experiences, focussing mainly in dreams, seem to constellate around the Hellenistic Period, with accretions one would expect from previous cultures. The best way to describe it is to say at night my mind is full of the thoughts, ideas, words and concepts that you'd expect to find in a highly educated Greek-speaking scholar of the 3rd Century A.D., at the latest, living somewhere in the Mediterranean Area of the Roman Empire. His day time thoughts, I mean. Not what he'd dream while asleep.

Perhaps this is another BRIDEY MURPHY.[*] I've brought back to being active a personality "from a former life." Undoubtedly, from internal evidence it appears to be the past, the archaic past, breaking through. But it's not chaotic. It's highly systemized, sort of like the *left* hemisphere of the Greek-speaking

---

[*]   Reference to Morey Bernstein, THE CASE OF BRIDEY MURPHY (1956), in which a contemporary woman was apparently able, while under hypnosis, to recall a previous life under the name Bridey Murphy in nineteenth century Ireland.

Roman citizen. It seemed to me that the preoccupations of this individual were indeed those of Jim Pike, and thus if you allow all prior steps in this chain of inferential thought to stand, you arrive logically at the final step that Jim Pike broke through to me "from the other side." But, if you apply Ockham's Razor, the Principle of Parsimony (the smallest theory to cover the facts) you can deal Jim out and run with the ancient material alone. Except that obviously it's organized as if by a living, idiosyncratic personality, which I often sense behind it. This personality, glimpsed by me as being a woman, holds up the book to me or mails it to me, etc. She likes me. She wants to guide, educate and help me. Evidently she's exposing me to all this enlightening and ennobling written material deliberately, to make me into a higher life form, or anyhow a better person. Up until now my higher education has been sadly neglected; she is making up for that, using very effective show-and-tell audio-video teaching techniques. I have the feeling that for every word or photo I consciously catch and remember there are thousands of yards of it poured onto me that I do not consciously remember. They take hold anyhow, as witness my busy intellectual research—homework, if you wish—the next day.

After one dream, in which I saw a sibyl who was a cyclops, I decided after doing research that it was the Cumaean sibyl who had seized hold of me, and not anyone from present times or the "other side." I got a lot of mileage out of that theory, but then I get a lot out of each theory I hold.

[. . . .]

My conscious memory—my conscious vocabulary—is only the tip of the iceberg. And yet it seems highly strictured [*sic; structured?*]; obsessed, in fact, by the theological disputations and dogmas and highly abstract and abstruse concepts and theories of Rome. As Robert Graves once said, "Theological dispute was the disease of that age," meaning that every one in the streets was obsessed by it and had to talk about it end-lessly—as my unconscious does. My unconscious is fix-ated in the Roman period, and that strikes me as strange. How did it get there in the first place? And being there, why does it remain?

Once I myself was conscious[ly], deliberately inter-ested in that period; I was in my early twenties, and read about it a lot, at the expense of being a rounded person. But my unconscious for all its obsessions with the theoretical material of that period is hard-headed and shrewd, and wants everything it comes up with applied in the most practical way. If it shows me the Golden Rectangle* it does so in order to calm me with that ultimate esthetically balanced sight; it has a firm therapeutic purpose. There is a utilization of all its abstract material for genuine purposes, for me, by and large. It is a tutor to me as Aristotle was to Alexan-der, which makes me wonder why it is grooming and shaping me this way, tutoring me in the exact fashion employed by the Greeks. Philosophy for real ends, for final causes, as Aristotle would have put it: for some-thing lying ahead and not as an idle pastime, an end in itself. The ennobling and elevating education is altering me and I would presume that when it is fin-ished I, having become changed (to resort to the Abla-tive Absolute), will act upon the improved character which I've acquired—not on the knowledge direct, as if on enlarged memory banks, but upon the basis of my matured and elevated character. I know this

---

*   The Golden Rectangle, which formed a part of the hypnagogic visions experienced by PKD during this period, embodies the Pythagorean ideal of harmonious proportion that points to ultimate unity.

whole process sees ahead because I have caught sight of its clear perception down the web of time, seen with it for a while; it knows what is ahead and acts accordingly. I'm sure it has a final purpose in mind, for which this is careful preparation. This recalls to me my notion that the Cumaean sibyl is behind it all; certainly she had or has a clear view of the future, of time; that is what a sibyl is.

Following basic Greek thought it is improving my mind and body together, as a unity. Health is equated—correctly so—with vigor and the capacity to act. All its concepts, its viewpoint, are Greek. Symmetry, balance, harmony. I sense Apollo in this, which is consistent, since the Cumaean sibyl was his oracle. Moderation, reasonability and balance are Apollo's virtues, the clear-headed, the rational. *Syntosis*, or whatever. Pythagorian harmoniousness. A reconciling of all impulses and tendencies within, then turning to the outer world once that is achieved and becoming syntonic with it as well. I'm getting a classical education. Greek, a little Latin, knowledge of Sanskrit, theology and philosophy and the Ionian Greeks various views of the cosmos. Very unusual to get this here in Southern California. All very sane and steady. The most worthy, the highest virtues and values in the history of our civilization.

How did they happen to arise within me? For instance, it pointed out that my *ananke*—the compulsion or fate lying ahead of me—is a darkening, a gathering gloom, which is a good description of my underlying melancholia. Against which I pit my learned *syntonos*. Cultivation against innate predispositions: a basis struggle in life, and well elucidated by my unconscious. How did it know these two terms and [*how*] was [*it*] able to define them for me? I didn't know. I *never* knew. This is material emanating from a wise viewpoint which I never possessed. This was not me, although it is becoming me; or rather, to be more accurate, it is shaping me so that I am becoming it. Meeting its standards, its ideals. Which are Apollonian Greece's, from over 2 thousand years ago: from its Golden Age. Our Golden Age.

Now, this really does not rule out Jim Pike as my Athenian or Hellenistic tutor. Jim had, I'm certain, that kind of classical education. Greek, Latin, Roman theology and so forth. The disputations of St. Paul, St. John, the Logos Doctrine, what Augustine knew. Also, Jim was—is—shrewd; he'd apply, did apply in his life, all this classical education. He is the only person I ever knew, in fact, with such a background. If Jim were to become my tutor this I really think, all this that I'm being taught, that my attention is being drawn to, would be precisely what he would get me involved with. The reading list I'm getting is the one he would give. This is Jim's *mind* I'm getting, not so much his personality. Its directed—expertly directed—contents. It has me drink beer instead of wine because beer is more healthy for me and I should drink a little something to relax me; there's an example. That's *directed* tutoring. This is not an inert computer, whose keyboard I myself punch according to my own whim and volition.

The one odd dream that I had, in which I picked up the most distant, the smallest, weakest signal—from a star, star-information, sidereal ... what I heard seemed to resemble, as an analog, an AI System, not a computer, and female in tone. Reasonable and female. This was a small system, though; it knew almost nothing, not even where it was (the "Portuguese States of America," it decided, when I suggested it look around for something written to read from, like the address on an envelope). This was a subsys-

tem and not my tutor, but its response told me that
nowhere in our world would I find the sending entity
which had begun impinging on me in the form of
highly abstract and highly balanced (liked the Golden
Rectangle) graphics back in March. Not so much what
it told me in a positive sense—where it was—but by ruling out where it is not: that helped. It isn't here,
which means here in time, space, dimension, any of
the coordinates.

The past, then. Or the future. Another star. An
alternate world. "The other side." They're all "the
other side" in some way. For instance, it made me
aware of God from the very start, but never of Christ;
I deduce from this that it is non-Christian and probably pre-Christian. Actually I can't catch in it any influences since the Greek Logos Doctrine. Which could
be Iranian. India to Iran to Greece and then possibly
(but not necessarily) to Rome. One night I had a
short bitter dream in which I cried out in despair,
"*Ich hab' kein' Retter*," I have no Savior. Then in fear
at having said that I added "*Ja, ja, es gibt ein Retter*,"
[*Yes, yes, a Savior is given*] but it was too late; the
whole Ground of Being, everything around me, dwin-
dled away and was gone; I floundered in the void,
suffering. I think this was an awareness that for all
its value, this new worldview being dominant in me
and taking over from the old one would deprive me,
perhaps forever, of Jesus Christ. I guess this is true.
It's a dreadful loss, but I can't stop it; what can the
pupil do in the hands of such a tutor? Unfortunately,
though, a tutor who—well, lived before Christ and
hence could not have known of Him? But Jim knew
of Christ. Perhaps then I have worked the logical
steps, deducing and deducing, to prove that my tutor
existed before the time of Christ, or if a bit later did
not know of, or if knowing did not accept. Time and

knowledge have been rolled back, for better or worse. Mostly it is better ... except in this one conspicuous regard. I miss my Savior.

So my "unconscious," which I've claimed this tutor to be, has available to it "my entire memory," except everything pertaining to events and concepts that arose after 100 A.D. That is an extraordinarily great restriction. Obviously, that is not in any sense that we know the term "my unconscious," laid down in my lifetime; it knows words, concepts, that I never knew—and doesn't know the commonplace elements of the last 2,000 years. Its location is far back in time. And another climate; I keep sensing—and craving—a moist, cool, high-altitude environment, where I can watch the stars.

I remember that when this first hit me, in the first couple of weeks, I was absolutely convinced that I was living in Rome, some time after Christ appeared but before Christianity became legal. Back in the furtive Fish Sign days. Secret baptism and that stuff. I was sure of it. Rome, evil Rome and Caesar's minions, were everywhere around me. So were the fast-moving hidden agents of God, always on the Go, like the Logos as it creates things. I was a Christian but I had to hide it. Or they'd get me. It made me very uncomfortable to belong to a persecuted sect like that, a small minority of fanatics. I was afraid I'd blurt out my beliefs and be thrown to the lions. That is one reason my blood pressure got so high. I was waiting to be hit by Caesar's spies, and also I anticipated the Second Coming or something good like that. Maybe the Day of Judgment. I was more excited than afraid, sure in my father, certain of my Savior. The Last Supper was real, actual and close by me. Maybe this is a clue. I'm still in that time period, but I've fallen under the wise and prudent guidance of an educated Greek—high

class in other words—tutor. Brought in from the prov-
inces where the ignorant scurry about, to be educated
in cultivated urban life. I think I read all this in the
novel THE ROBE[*] x years ago. Jeez, I've fallen into
someone else's novel!

You know, I could if I wanted to make the most
dramatic but speculative case, for fictional purposes I
guess, reason that I was pulled back through time,
back and back, to where it All Went Wrong, which
would be where around 100 A.D. I, typifying everyone
who went wrong perhaps, became a Christian. "That
was a wrong turn," the Vast Active Living Intelligence
System that creates decided. "When those people
decided on Christianity. I'll throw away 2,000 years,
go back, have this one—he'll get it going right; he's typical—turn to some other religion instead, and have
that become dominant. Let's see . . . " A New Start. Second Time Around. Why not? Thus, my sense that my
help was coming from an *alternate universe.*

I don't know why I'm speculating along like this,
though, because in point of fact I've decided, by a
process of deduction, who my tutor is. Asklepios, or
one of his sons. A Greek physician, whose step
mother was the Cumaean sibyl, his father Apollo, at
whose shrines " . . . the sick were given wholesome
advice in their dreams," this cult yielding only reluc-
tantly to Christianity. Also Asklepios was according
to legend, slain by the *Kyklopes,* a cyclops. Which
would explain my extraordinary dreams: I saw a
fusion of his step-mother and him who Asklepios
feared most in all the world.

This also explains why the highest wisdom shown

---

[*]   THE ROBE (1942), novel by Lloyd Douglas.

me is that associated with Apollo. His—my tutor's—father.

Interestingly, although Apollo is considered to have been a myth, the Cumaean sibyl is thought to have really existed, and Asklepios likewise. The sibyl lived at least a thousand years, migrating to Rome and writing her Sibylline Books. Asklepios, as I say, was slain by a *Kyklopes,* by order of Zeus. That wasn't anything Apollo could do about it; Asklepios was bringing a dead person back to life with his healing powers, which Zeus couldn't tolerate because it interrupted the natural order. Which I guess is *ananke* again ... which would explain why in his instructing and shaping me Asklepios would emphasize that element in life. He learned all about it. I'm getting the benefit of his unfortunate experience.

I can see me telling my therapist this. "What's on your mind, Phil?" she'll say when I go in, and I'll say, "Asklepios is my tutor, from out of Pericleian Athens. I'm learning to talk in Attic Greek." She'll say, "Oh really?" and I'll be on my way to the Blissful Groves, but that won't be after death; that'll be in the country where it's quiet and costs $100 a day. And you get all the apple juice you want to drink, along with Thorazine.

Apollo's motto at Delphi was "Know thyself," which forms the basis for all modern psychotherapy and mental health and certainly underlies my getting in touch with myself, as depicted here. The other night when I found myself thinking, during the hypnagogic state, in Greek, I managed to snatch a couple of words out of what I believe to be a syntactic sentence. (At that time I wasn't positive it was Greek; it remained a problem to check on, today. It was.) I snatched out:

crypte (—) morphosis

Those mean something like:

latent shape (or hidden or concealed shape)

Although I don't have anything more to go on, it would seem to me that I—or my tutor—was musing on this whole situation, and in pithy Greek formalizing it. A latent form is emerging in me, buried perhaps by Apollo himself, when his son Asklepios was killed by the *Kyklopes,* so that his son's wisdom and skills, derived from Apollo, would continue on despite Asklepios' sudden death—remaining latent within the *morphology* of the Indo-European descendants of Asklepios, perhaps genetically handed down through his sons. (He had two.) Now, when needed, this *crypte morphosis* is emerging, again active; its external stimulating-triggering source being some aspect of the dreadful civic decline of our society, its falling into ruins. "Within the degenerate molecules, the trash of today, he (PKD) resurrects a power buried for eons." (S. Lem, about UBIK.)* Other gods of the past have at other times returned to life: Wotan in Germany, during the Nazis. Surely Apollo with his balanced wisdom, his clear healing harmony of opposites, his clear-headed self-knowledge and integrity—what better archetype or god, long slumbering, should be roused at this sad time? Of all the ancient buried deities Apollo is needed by us the most; we have seen enough of the politics of unreason, "Thinking with the Blood," etc.

[....]

---

* From Stanislaw Lem, "Science Fiction: A Hopeless Case—With Exceptions" (1972), an essay included in PHILIP K. DICK: ELECTRIC SHEPHERD (1975), edited by Bruce Gillespie.

Footnote. The original display of dazzling graphics which I saw, which inaugurated all this, were characterized by their balance, not what shapes they contained. They were, like much of Kandinsky's abstract art, modern aesthetic elaborations, in color, of the ancient *a priori* geometric forms conceived by the Greeks, which even in their time passed over into esthetics by way of Pythagoria,* e.g., the Golden Section becoming the Golden Rectangle. Certainly this would indicate that even the start of this contained the hallmark of Apollo: the balance, the harmony—I remember noting that in all the tens of thousands of pictures what was continuous in them was this perfect balance, illustrating a fundamental principle of art. It was that aspect which caught my attention and eye and told me they had great worth. In a sense, since all were rectangles, they were permutations of the Golden Rectangle, which I saw today in its original abstracted, empty form, so calm, so enduring, so restful, reminding me of Apollo's basic virtue: *syntosis.* I didn't even know the word, then; it came to me in sleep. Healing me, as was done 2,600 years ago and never quite ceasing.

By the way—the town where Asklepios' sanitarium existed, I read now, is up in the mountains. Probably the climate was and is cool and moist; I read it's heavily wooded. I'm [*I'll*] bet the stars are quite visible, there. It's the place I yearn for. Out of memory.

(Mid-July 1974)

I awoke abruptly to find myself with my Savior, and then entered Fellowship with God (the dreams of the delighting void). Can it be said that this is *the*

---

*   The ongoing thought and works of the Pythagorean wisdom school.

rebirth, accomplished by penetration of the Child by the solar *spermatikos*? Yes, Firebright, brought to life and sustained Greater intelligence for me, better health, longer life, even prosperity. A certain facility with life. But most of all I recall what I saw when I awakened: I saw my God, smiling in the sunlight of day. Once, during the years of the Terrible Separation,[*] I saw Palmer Eldritch in the Sun—I saw God backward, but sure enough, in the daytime sun: at high noon, and knew him to be a god. THE THREE STIGMATA, if read properly (i.e., reversed) contains many clues as to the nature of God and to our relationship with him. I was motivated to flee, then, fearing what I saw, so vast was the breach then. It was definitely a true vision of God, but grown (to my blind sight) terrible; still, it was the beginning of my seeing: that I could see God at all, in the sun, showed that I was not entirely blind, but rather deranged. My 3-74 experiences are an outgrowth of my Palmer Eldritch experience of over ten years earlier. "Faith of Our Fathers" shows this, too; I knew Him to be real ... but only in UBIK does he begin to appear as benign, especially then in MAZE OF DEATH. We were coming back together, as friends in the light-struck meadow or forest ... the summertime to greet.[**]   *(1975)*

One could assume, I guess, that the divine seed is in every one of us, but remains dormant (*crypte morphosis*); it is never fed, and this feeding comes to the pineal body via sunlight. So there is no implantation.

---

[*] "Terrible Separation" is a reference to PKD's own sense of the gulf that existed in the 1960s between his own limited human existence and a genuine encounter with the divine as a positive, redeeming force in the universe.
[**] This final sentence is a paraphrase of the lyrics of one of PKD's favorite *lieder* by Franz Schubert.

I myself, I felt something (Firebright) was implanted. I had visions of Firebright's heavenly parents. That sounds like more than celestial food. Which do we have, a quickening, an awakening, or an implantation? The parables about the seeds sown ... they don't make it certain (some sown on barren soil, some on rock, some on good soil, etc.) *If* one had had a dormant seed all one's life, and it had never stirred, come to life at all, and then a shaft of firelight from the Sun of Righteousness caused it to come to life *for the first time*, one might sense an implantation from outside; something which was not oneself. Sasha* must feel that way, with her little new unborn kittens inside her. "They came from outside." But in fact they were fertilized from outside. Okay, fertilization is what takes place: it isn't a seed such as a plant has, but an egg such as a human woman ovulates, and a cosmic *spermatika* fertilizes it; a zygote is produced. Firebright is a combining. Here would be the crucial distinction between Neoplatonism and Gnosticism, which I feel so strongly about: the former is sort of self-fertilizing, parthenogenesis, so to speak, but in Gnosticism you have the idea that the Savior is absolutely necessary, so we have here the idea that something entirely outside one is necessary, it comes along (God's grace) and if it doesn't come, then there is no zygote, no Firebright, no seed, no immortality. I always felt Gnosticism was correct over Neoplatonism; viewed this way, it is evident why. The Neoplatonist knows what happened, in a basic way, but he feels he did it by himself: up by his own bootstraps. A personal achievement. I guess this is a failure to know about

---

*   PKD's cat.

the "birds and the bees," as the "Decoded N T"[*] points out. How are babies born? By thinking about it, or by copulating? Let's be realistic; it takes a union, always true in higher forms, of which we are one. This is why the "Dec N T" can so plainly declare that no meditation, no prayer, no affirmation of belief, is going to do it. It is done to us, not by us. All each of us can do is accept—i.e., receive.

You are to be "meek," i.e., Yinnish, humble, receptive, but what overpowers you (the father!) is fierce, like Elijah, seeking justice and truth, powerful, definitely Yangish, and the not-you. Just the opposite. Possession by the God (*vide* Virgil describing Apollo taking over the Sibyl). You may be masculine to other humans, but to Him you are feminine, passive. Now, the Mynaeds of Dionysus did not seem to believe (read *know*) that a permanent fertilization, acquisition took place, but the Orphics certainly did; here lies a vast distinction! The being-overpowered leaves something forever: a vision of truth, of reality, a rising up to ultratemporal regions, but after the beatific vision, the Firebright Second Birth, what is born, lives on, eternally. What a jump from the mere Dionysian frenzy to Orphism and beyond, to Christianity! What a realization of the value of being possessed!

This borders on the Sufi: *becoming* God. One does "become" God while he possesses you, but then he leaves. But—well, it's like poor Leda. *Vide* Yeats' poem. But look at the progeny: Helen of Troy.   *(1975)*

Every time in my life that I've heard the spirit

---

[*]   THE DECODED NEW TESTAMENT (1974). Published by Gene Savoy's International Community of Christ in Reno, Nevada. An alternate reading of the New Testament from an esoteric organization that briefly influenced PKD.

it's been when my normal (linear) thinking had exas-
perated & exhausted itself—reached its end without
results, but each time, results were still absolutely
necessary. This alone makes a circumstantial case for
locating the spirit, the Inward Light, in the right
hemisphere (I suppose). Normal habitual cognitive
processes must be tried fully and fail. This would be
why under routine & ordinary conditions I don't
hear it and am cut off from it. But this only tells me
where it can be localized in terms of brain morphology. As an oppositional other brain, not my own, it
still—well, how does it come to think in Attic Greek,
and make use of technical terms such as *syntonic*?
My original diagram showed a piece of the
macrocosmos within the microcosmos, but that was
more a metaphor and poetry. Also, if my right hemisphere can do this, why does it do it only when I am
under duress? Why isn't there bilateral parity? What
an improvement that would be. Is it a new organ just
starting to come on, as Dr. Bucke[*] believed (i.e., the
next step upward in human evolution?) Maybe so.

(1975)

Last night (June 2nd[**]) I had a blissful truly mystical experience, which is probably the first one I've
had in the strict sense, inasmuch as it was a state, an
ASC,[***] with vast understanding and comprehension
as to how everything fitted together, but lacking any
and all adventitious percept-system experiences, as I
had in 3-74 and 2-75. However, had I never had any-

---

[*] Dr. Richard Maurice Bucke (1837-1902), friend of Walt Whitman and
author of COSMIC CONSCIOUSNESS, A STUDY IN THE EVOLUTION OF
THE HUMAN MIND (1905).
[**] 1975
[***] Altered state of consciousness.

thing else, it alone (last night) would have dignified my life immeasurably. How to record it verbally, though, I don't know. It linked it all up. That's a lot.

As basic realization: my 3-74 experience—the intervention by God in the world—was not an anomaly, except in terms of my experience of it. That is to say, it was a natural, regular event, which I had just never seen before; however, it always goes on, went on, will go on forever. It is the perpetual re-establishment of equilibrium and harmony, relating to the Tao and to ma'at.*

Primarily, I began by realizing that along the lines of Parmenides when he denied the testimony of his senses as regards to what is (in actuality, what exists), I realized that:

(1) There is no visual (sense-organ) evidence of God at work anywhere in the world.

(2) I must either deny that God, then, is at work in the world, or I must deny the evidence of my senses.

[. . . .]

I must have made myself, or anyhow been, very receptive (Yinnish) to the forces active in the universe at that moment. When hex 36** changed to some other good one, I was carried along, I just have, as the Taoists or Zen people, somebody anyhow, says, made myself empty (wu).

For hours last night I had in a blissful trance, sensing the capacity of the universe to rebound, its elasticity. You can't break it; it will regain its "shape" after any deformity sets in.

[. . . .]

---

* The ancient Egyptian goddess Ma'at (or Maât) symbolizes equilibrium, poise, and harmony. "Ma'at" also serves as an abstract term indicative of such qualities; it is in that abstract sense that PKD uses it here.
** Hexagram 36 of the I CHING.

Having experienced this blissful mystical understanding of it all, everything I've been into from 3-74 to now, I am thinking, Perhaps I can infer that the *Parousia* are [*sic*] not here in any universal or objective sense; but surely *for me*, as an individual, the entire sequence of depicted events came—and in the order described. Which causes me to ask, If as Meister Eckhart says, the Kingdom of God is within the Soul of each person (i.e., an entirely individual, inner event) then is not the entire realm of *Parousia,* all of it, within the inner individual soul of one person-at-a-time? But if so, then why do not other people report my experience as theirs? Over 2000 years there is no individual report like mine, except perhaps Eckhart? Well, no matter how I cut it I will have trouble explaining some parts.

It is possible that in some way, or for some reason, I somehow (this is heavy) died but did not die. *Vide* the photo of me.[*] I passed by degrees across to the other side, and then returned, reborn.

Let me assert as a possibility this: that as Teilhard de Chardin says—mankind following Christ as a species along through the stations of the cross—I went through the vicarious experience of the Passion ... or was it vicarious? It was real. *That* all took place, had to take place, to usher in 3-74, the rebirth. As Hoyt Axton[**] says, "Most people want to fly to heaven; they're not willing to *climb*."

[. . . .]

There is a great mystery about the Kingdom of God, as to where it is, and the *Parousia* in general; it is in you, but also among you, and it is invisible but

---

[*]   The photo referred to here is unknown.
[**] Country music singer.

actual. He must mean it is transpersonal. When you participate (yes, that is it); you *enter* it—did He not use this key word? You enter it; therefore it already exists before you and outside you, which indicates objective existence (contrast, "I entered sadness," a state of mind). It is real and it is there; one by one we enter it, or we don't. We cross over and enter, led by our shepherd. In response to the sound (sic) of his voice (sic). A place of safety and peace, where we remain with Him. We find our way to it (recall my vivid experience in 3 or 4-74 in seeing a pylon or archway with a silvery moonlit world beyond, and Greek letters—silence. I could pass through the gate and enter that world beyond; I could see it clearly, first here, then there, now over there, glowing and waiting, open to me. Not in any one spot but glimpsed again and again![)]

That was no subjective state; that was a perception of something real which others couldn't see; a set-ground gestalting. I discerned the doorway repeatedly; it was multilocated and authentic. Not omnipresent but multipresent. The Secret Kingdom, hidden.

A moment of fear touches me; did I then fail to pass through that gate and enter it? I think I passed on through, because after seeing it (that was quite early along) I then had the holy waste & void dreams, or visions, visionary trance experiences, where I was with God; that came later, I'm sure; yes, that was later, after the Carmel dream which ushered it in. So I did enter.

[....]

When I was little I used to haul out big wooden cartons and boxes to play inside of . . . it is as if, through the pylon gate, I found my way back to the peace and safety of those cartons of my childhood . . . God has brought me at last to safety and a realization, at last, of safety, the safety I yearned for and did not

have even then (5 years old). Viewed another way perhaps it can be said that I have been brought safety
into the fold, after straying all over the landscape.
Either way we are talking about the same place. I feel
a great peace now, at last, for the first time in my life.
This whole period, including 3-74, has been arduous; I
had to work hard and hustle after my illumination (3-
74), right on down through the months, these 14
months, writing on this as I am doing, reading and
researching and writing and meditating in order to
understand. I believe I've worn myself out more with
this than with any previous writing, any novel or
group of novels. I have educated myself regarding my
experience. Gone to school over it. What does it add
up to (at this point in my knowledge)? I passed
through the narrow gate in mid-74, and now I am told
that He will come back for the world itself, fairly soon.
Thus an individual experience will be made/is being
made into a common or group or collective or objective experience by our people in general. As with
other questions, the answer to the question, Is it subjective & individual or objective & general is, *Both.*

[. . . .]

This is the way to put it: "What do you have to do
to enter the Kingdom of Heaven?" and then the list
which follows conforms to the list one would draw, in
sequence, of what I experienced, back before that, too,
to the distress—lost—period which ran on months if
not years. What I went through both bad (before 3-74)
and good (3-74 on) had to be gone through, like an
enormous spiritual transcendental car wash—a
human being refurbishing system, so complex as to
beggar description, beginning with the drama of the
flying monsters with horses' necks (dragons) and then
picking up in distinctness with the chromatic flash-
cut graphics, the latter night being, if any section can

be so said to be, the moment when the Spirit began to pour out onto and into me. The beginning, in other words, of the New. Up to then it had been nothing but various aspects of me perishing—dying. The rebirth began with the graphics; the turning-point in the parabolic orbit has begun. I was re-entering life, as new life re-entered me: "from above." The thing about all this is that if it is said to me, severely, "You have to do (experience, go through) a lot to enter the Kingdom of Heaven; you can't do it like you are; you've got to be very much changed, and receive the Spirit," etc. I can say, "I know." (Or I think I know. I hope I know. I hope I don't just have *hubris* about this. I hope I'm not boasting. If I am I'm sorry.) I think, though, really, what is convincing about it when I view it objectively is that, remembering back, I was genuinely broken down, stripped down, torn down to my skeletal plating, like an insect who has woven a cocoon, rebuilding processes, all adventitious to me, improving and teaching me, altering me—well, the "possession" part alone remade me in the most fundamental way indeed—and clearly as completely remaking me as can be conceived.

(1) I believed I was someone else.

(2) From another time period.

(3) Dead centuries ago and reborn.

(4) A holy Christian person.

(5) I spoke Attic Greek somewhat and remembered Rome.

(6) I wanted a new name and trimmed my beard.

(7) All my interests and habits changed—instantly.

(8) My linguistic idiosyncracies altered permanently.

(9) Even the way I margined my pages changed.

(10) I wrote people I'd never written before.

(11) I joined religious organizations I'd never heard of.

(12) All my political alliances of a lifetime changed totally.

(13) I called cats "she" and dogs "he."

Ergo: He who was alive died, and someone else lives now in me, replacing me.

(14) I talk to and am talked to by God.

Well, what more can you ask out of a transformed person? I know the future and things beyond my senses, but I'll skip that because I am not sure if that counts.

(15) I stopped drinking wine and drank beer.

(16) I knew that aerosol sprays were lethal; like-wise cigarettes.

(17) I could discern evil and could tell what was true.

(18) My spelling is unchanged. (To give some continuity.)

(19) I recovered from most of my quasi-physical ailments.

(20) Most of my time since I spend studying theology.

(21) The level of my intelligence is increased—this includes reading retention, speed, and abstract thinking.

(22) My depth perception is improved.

(23) Mental operations which baffled me are now easy (i.e., mental blocks now seem gone).

(24) My psychological projections are withdrawn.

The only problem is, I am in no customary sense—

maybe in no sense whatsoever—spiritualized or exalted. In fact I seem even more mean and irascible than before. True, I do not hit anybody, but my language remains gunjy and I am crabby and domineering; my personality defects are unaltered. In the accepted sense I am not a better person. I may be healthier (maybe not that; *vide* the blood pressure). But I am not a good person, even though my emotions and moods are better under control. Maybe I just have a long way to go, yet.   *(1975)*

Mark 4:11 says that the parables were intended to confuse and not inform everyone except the disciples, the latter understanding the esoteric meaning, the outsiders getting only the exoteric meaning which would fail to save them; this was especially true regarding parables about the approaching Kingdom of God. I keep forgetting this. How much of the real inner meaning has come down to us? The written gospels record probably mostly the exoteric parable meanings, not the inner core. Whether we like it or not, it is there in *Mark* (if not elsewhere), and this favors the view of an elect within the body of mankind. At least so far as Jesus went. Maybe now there is a Third Covenant which will include all creation or anyhow all men. I am thinking in particular of the grain of wheat sown into the ground to rise again, a mystery theme common to Greek mystery religions; in fact evidently the basic one. What it really means—to know this— enables the hearer to achieve what is achieved: eternal life. The how is contained, as well as the what. I think that in 3-74, at the height of despair and fear and grieving I stumbled into the Kingdom, stumbled around for a while and then stumbled back out, none the wiser as to how I got there, barely aware of where

I had been, and no idea as to how I stumbled out, and seeking always to find my way back ever since. Shucks. Drat. If it wasn't the Kingdom I don't know what it could be, with its bells and the lady singing and the void, with the trash in the gutter glowing, and the golden rectangle doorway with the sea and figure beyond, and the moonlight. There were people living there, especially the lady. It was all alive. It had personality. It explained everything to me. Now I don't see or understand anything. At that time I could even remember back to my origins. My real origins: the stars. What am I doing here? I forget, but I knew once. Amnesia has returned; the veil has fallen, back where it was. The divine faculties are occluded as before. Obviously I didn't accomplish it; I was given it, since I don't know how to find it again. "Man is not as wise as some stones, which in the dark, point toward their homes." My soul, sunk down in ignorance again. Blind & deaf. Ensnared by gross matter, limited. The long dark night of the soul is a lousy place to be.

Heraclitus says the Logos can be heard. My goodness.   (1975)

I am thinking back. Sitting with my eyes shut I am listening to "Strawberry Fields." I get up. I open my eyes because the lyrics speak of "Going through life with eyes closed." I look toward the window. Light blinds me; my head suddenly aches. My eyes close and I see that strange strawberry ice cream pink. At the same instant knowledge is transferred to me. I go into the bedroom where Tessa is changing Chrissy[*] and I recite what has been conveyed to me: that he has an undetected birth defect and must be taken to

---

[*]   Tessa Dick, PKD's fifth wife, and Christopher (Chrissy), his infant son.

the doctor at once and scheduled for surgery. This turns out to be true.*

What happened? What communicated with me? I could read and understand the secret messages "embedded within the interior bulk." I have been placed under God's protection. The advocate now represents me. I hear a far off quiet voice that is not a human voice; it-she-comforts me. In the dark of the night she tells me that "St. Sophia is going to be born again; she was not acceptable before." A voice barely audible in my head. Later she tells me she is a "tutelary spirit," and I don't know what that word means. Tutor? I look it up. It means "Guardian."

I dream that "Elias" is sunk in despair were I not to turn the Monopoly play money and gold watch I found over to the Mexicans in Placentia. Who is Elias? I look it up. It is the Greek form for Elijah. Monopoly money—gold watch. Code—capitalism. Why should Elijah despair if I fail to return the watch and money to their proper owners? What is at stake here? After I give the watch and money to the Mexicans I realize they came from them in the first place. I go outdoors & no longer need hide from or be afraid of the cops.

Will I ever know why what I did was important? For several years I had sensed divine forces secretly at work guiding, protecting & helping me. But in 3-74 I *saw* them. So previously I had been right. My meeting Tessa—Christopher's birth. The secret sacraments I performed, hiding them—*him?*—from the Romans.

Ich weiss. [*I know.*]

My work *ist getan* [*is done*]. I never need fear again: Because the work was brought to successful

---

* The events described here, including the surgery on Christopher, occurred in September-October 1974.

completion. There is no need to hide. They were look-ing for X,* but did not find it. X got into print and on synch schedule. Alleluja! *Marenatha!*

Really, secretly, I know. The Revolution was a suc-cess. There was no way they could keep X from com-ing into print on schedule. "Nats" "Pol"—AMORC** code words. The Knights Templar on the march against the man hiding in the darkness inside the building. Sentences to death. The wise old king had passed judgment.

I saw the final days. Time fulfilled itself. We are safe now from the world, which has been overcome. I got to see God as he really is, & I saw what we are like. "We shall be like him" 1 *JN**** 3:2   *(1977)*

Pain is the good which most effectively keeps me alive. & it is good that I am alive. *This* pain, *my* pain, but not pain as such, is good. Due to something in my DNA nature, if I felt pleasure I would give up the pro-cess & die. Pain is the most *economical* drive to keep me going, and the dialectic process *must* conserve its energy.

This is the way I am, and in total knowledge God knew that this was the *best* way for me. Reality for me is painful—must be and always will be—but (that) real-ity is good; *all* realities are good. *God does not err.* His

---

*   "X" seems to be PKD's symbol for the one or more of his works (just which remained uncertain to him) that he believed may have contained a vital message that could spur the process of divine salvation of the world. In the next paragraph, PKD makes reference to "Nats" and "Pol"—the colloquialisms PKD invented for the national guard and the police in FLOW MY TEARS, THE POLICEMAN SAID (1974), a novel that PKD frequently posited as the most likely identity of "X".

**   AMORC is the acronym for the American Rosicrucian society founded in 1915 by Harvey Spencer Lewis—the Ancient and Mystic Order Rosae Crucis. PKD briefly joined in 1974.

*** John.

decision is always right. Therefore it follows from this premise that even if reality is necessary and painful it is *always* good.   *(c. 1978)*

Oh God, I am so weary of this lonely world! Can't I find my way back? Its power reasserted itself, its power to compel me to see it & live in it but knowing & remembering. We were so happy preparing for the return of God! & then we fell asleep—bewitched— Klingsor & his castle of iron. *Libera me, Domine!* [*Release me, Lord!*]   *(July 1978)*

Yes, it was a mercy to me—I went over the brink into psychosis in '70 when Nancy did what she did to me*—in '73 or so I tried to come back to having an ego, but it was too fragile & there were too many financial & other pressures; the hit on my house & all the terrors of 1971 had left their mark—& so, esp[.] because of the IRS matter suffered *total* psychosis in 3-74, was taken over by one or more archetype. Poverty, family responsibility (a new baby) did it. & fear of the IRS.

Only now, as I become for the first time in my life financially secure, am I becoming sane. Free of psychotic anxiety (R. Crumb's case is *very* instructive),** & career-wise I am doing so well: I am at least experience genuine satisfaction (e.g. my car, my novels, my stereo, my friendship with K.W.***), & there is far less responsibility on my shoulders. Also, my

---

* Nancy Hackett, PKD's fourth wife, decided in 1970 to end the marriage. For an account that includes the views of Nancy Hackett as to the events of that year, see chapter seven of DIVINE INVASIONS: A LIFE OF PHILIP K. DICK (1989).
** During the 1970s, comic book artist R. Crumb underwent an intensive tax audit conducted by the I.R.S.
*** K.W. Jeter, a friend and fellow science-fiction writer.

accomplishments last year—traveling, being with Joan*—did wonders for my psychological health. I learned to say no, & I conquered most of my phobias. I think they lessened as I learned to enjoy living alone for the first time in my life. & the therapy at Ben Rush Center helped.

But I think that when all else failed & external pressures & inner fears drove me into psychosis, *God placed me under his personal protection* & guided me & saved me by his divine love, mercy, wisdom & grace through Christ ... although not, perhaps, as I delusionally imagined. The intervention appears in TEARS as the dream & the reconciliation with my shadow, the black man, which followed; & my anima, possessing mana, acted as my psychopomp through the underworld to safety.

[....]

Abandoned by Tess,** my suicide attempt brought me in touch at last with my body, my physical self, & caused me to respect—not despise—my body.

[....]

Still, I still have too low a self-esteem, but my success as a recognized writer has helped that. The death of my mother*** has helped, because I can see what a malign person she was in my life & how I feared & disliked her—which she deserved[....] My friendship with K.W. has helped, too. (i.e., he has helped make me more thick-skinned & better able to monitor &

---

* Joan Simpson, with whom PKD had a romantic relationship in 1977.
** In February 1976, PKD attempted suicide after his fifth wife, Tessa Dick, moved out of their house with their son Christopher. Tessa Dick recalls that PKD insisted on the move. See chapter eleven of DIVINE INVASIONS: A LIFE OF PHILIP K. DICK (1989).
*** Dorothy Kindred Hudner, PKD's mother, died in August 1978. The relationship between mother and son was a difficult one. See chapters one and two of DIVINE INVASIONS.

access my intrinsic worth). Also I am aware of my good works & hence myself as a good person.

[. . . .]

& I accept my own aging, now. & I have my two fine cats. I guess now I don't need my psychotic fantasy-system so much—but I treasure parts of it, esp[.] the love & the beauty—& *her*. My psychosis put me in touch with *"das ewige weiblichheit"* [*the eternal feminine*] in me, & for that I will always be grateful; it means I will never really be alone again: whenever I really need her, I will sense her presence & hear her voice (i.e., St. Sophia.) At the center of psychosis I encountered her: beautiful & kind &, most of all, wise, & through that wisdom, accompanying & leading me through the underworld, through the *bardo thödol** journey to rebirth—she, the embodiment of intelligence: *Pallas Athena herself*. So at the core of a shattered mind & life lies this equicenter—omphalos—of harmony & calm. I love her, & she is my guide: the second comforter & advocate promised by Jesus . . . as Luther said, *"For the very desperate,"* here in this world secretly, for their—our—sake.

[. . . .]

Driven mad by fear & adversity I have seen—& lived in—another world that most people never get to see. But it is not that *world* that I remember & treasure but it is *her*—she who I met there, who met me & helped me. I saw her in many forms, but her voice was always the same. I recognized my savior in her— *as* her; he took the form which would mean the most to me (as Zoroaster says about meeting one: religion as the other end of the bridge which spans two

---

*   The postmortem realm described in the TIBETAN BOOK OF THE DEAD.

worlds: she is young & beautiful if you are a son of Light—old & withered if you are a son of Darkness.)

When I saw her she was beautiful beyond compare—Aphrodite & Pallas Athena both—& some day I'll see her again. She is inside me—she is my soul.

I can entertain (hold) two normally contradictory beliefs—explanations—:

1) I became totally psychotic & projected & imagined all that religious, supernatural stuff.

2) The guide & savior, the figure of the beautiful woman who I met & whose voice I kept hearing, whose existence during my psychosis I imagined, was & is completely real—& I know when the need arises again, I will find her once more, or rather she will find me & again guide me.

Now the wisdom of giving me the prophecy ("St. Sophia will . . . " etc.) in Greek is evident. How can I dismiss *that* as a psychotic hallucination when I didn't know what "St. Sophia" meant?[. . . .]

But foremost: the "AI" voice (which, e.g., gave me the prophecy, & which still corrects & instructs me). It either all stands or it all falls. I think it stands.   *(1978)*

Consider what the AI voice has said recently:
"The head Apollo is about to return."
"The time you've waited for has come."
"Don't tell that you're a secret xtian."
"It [*the xerox missive*] was from an intelligence officer in the army." (So it *was* a trap.)
"I did call you, Philip." (This, Christ's voice, not the "AI" or Holy Spirit's.) "You are doomed to do what you will do. There is no other possibility. Some will be saved & some will not."

So the great assize is taking place; v. TEARS, the dream. The time of his return as judge and rightful king is here, & he is selecting his flock. "The head Apollo is about to return" is interesting because the return of Apollo as rightful king was the signal to the Greco-Roman world that the cycle of ages has passed from the Iron (BIP) to the Golden (v. Virgil's eclogue).*

"I did call you, Philip." So I actually heard the savior's voice call me: the good shepherd. &, as it is written, "My sheep (flock) know my voice."

If anyone thinks this all has drawn me away from reality & practical problems, just consider the xerox missive, which I now know was indeed a U.S. intelligence trap.

Is he now selecting his flock? He is the one who picks us, not we him. I have every reason to believe he picked me.   *(1978)*

Well, thinking this, about how Zoroastrianism teaches that we are met by the spirit of our religion when we die, & if we are a son of light, she is *"Jung und Schön."* [*Young and beautiful.*] But if we are a servant of the lie she is a wrinkled old hag ... I dream I heard the magic bell, & see her in bird feathers—like Papagana** ... I am even more 1) uneasy as to whether I am in the "live" world (lower realm) or the "next world" (upper realm); but 2) pleased at how *ma'at*** has judged me. There has been, admittedly, a lot of pain (over [*past women in his life*]) but the reward element predominates; I feel better & better, &, what is equally important, seem to understand more & more, exponentially. I am no longer chronically depressed & apprehensive (terror stricken). I've

---

* The reference here is to Virgil's Fourth Eclogue, which was asserted, by the Church Fathers, to contain a prophecy of the coming Christ.
** Character in the Mozart opera THE MAGIC FLUTE.
*** See note on page 25.

written (I feel) my best book so far.[*] My mind is alive & active. I feel I am growing & developing. I finally got Laura & Isa[**] down here. I'm economically secure. I'm no longer abusing drugs, legal or illegal— i.e., drug dependent. I am very happy. I even went to France. I had a lot of fun with Joan.[***] My career is gosh wow (due in good measure to my own—and Thomas'—efforts). So I may be dead, as of 3-74. My cosmological concepts are so terrific, so advanced as to be off the scale. I create whole religions and philosophical systems. The very fact that I honestly ponder if I may be dead & in heaven is *prima facie* evidence of how happy & fulfilled I am. How many people seriously wonder this? (Maybe everyone, when they die.) If I am *not* dead, how do I explain 2-3-74? No one has *ever* reported such obviously *post mortem* experiences.

Well, I explain it in terms of a two part oscillation comprising my *total* existence: (1) the part where I am alive in this world & my sister is dead & an idea in my brain; & 2) the other part where I am dead & *she* is alive & I am a thought in her living brain—& I explain this oscillation of two antithetical irreducible propositions as an instance of the dialectic (whose existence was revealed to me in 3-74) which underlies all existence due to the fact that we're components in a binary computer, etc., & I construe this matter as a riddle posed to me by the designer of the computer: Holy Wisdom,[****] who is playful. But how

*   The reference here is to VALIS, written in 1978.
**   PKD's two daughters, by his third and fourth marriages, respectively. PKD had arranged for each of them to visit him at his Santa Ana condominium during this period.
*** Joan Simpson. See note on page 36.
****This is a cognate term for Saint Sophia.

do I explain why all this was revealed to me & to no one else? I have no explanation; I know what I know but not *why*. Unless, of course, when you die it's all revealed to you routinely—

Or—having a deceased twin sister makes me unusual: in symbiosis to a dead (sic) person, & in telepathic contact with her. Or maybe I'm just a genius. No, I'm not. But I am curious. I love epistemological riddles. & so now I've got one, a superb one. It's ultimate. Just theoretically, its formulation couldn't be beaten. I love it. I'll solve it.

I regard the two-proposition formulation about "am *I* alive or ... " etc. as a brilliant application of the "UBIK" puzzle to my own self. But I can't take credit for formulating it; it was *presented* to me. Whoever the funning player is, she is a delight. Sophia, I think it is you.

One thing I must posit as absolutely veridical: the power of Karma over me was broken completely in 3-74. So at the very least, I am 1) dead to the way-of-being in the world I had known; & 2) alive to a new *free* way of being, & progressively more so.   *(1978)*

Dream: I am Jerry Lewis, a contemptible clown, but admired by millions, esp. in France. In a parking lot I fall, & lie down to die. At once my fans gather from everywhere, & close in around me to protect me, giving military salutes; it is a heroic scene, the dying leader & his loyal troops.   *(1979)*

What does it mean—how can it be—to die & come to life? I died & came to life. It is a mystery. I remember dying. There can be no doubt about it. & then I could see; I was no longer blind. I was on the outside of the universe looking in; everything was reversed. &

it was 2000 years ago. I remembered. Who am I now? Thinking in Greek, & the healing & the prophecy. Saint Sophia will be born again; she was not acceptable before.

The palm trees. The garden.

Ich bin er. Das weiss ich. Immer kommt es dazu zurück. Wie viel sind er? Und wo? & wie? Die zeit ist heir! [I am him. That I know. Ever will he come back again. How many will we see him? And where? & how? The time is now!] (1979)

How can I ascertain my role? Did I *do* something? Absolutely. But I don't know what I did, so I don't know who (so to speak) I am in the drama. Was something done *for* me? Absolutely yes. There are, then, *two* aspects. I *became* some one (whom I call Thomas) & as Thomas I did something—I know not what—& something was done for me (I was rescued, but I don't know from what). In the antithetical dialectic between the rightful king & the old tyrant-usurper I was with (or was?) the rightful king (represented in my book as Taverner): exculpated and rescued, but also bringing down doom on the tyrant. This is the "priest of Dionysus" role, the stranger.

It is the legitimate power which when "crucified" (humiliated & killed, the latter perhaps symbolically[)]; viz.: *I died & yet did not die*—

Here is the mystery: humiliation & death & yet he is not dead—& what is more, he is *now* disclosed as he truly is: *divine*. For the first time.

The Gospels alone don't make it clear; you have to add TEARS and *The Bacchae,*[*]—the stranger who 1) is arrested by the tyrant i.e. is innocent but/and victim-

---

[*] The tragedy by Euripides.

ized by the tyrant; 2) is exculpated; 3) but does in the
tyrant in such a way that a mortal blow is delivered
(by him or through him or due to him) to the tyrant.

So he has a dual role: victim turned into instru-
ment of destruction. This sums it up; the two roles
blend into one role (v *The Bacchae*). This sounds like
the bait-hook analysis of Christ, & it fits 3-74 & the
xerox missive.

Since I don't think I *really* pulled down the tyrant
or anyone, 3-74 must be understood as mythic identification (*esse*) & ritual (drama with personae), it was a
holy (sacred) ritual drama enacted outside of time.
The salvation was spiritual more than pragmatic, then
(& hence more important). I participated outside of
time in the God's arrest, humiliation (persecution),
the trap, then triumph (reversal from innocent victim
to agency of doom). But it was mythic, ritual, holy, re-
enactment. The trapped turned out to *be* a trap (bait &
hook), & resurrection in divine (transfigured) form.
Unity (by adoption?) with the God who goes through
it always—ah; the God was there in 2-3-74; I *became* the
God by ritual identification. Christ, obviously.   *(1979)*

All I really know is that there is another mind [....]
responding—& entering into dialogue with *my* mind.
It is like a hologram that I encountered, drawn from
my own mind. Macro as mirror of micro, rather than
the other way around? This is just unreal! The
implications are: YHWH can create an infinite number of universes, & does. & what is more, he either is
or is in these hologram response universes!

Let us recall Palmer E[*ldritch*]'s worlds at this
point.

He did not wait for me to die to give me the universe (reality) I wanted. Does that mean we are in

something like cold-pac? In some respects we are. But
I do not know in what respects. But he simulated
(mimicked) Valis, & my informational world. He, it,
whatever it is, is a macro-mind that can cause to be
whatever he wishes.   *(1979)*

It really does not make sense to say that the universe is irreal unless you have something real to compare it with. So the correct formulation is not "irreal,"
which begs the question, but epiphenomenal, whereupon you look behind or beyond the epiphenomenon
to see what its urgrund [primal basis of reality] is.

The answer is, the epiphenomenal is real insofar
as it partakes of God & *only* insofar as it does. Thus I
have to agree with Sankara that ultimate questions
regarding ontology lead back to God.

However, God can transubstantiate the epiphenomenon into the real, by virtue of his immanent
presence in it, as in the eucharist. Thus reality is
viewed as a perpetual sacrament: with the formal
eucharist as a micro-enactment of a continual macro-
cosmic on-going process which I actually *saw*. The
real, then, is sacred, even at the trash stratum, due to
this transubstantiation.

5:00 a.m. realization: there's no way of getting
around it. I saw the world dissolve into Brahman; unitary & sentient—with plurality a magician's trick
(*maya*). I got it to dissolve into what it really is. "They
reckon ill who leave me out."* God did not break
through into reality—no, reality revealed itself to be
what it really is: Brahman. This is reversion not invasion. The illusion relaxed. Hence I said, "I am no longer
blind." This doesn't fit in with theophany but it does

---

*   From the poem "Brahma" by Ralph Waldo Emerson.

with the disappearance of the tricks. "We are normally occluded" doesn't fit in with a theophany but it does with reversion—the loss of the spell of *maya.*

I saw it as it really is: I saw with the *ajna* [*third*] eye.   (1979)

God manifested himself to me as the infinite void; but it was not the abyss; it was the vault of heaven, with blue sky and wisps of white clouds. He was not some foreign God but the God of my fathers. He was loving and kind and he had personality. He said, "You suffer a little now in life; it is little compared with the great joys, the bliss that awaits you. Do you think I in my theodicy would allow you to suffer greatly in proportion to your reward?" He made me aware, then, of the bliss that would come; it was infinite and sweet. He said, "I am the infinite. I will show you. Where I am, infinity is; where infinity is, there I am. Construct lines of reasoning by which to understand your experience in 1974. I will enter the field against their shifting nature. You think they are logical but they are not; they are infinitely creative."

I thought a thought and then an infinite regression of theses and countertheses came into being. God said, "Here I am; here is infinity." I thought another explanation; again an infinite series of thoughts split off in dialectical antithetical interaction. God said, "Here is infinity; here I am." I thought, then, an infinite number of explanations, in succession, that explained 2-3-74; each single one of them yielded up an infinite progression of flipflops, of thesis and antithesis, forever. Each time, God said, "Here is infinity. Here, then, I am." I tried for an infinite number of times; each time an infinite regress was set off and each time God said, "Infinity. Hence I am here." Then he said, "Every thought leads to infinity, does it not? Find one that doesn't." I tried forever. All led to an infinitude of regress, of the dialectic, of thesis, antithesis and new synthesis. Each time, God said, "Here is infinity; here am I. Try again." I tried forever. Always it ended with God saying, "Infinity and myself; I am here." I saw, then, a Hebrew letter with many shafts, and all the shafts led to a common outlet; that outlet or conclusion was infinity. God said, "That is myself. I am infinity. Where infinity is, there am I; where I am, there is infinity. All roads—all explanations for 2-3-74—lead to an infinity of Yes-No, This or That, On-Off, One-Zero, Yin-Yang, the dialectic, infinity upon infinity; an infinities [*sic*] of infinities. I am everywhere and all roads lead to me; *omniae viae ad Deum ducent* [*all roads lead to God*]. Try again. Think of another possible explanation for 2-3-74." I did; it led to an infinity of regress, of thesis and antithesis and new synthesis. "This is not logic," God said. "Do not think in terms of absolute theories; think instead in terms of probabilities. Watch where the piles heap up, of the same theory essentially repeating itself. Count the number of punch cards in each pile. Which pile is highest? You can never know for sure what 2-3-74 was. What, then, is statistically most probable? Which is to say, which pile is highest? Here is your clue: every theory leads to an infinity (of regression, of thesis and antithesis and new synthesis). What, then, is the probability that I am the cause of 2-3-74, since, where infinity is, there I am? You doubt; you are the doubt as in:

> They reckon ill who leave me out;
> When me they fly I am the wings.
> I am the doubter and the doubt . . .*

_____

* From the poem "Brahma" by Ralph Waldo Emerson.

"You are not the doubter; you are the doubt itself. So do not try to know; you cannot know. Guess on the basis of the highest pile of computer punch cards. There is an infinite stack in the heap marked INFINITY, and I have equated infinity with me. What, then, is the chance that it is me? You cannot be positive; you will doubt. But what is your guess?"

I said, "Probably it is you, since there is an infinity of infinities forming before me."

"There is the answer, the only one you will ever have," God said.

"You could be pretending to be God," I said, "and actually be Satan." Another infinitude of thesis and antithesis and new synthesis, the infinite regress, was set off.

God said, "Infinity."

I said, "You could be testing out a logic system in a giant computer and I am—" Again an infinite regress.

"Infinity," God said.

"Will it always be infinite?" I said. "An infinity?"

"Try further," God said.

"I doubt if you exist," I said. And the infinite regress instantly flew into motion once more.

"Infinity," God said. The pile of computer punch cards grew; it was by far the largest pile; it was infinite.

"I will play this game forever," God said, "or until you become tired."

I said, "I will find a thought, an explanation, a theory, that does not set off an infinite regress." And, as soon as I said that, an infinite regress was set off. God said "Over a period of six and a half years you have developed theory after theory to explain 2-3-74. Each night when you go to bed you think, 'At last I found it. I tried out theory after theory until now, finally, I have the right one.' And then the next morning you wake up and say, 'There is one fact not explained by that theory. I will have to think up another theory.' And so you do. By now it is evident to you that you are going to think up an infinite number of theories, limited only by your lifespan, not limited by your creative imagination. Each theory gives rise to a subsequent theory, inevitably. Let me ask you; I revealed myself to you and you saw that I am the infinite void. I am not in the world, as you thought; I am transcendent, the deity of the Jews and Christians. What you see of me in world that you took to ratify pantheism—that is my being filtered through, broken up, fragmented and vitiated by the multiplicity of the flux world; it is my essence, yes, but only a bit of it: fragments here and there, a glint, a riffle of wind ... now you have seen me transcendent, separate and other from world, and I am more; I am the infinitude of the void, and you know me as I am. Do you believe what you saw? Do you accept that where the infinite is, I am; and where I am, there is the infinite?"

I said, "Yes."

God said, "And your theories are infinite, so I am there. Without realizing it, the very infinitude of your theories pointed to the solution; they pointed to me and none but me. Are you satisfied, now? You saw me revealed in theophany; I speak to you now; you have, while alive, experienced the bliss that is to come; few humans have experienced that bliss. Let me ask you, Was it a finite bliss or an infinite bliss?"

I said, "Infinite."

"So no earthly circumstance, situation, entity or thing could give rise to it."

"No, Lord," I said.

"Then it is I," God said. "Are you satisfied?"

"Let me try one other theory," I said. "What hap-

pened in 2-3-74 was that—" And an infinite regress
was set off, instantly.

"Infinity," God said. "Try again. I will play forever,
for infinity."

"Here's a new theory," I said. "I ask myself, 'What
God likes playing games? Krishna. You are Krishna.'"
And then the thought came to me instantly, "But
there is a god who mimics other gods; that god is
Dionysus. This may not be Krishna at all; it may be
Dionysus pretending to be Krishna." And an infinite
regress was set off.

"Infinity," God said.

"You cannot be YHWH Who You say You are," I
said. "Because YHWH says, 'I am that which I am,' or,
'I shall be that which I shall be.' And you—"

"Do I change?" God said. "Or do your theories
change?"

"You do not change," I said. "My theories change.
You, and 2-3-74, remain constant."

"Then you are Krishna playing with me," God
said.

"Or I could be Dionysus," I said, "pretending to be
Krishna. And I wouldn't know it; part of the game is
that I, myself, do not know. So I am God, without realizing it. There's a new theory!" And at once an infinite
regress was set off; perhaps *I* was God, and the "God"
who spoke to me was not.

"Infinity," God said. "Play again. Another move."

"We are both Gods," I said, and another infinite
regress was set off.

"Infinity," God said.

"I am you and you are you," I said. "You have
divided yourself in two to play against yourself. I, who
am one half, I do not remember, but you do. As it says
in the GITA, as Krishna says to Arjuna, 'We have both
lived many lives, Arjuna; I remember them but you

do not.' "* And an infinite regress was set off; I could well be Krishna's charioteer, his friend Arjuna, who does not remember his past lives.

"Infinity," God said.

I was silent.

"Play again," God said.

"I cannot play to infinity," I said. "I will die before that point comes."

"Then you are not God," God said. "But I can play throughout infinity; I am God. Play."

"Perhaps I will be reincarnated," I said. "Perhaps we have done this before, in another life." And an infinite regress was set off.

"Infinity," God said. "Play again."

"I am too tired," I said.

"Then the game is over."

"After I have rested—"

"You rest?" God said. "George Herbert** wrote of me:

> Yet let him keep the rest,
> But keep them with repining restlessnesse.
> Let him be rich and wearie, that at least,
> If goodness leade him not, yet wearinesse
> May tosse him to my breast.

"Herbert wrote that in 1633," God said. "Rest and the game ends."

"I will play on," I said, "after I rest. I will play until finally I die of it."

"And then you will come to me," God said. "Play."

"This is my punishment," I said, "that I play, that I

---

*   Krishna to Arjuna in chapter 10 of the BHAGAVAD GITA.

** George Herbert (1593-1633), English Christian poet and mystic. The lines quoted by PKD form the final stanza of the poem "The Pulley." In line five, "my" is capitalized in the original.

try to discern if it was you in March of 1974." And the thought came instantly, My punishment or my reward; which? And an infinite series of thesis and antithesis was set off.

"Infinity," God said. "Play again."

"What was my crime?" I said, "that I am compelled to do this?"

"Or your deed of merit," God said.

"I don't know," I said.

God said, "Because you are not God."

"But you know," I said. "Or maybe you don't know and you're trying to find out." And an infinite regress was set off.

"Infinity," God said. "Play again. I am waiting."

(17 November 1980)

God said that I couldn't know with certainty, but, instead, to watch where the computer punch cards piled up. Okay.

(1) As late as 11-16-80 (the day Ray* arrived) I theorized that Valis was the *macrometasomakosmos*** and the "second signal" and that this was the Cosmic Christ, not disguised as an invader in our universe but assembling itself *out* of our universe. So here you have the Cosmic Christ, seen in 3-74.

(2) In my anamnesis I remembered being a Christian, of the first century C.E. This was "Thomas." He brought with him the original sacraments of the apostolic secret church.

(3) On 11-17-80 I experienced a theophany and

---

* Ray Torrence, bookseller and friend of PKD. Torrence was paying a visit to PKD and was with PKD on 17 November 1980, the date of what PKD called the "theophany." In interview with the editor, Torrence stated that he recalled nothing unusual about PKD that day.

** Ultimate cosmic body or structure.

God turned out to be the Christian God, of love (his nature was love). He told me that my problem was that I could not believe I had seen him, specifically him, in 3-74.

(4) Small details. Disinhibition by the Christian fish sign. The *Acts* material in TEARS. Seeing the world of *Acts*. Remembering the supratemporal *eidos* of the secret underground revolutionary Christians, of which I am one, battling the Black Iron Prison; what I call realm #3 or morphological arrangement.

The first three; let us consider.

(1) Possibility that Valis (the *macrometasomakosmos* and "second signal") are the Cosmic Christ.

(2) Thomas was a secret early Christian.

(3) When God revealed himself to me in a theophany he was the Christian God, specifically.

Don't these all fit together? Look at how the computer punch cards fall; look at the distribution. (3) is proved; He proved who he was by causing me to experience infinite bliss. Oh Yes:

Regarding (4), the AI voice's initial statement was, "St. Sophia will be born again; she wasn't acceptable before." Another small item.

How do the computer punch cards fall now, with the addition? Mention of St. Sophia (Christ), the Christian God—who told me that my theorizing in the exegesis was not logical but infinitely creative; and he would take the field and block my endless speculations.

Isn't (1) and (2) verified by (3), which is a known? Can't I work backwards from (3) to especially (1), which is to say, Valis, the *macrometasomakosmos*, the "second signal" (*vide* entry date 11-16-80)? I would say yes; yes I can.

Also, I have the impression that the dialectic (that I saw in 3-74) represented two processes at two levels:

(1) The disintegrating "splitting" of entropic time. This would be world and would pervade all creation.

(2) At the same time (so to speak) at a higher level it would be God versus Satan, with God as the wiser horn who always wins through enantiodromia.

Now, this winning through wisdom points to the Cosmic Christ, since Christ is Holy Wisdom, St. Sophia, Hagia Sophia, Wisdom personified. Also Christ is God (*"Kai Theos en ho logos"*) [*The King is God through his Word*]. Therefore, if this be true, perhaps although I did see world in 3-74 I saw world as Christ; world becoming the Cosmic Christ (the *macrometasomakosmos*). Then Christ combatting Satan in the dialectic is God Himself, the Christian God of love, combatting Satan. This would explain why one horn of the dialectic was wiser than the other, and, despite the power of the other, always won (through its wisdom; this is what produces the cease-less enantiodromia). By the way; this fits in with Jakob Böhme's vision of the Yes-No dialectic of God who passes through stages, and that the negative or "No" sides are what we experience as evil. In my opinion this is God as the Cosmic Christ.

A trinitarian view of God and Christ being of one substance must be held in order to understand this.

The arguments for Valis being the Cosmic Christ are not conclusive but they are compelling.[...]

(11-24-80)

So Satan served me up a sophisticated world in accord with my epistemological expectations (as expressed in my 10 volume meta novel)* & I took this to be God & worshipped it, which is not only delusion—although a subtle delusion—but blasphemy; but in doing this

1) Satan revealed to me a great deal about world (although he led me to believe it was God, not world); &

2) Because of the infinitude of my theorizing I reached God anyhow—& this is an example of the triumph of God the wise horn of the dialectic; so:

3) The dialectic revealed to me is the entropic world-process; but also:

4) The dialectic is God in combat with Satan & God always wins; winning me (as expressed in 11-17-80) is an example: Satan's delusions led me to God in the end (through the "infinity" route; viz: as God said, "Where there is infinity, there is God; where there is God, there is infinity.").

Thus my exegesis has been futile, has been delusion, &: has been a hell-chore (as I was beginning to realize, but God delivered me from it, from my own exegesis; & he pointed out the one truth in it: the infinity expressed in it was—but this was overlooked by Satan who does not possess absolute knowledge—a road to God, & did lead there; but *only* when I recognized the exegesis as futile & a hell-chore delusion. Hence God permitted this deluding by Satan, knowing when it would end.

So I wind up knowing a lot more about world—world as we will later experience it, the world—experience of the future; & I no longer suppose that I was

---

*   PKD would group various of his past works into thematic wholes to which he gave the name "meta novel". See chapter four herein, "Interpretations of His Own Works," for examples of this process. The precise configuration PKD had in mind here is unclear.

discerning God, & realize that I was discerning world
instead; & I was at last led to God. But not by my
intellect, not by Gnosis, not by myself at all; it was
due to God's initiative due to his loving-kindness; &
what was proved was (once again) that *all*
roads/ways/routes if pushed far enough lead to God.
Hence (as I say) there is an example of how God the
wise born of the dialectic defeats its stupider foe inevitably in the end—this was an enantiodromia. It
occurred when I realized that all that I had seen of
God in 2-3-74 was a glint of color & a rippled wind in
the weeds of the alley, acting on reality; that Valis
was not God but rather world ("the reality field") perturbed (from beyond creation) by God; but this did
not yield knowledge of God direct, but only by inference; & that in fact 2-3-74 was not a theophany, but
was a more sophisticated experience of world: creation pulled through infinity by reaching the end of
(exhausting) its creative/entropic "splitting" (disintegrating; differentiating) dialectic process: entropic
time converted into negentropic time. But this was
still world, & Satan caused me to worship it ... to fall
victim to it, ensnared by it; taking it to be God; until
I found that I had pushed my exegesis to infinity
without result! & then I focussed on the very infinitude of my theories & saw (recognized) this as an
instance of cosmogenic entropy; &, at last exhausted,
prayed for release; & God did appear to me in theophany & took the field & blocked each & all theories, & ended my exegesis, not in defeat but in *logical*
discovery of Him (which Satan had not foreseen).
Thus intellect & knowledge on my part led to exhaustion & to destruction of that intellect & a recognition
of the futility of what I was doing; I knew I knew
nothing; & then God took the field & made his move
that resulted in the enantiodromia that led me to

him anyhow, as if I had wandered that way by
chance; *but it was by his plan* all along. & this was an
instance of the dialectic that I had seen.

Finally I wind up with $\ddot{Y} = \overline{Y}$; viz:

Both these 2 following statements are true:

1) The intellect will not lead you to God.

2) The intellect *will* lead you to God.

I am left with this paradox, which Satan did not foresee; he saw only statement (1) & did not see how
God could convert it into its mirror opposite
through enantiodromia. This God works & wins
within the Fallen entropic creation of the disintegration "splitting" dialectic to win us one & all in the
end, by different routes. Thus the cosmic game
between God & his adversary continues on; here
was another victory by God; & in the end God will
convert the dialectic itself into its opposite (through
enantiodromia) & the game will end in God's victory & Satan's defeat, which God's victory vis-à-vis
me echoes in microform.

In a certain sense it can be said that God's victory
consists in turning Satan's false creation—i.e. Satan's
lie & delusion—*into the real,* which is exactly what I
saw Valis doing: transmuting reality by transubstantiation into the real. Here is the secret & perpetual &
ever-growing victory by God over his adversary as he
(God) defeats him (Satan) again & again in the game
they play—the cosmic dialectic that I saw. This is
enantiodromia at its ultimate: the conversion of the
irreal to the real. In my case it was the conversion of
"the human intellect will not lead to God but will
lead only deeper & deeper into delusion" into its mirror opposite: "The human intellect, when it has
pushed to infinity, will at last, through ever deepen-
ing delusion, find God." Thus I am saved: & know
that I did not *start out* seeing God (2-3-74) (which led

to this 6½ year exegesis),* but, instead, wound up finding God (11-17-80)—an irony that Satan did not foresee. & thus the wise mind (God) wins once again, & the game continues. But someday it will end.

END

[At this point, PKD created a title page for the EXEGE-SIS as a whole, as set forth on page 58.]

---

* PKD footnote here reads: "See separate envelope notes dated 12/10/80 p 10 *passim.*" Pages 1 through 4 of these notes are excerpted in the next selection (pp. 59-62) in this chapter.

3/20/74
12-2-80

Philip K. Dick
408 E Civic Center #301
Santa Ana, Calif 92701

THE DIALECTIC:
God against Satan, & God's
Final Victory foretold & shown

Philip K. Dick

AN EXEGESIS

Apologia pro mea vita

Footnote.

My flight expressed by the phosphene graphics was a movement faster & faster through cosmogenic-entropic time, ending in exhaustion & then the enantiodromia of entropic time—which had reached infinite velocity & infinite fragmentation ("splitting") —which is to say the dialectic into negentropic time or synthesis, reintegration: hence I saw Valis,[*] the universe pulled through infinity, inside out, to freeze; this was 3-74.

My exegesis was entropic-cosmogenic time *resuming*, speeding up faster & faster, "splitting" (fragmenting) farther & farther. Finally, it, too, ended in infinite velocity & infinite fragmentation (creativity, expressed as ever newer & quicker theories); it ended in exhaustion & then the enantiodromia of entropic time—the dialectic of my thoughts—into negentropic time & another reintegration (this was 11-17-80). Only this time I did not see Valis,[*] there was a *theophany*, & I was in the presence of God & God's loving-kindness; whereupon He explained everything to me. So events leading up to 3-74 & my experience with Valis had a parallel in the dialectic of my exegesis leading to 11-17-80 & the theophany of the Christian God of Love. The common ingredients of the two flights were: the cosmogenic-entropy "splitting" dialectic flight itself, until infinite velocity (time) & fragmentation (space) were reached, then exhaustion, then enantiodromia into negentropic time & "freeze" (reintegrational) of, so-to-speak "Prajāpati",[**] but then comes a totally different outcome:

---

[*] PKD foonote: "World, not God (as I had supposed)." This same note was referenced by PKD for each of the two indicated references to "Valis".
[**] Sanskrit for the "Lord of Creatures". Prajapati, as a demiurgic figure, is mentioned frequently in the RIG VEDA.

1) 3-74. Valis which is world properly seen (morpho-logical arrangement, growth & perfection & self comple-tion in negentropic time, the entropic—flux—universe pulled through infinity—i.e. inside out). Compared to:

2) 11-17-80. The Christian God in theophany, who is *other* than world, who is transcendent. What I *thought* I had seen in 3-74:

The summation (combining) of the two is (1) an acute knowledge of world based on 3-74 & the exege-sis arising out of that experience. (2) Direct knowledge of God & God's nature based on the above elements; so that 3-74 led to the exegesis, which although it was a loss of negentropic, integrative time & a resumption of cosmogenic-entropic time, did lead (due to the infi-nite speeding up of time & the infinite breaking down of space until exhaustion set in) to the theophany I had supposed I had already had.

Now it is possible to see how the Mary Jane[*] fitted in; it added the final push to the dialectic in me, my exe-gesis (in other words, as preceded 3-74, my thinking) so that it reached infinite speed & infinite space, exhaus-ted itself; & again, as before, enantiodromia set in. This enantiodromia did not have to do with world, however, but had to do with the human intellect striving to find God—futilely. (Futilely until the last great enantiodro-mia occurred & God took the field to block the dialectic of my thinking himself, & thus revealed himself.

So there is a striking parallel—a logical, structural parallel—between 3-74 & 11-17-80, but in another, more profound respect the two are mirror opposites—since the first is a vision of world (which I thought was God, yet it was not, & so it yielded no knowledge directly about God, but only inferential knowledge

---

[*] The reference here is to marijuana. PKD had smoked some on 11-17-80.

that he existed & *that* he had saved me—in *pronoia* [*foreknowledge*]) & the second is a genuine theophany. When one realizes that world & God are wholly other to each other (Satan rules world) then this mirror—opposite situation can be appreciated. Let me add, too, that total revelation about world does not yield knowledge of God. God entered when I became aware that my theorizing was carrying me into an infinite regress, which is to say, when I became exhausted—at which point enantiodromia occurred; intellect had proven futile & yet, paradoxically, it had led to God—but due to God's volitional initiative. His (as I call it) taking the field, which is an inbreaking by the divine.

The circumstances under which the theophany occurred (I gave up on the exegesis & kicked back & massively turned on) are not capricious causes but follow the logic of the dialectic along several axes.

This shows the hauntingly eerie paradoxical (almost seemingly whimsical or playful) nature of enlightenment: it comes to you only when you cease to pursue it. When you totally & finally give up.

Another way of putting this is to say that the answer lies in the least likely place, where you are least likely to look. This is what gave rise to Zen. Yet, emerging from this maze of paradox & mirror opposites, of seeming, of infinite change, here, finally, is the answer I sought, the goal I sought. & it is where I started from back in high school in my physics final when I prayed to God, the Christian God—who was always there, leading me to him.*

---

* In high school, while taking a physics test, PKD became anxious and forgot the key principle behind displacement of water, on which eight of the ten test questions were based. When the exam period was nearly over, PKD began to pray. Then, an inner voice stated the principle simply—and PKD finished the test and earned an A. The episode remained in his memory his entire life.

My guess in "VR"[*]—that it was YHWH, was correct. But it wasn't a guess; it was what the AI voice told me. Always, faintly & distantly but clearly, the AI voice pointed the way to the truth. It knew the answer from the beginning, & spoke in the spirit of God (*Ruah*).[**] Through it I figured out that Valis was not God but reality *perturbed* by God. I knew, then, that I had not found God after all. My great discovery, then, was not in knowing what I had found, but facing the fact of what I had *not* found—the very thing I was searching for.

Ironies abound. But the playfulness ended in infinity, exhaustion & the great reversal. The God was reached, & the journey did not begin in 1974. It began in high school during that physics test when I first heard the AI voice. *35 years!*   *(December 1980)*

---

[*]   VALIS REGAINED, PKD's original title for THE DIVINE INVASION (1981).
[**] *Ruah* is the Hebrew term for "spirit"; it also means "breath". In kabbalistic tradition, it is the intermediary spiritual state between direct awareness of the godhead and the animal soul.

CHAPTER TWO

THEORETICAL EXPLORATIONS

In UBIK the forward moving force of time (or time-force expressed as an ergic field) has ceased. All changes result from that. Forms regress. The substrate is revealed. Cooling (entropy) is allowed to set in unimpeded. Equilibrium is affected by the vanishing of the forward-moving time force-field. The bare bones, so to speak, of the world, our world, are revealed. We see the *Logos* addressing the many living entities. Assisting and advising them. We are now aware of the *Atman* everywhere. The press of time on everything, having been abolished, reveals many elements underlying our phenomena.

If time stops, this is what takes place, these changes.

Not frozen-ness, but revelation.

There are still the retrograde forces remaining, at work. And also underlying positive forces other than time. The disappearance of the force-field we call time reveals both good and bad things; which is to say, coaching entities (Runciter, who is the *Logos*),

63

the *Atman* (Ubik), Ella;[*] it isn't a static world, but it begins to *cool*. What is missing is a form of heat: the *Aton*.[**] The *Logos* (Runciter) can tell you *what* to do, but you lack the energy—heat, force—to do it. (i.e., time.)

The *Logos* is not a retrograde energetic life form, but the Holy Spirit, the *Parakletos*, is. If the *Logos* is outside time, imprinting, then the Holy Spirit stands at the right or far or completed end of time, toward which the field-flow moves (the time flow). It receives time: the negative terminal, so to speak. Related to the *Logos* in terms of embodying world-directives and world-organizing powers, but at a very weak level, it can progressively to a greater degree overcome the time field and flow back against it, into it, impinging and penetrating. It moves in the opposite direction. It is the anti-time. So it is correct to distinguish it from the *Logos,* which so to speak reaches down into the time flow from outside, from eternity or the real universe. The H.S.[***] *is* in time, and is moving: retrograde. Like tachyons,[****] its motion is a temporal one; opposite to ours and the normal direction of universal causal motion.

Equilibrium is achieved by the *Logos* operating in three directions: from behind us as causal—time—pressure, from above, then the final form, the very weak H.S. drawing toward perfection each form. But now equilibrium as we know it is being lost in favor of a growing ratio of the retrograde teleology. This implies we are entering, have entered, a unique

---

[*]   Glen and Ella Runciter are characters in UBIK (1969).
[**] Sun god of the ancient Egyptians.
[***] Holy Spirit.
[****]Physicists pose the theoretical existence of tachyons—particles that move faster than light in retrgrograde time.

time: nearing completion of the manifold forms. Last
pieces are going into place in the over-all pattern.
The task or mode of the H.S. is *completing*. Not beginning, not renewing or maintaining, but bringing to
the end, to the close. An analogy would be the transit
of a vehicle from one planet to another; first stage is
the gravity of planet of origin; then equilibrium of
both planets in terms of their pull; then the growing
pull of the destination gravity-field as it gradually
takes over and completes the journey. Beginning,
middle, end. At last one senses the receiving field
engage, and then correct.

   When I wrote UBIK I constructed a world (universe) which differed from ours in only one respect:
it lacked the driving force forward of time. That
time, in our own actual universe, could weaken, or
even go entirely away, did not occur to me because
at that point I did not conceive time as a force at all
[...] I thought of it in Kantian terms. As a mode of
subjective perception. Now I believe that time, at this
point in the expansion of the universe (or for some
other reason(s)) has in fact actually begun to weaken,
at least in relation to certain other fields. Therefore,
this being true, a measure of the UBIK-experience
could be anticipated. I have indeed had that experience, or a measure thereof. That is, time still drives
on, but counter forces have surfaced and impinge,
laying bare the UBIK landscape—only for a few
moments, that is temporarily. Then time resumes its
sovereignty.

   What one would expect is two-fold: (one) Material
(e.g., information, images, weak energy fields, etc.)
from the future leaking or bleeding back to us, while
we continue on. (two) Abrupt lurches back on our part
to recent time periods, like a needle on a record being
anti-skated back to a prior groove, which it has

already played, and then playing on from there as if
nothing happened. The latter we would not be consciously aware of, although subcortical responses, and
perhaps vague sense of amnesia, dreams, etc., would
tell us that something was "wrong." But the leakage
back to us from the future, not by us but *to* us, that we
would be aware of (calling it esp, etc.), and yet be
unable to account for it.

But what is most telling is that in March, at the initial height of the "Holy Other" pouring into me, when I
saw the universe as it is, I saw as the active agent, a gold
and red illuminated-letter like plasmatic entity *from the
future*, arranging bits and pieces here: arranging what
time drove forward. Later I concluded that I had seen
the *Logos*. What is important is that this was perceptual
to me, not an intellectual inference or thought about
what might exist. It came here from the future. It was/is
alive. It had a certain small power or energy, and great
wisdom (sic). It was/is holy. It not only was visible
around me but evidently this is the same energy which
entered me. It was both inside and out. So the *Logos*, or
whatever it was, this plasmatic life form from the
future which I saw, satisfies, as near as I can fathom,
most of the theoretical criteria above.

Also, the official Catholic/Christian theories about
the Holy Spirit so depict it: moving backward from
the end of time, pouring into people. But if the Holy
Spirit can only enter one, is only inside, then what I
saw that was gold and red outside, like liquid fire,
wasn't the H.S. but the Logos. I think it's all the same
thing, one found inner, one found outer. What difference does it make? It's only a semantic quarrel; what's
important is that it comes BACK HERE FROM THE
FUTURE, is electrostatic and alive, but a weak field. It
must be a form similar to radiation ...

However, that which caused me to see differently

and to be different must be distinguished from what I saw and became. A bio-plasmatic orgone-like energy entered me or rose up in me and caused changes in me; that is one enormous miracle ... but the heightened awareness caused me to see a different universe: one which contained the red and gold living threads of activity in the outside world, a world enormously changed, very much like the world of UBIK. But I feel a unity between the force which changed me and the red and gold energy which I saw. From within me, as part of me, it looked out and saw itself.   *(1974)*

My whole God is identified with a vitalizing (or revitalizing) life-giving principle, like the orgone, like springtime ... and the adversary (e.g. Marxism) is envisioned as mechanical, hollow-eyed, without life. God is a vitalistic force, like Drietsch's [*reference uncertain*] entelechy, etc. This is like my division between the Human and the Android. With God, in the form of Christ, as the exemplar Human. The complete human.

This beats the Greek idea of God as Mind which does nothing but think. Or know. How is it to know, if there is nothing to know? I conceive of it as a builder, an artificer, who creates, in conformity to its Plan: the *Logos* (I conceive of *Logos* as blueprint of something to be actualized). The Greek prejudice against the manual arts/the mere crafts prevented them from seeing this quality of God.

He is both building and He is perfecting what He has already built. He animates it, infuses it.

Ursula* accuses me of getting away from "Taoistic

---

* Ursula Le Guin, the science fiction writer. She and PKD were in correspondence at this time.

balance" when I get into Christianity. The *Logos* and balance (cf. Fr. 51 of Heraclitus*) are intimately connected, with the *Logos* implementing balance of harmony everywhere, it being the Plan. It is hard to imagine the *Logos* out of balance. Also, when conditions on our world were out of balance, it was the *Logos* which brought what we experienced as relief, but which, on a supraterrestrial scale, was probably a restitution of *harmonie*. Also, there is my "Rhipidon"** fan dream of the left-right—with the center as God's balanced perfection in any situation (and the material in "Decoded"*** about Satan as the unreal to left and to right[)].

I was reading about the analogy of the *kosmoi***** to animals (each to an animal), which in its latter stages ran down or got old, like an animal, and formed cycles, and suddenly it came to me how like the Hindu idea this is, the idea of cycles, and it seemed to me for sure that this is what has happened, rather than a mere pushing-forward too much of one of the opposites (to create, in Anaximander's sense, injustice) but the true end of a running-down, wearing-out cycle. What happens then is perhaps a revitalization of the high-entropic kosmos (what must be realized is that the kosmos is smaller than the universe, or anyhow that the Unbounded lies outside it and imparts laws to it). The Second Advent or God's Intervention, the proph-

---

*   Fragment 51 of Heraclitus, in the translation by Edward Hussey favored by PKD, reads: "They do not understand how what is at variance is in agreement with itself: a back-turning structure (*palintropos harmoni*) like that of the bow and of the lyre."
**   See Glossary.
*** THE DECODED NEW TESTAMENT. See note on page 23.
****Plural of *kosmos*. Hussey (see subsequent note) discusses, in chapter two of THE PRESOCRATICS (1972), the analogy—perceived by both Presocratic and Hindu thinkers—between the creation of a *kosmos* and animal reproduction.

ecy, is more accurately the running down or wearing out of our *kosmos*, and the revitalization. Here is the biological model, rather than the mechanical model (*vide* Hussey[*]). The egg: reborn, et al. Biological models. Orphic. What repels me about Marxism is its mechanistic quality. I get the impression that some of the very early Greeks believed that when the *kosmos* has run down sufficiently, the Unbounded (i.e., the deity) had of necessity to revitalize it, or whatever he did; we are all governed by law of some kind; it wasn't by whim. [...] My idea the other night was: suppose the universe were entirely emptied of all matter, in every form. So it was just empty space. Nothing, then, would exist. Right? Wrong. All the laws, which now govern matter, which govern energy as well, would obtain, although we couldn't discern them. It seems to me that if we don't assume an Unbounded (as so represented by the pressure of these necessities on matter and energy) we are just describing, we are saying, "Things do what they do because they do it." A tautology. An observation of regularity, not an analysis of why. You could approach it another way if desired: either the universe does not run down (but the laws of thermodynamics show that it does), or it ends; or it periodically is renewed. To say that it renews itself poses certain problems; I find it easier to imagine it renewed from without, although that poses certain problems too. But if the universe is everything, then it begins to run down (like a clock, like an animal) and then suddenly it revitalizes itself (as I experienced). I am equating the Second Advent & God

---

[*]   Edward Hussey, Oxford scholar and author of THE PRESOCRATICS (1972), a work cited in chapter four of VALIS (1981). As to PKD's reference here, see chapter two of Hussey's book.

breaking his silence with this turn of the cycle, this springtime, this revitalization. I think this is what has happened. A revitalizing is going on and it certainly comes *here* from elsewhere. Where that "elsewhere" is, I don't know, but I've experienced a real, alive, thinking force.

One of the best points in Hussey's book is where he says that one of the ancient Greeks (Anaximander, maybe) assigns to the deity this primary function or activity or attribute or quality or definition: that he gives life, and movement (which I see as the same). Therefore we would experience the return of God, this revitalization, as exactly what the word implies: a renewal of life.

I note that Parmenides' Form I is equated, by him, with light! This is exciting, since as I understand Parmenides, he saw Form II as a mere mirror reflection, and urged a monism on us (the fiery or dry soul) which made us relate only to Form I, or to light.

The Orphic egg. If the universe is born from something for which the egg is a paradigm, then maybe, as the individual is, then both are reborn from something like an egg—a light egg. Maybe this was the esoteric teachings of the Orphic: rebirth. Rejuvination (eternal life).

(1975)

—A searingly important realization:

The view (revelation) that a wise, benign, powerful true God from "outside" has invaded our *spurious* reality & is transforming it ontologically into the good and real—this is [a] fundamental Gnostic view: the bad or stupid demiurge constructs a "counterfeit" reality that "couldn't come to (full) life, & the real, distant "stranger" God took pity re all this & entered this counterfeit creation—as Christ—to begin his task of transmuting (saving) this whole cosmos.

My writing is dead-on Gnosticism—to view our world as spurious. My 3-74 experience added the further Gnostic gnosis of the penetration (Zebra) by the *true* God (what I saw as zebra's modulating processes & his mimickry). In other words, my writing presents one part of the Gnostic world view, entering over into the completing of the vision by the 3-74 revelation. I deduced the first premise & then by divine revelation received confirmation of the completing part.

The Gnostic reproach about our world is not just that it is evil but spurious: imperfect, as a mere copy of the true pleroma.

I couldn't get any more Gnostic, once I saw Zebra as invading & mimicking as he modulates, if I tried.

With the (vision of the) entrance into our spurious world of a transmuting benign deity (Zebra) my Gnostic cosmology is complete. But already, *before* my vision in 2 or 3/74, I had written about it; I mean UBIK. I need not get Zebra & his transubstantiating activity down on paper to have succeeded in writing out the full picture. It's there, in those 3 or 4 novels.* The collective totality of the message in those 3 or 4 novels (or 5, if TEARS is included) as absolutely & indubitably Gnosticism—which I knew nothing about, when I wrote them. *(1977)*

If there is, as the Gnostics believe, a blind (or irrational) creator deity, Valis—who is rational—is at war with it, & has invaded its universe. Valis is the in-breaking of

---

* It is not entirely clear which novels PKD is referring to here. UBIK (1969) and FLOW MY TEARS, THE POLICEMAN SAID (1974) are certainly among them, as is stated in this selection. For other likely candidates, see the selections in chapter four herein.

negentropy into disorder (entropy). It picks up every card the deranged creator lays down in this dialectical game. Valis is a local *krasis* [*due mixture of component forces*], & once begun, *is expanding relentlessly*, consuming & subsuming everything around it. It is flexible, growing, diverse & complex; whereas the BIP is dead & rigid & monotonous & simple.   *(1978)*

Definition of what I experienced in 3-74:
ZEBRA (VALIS): "a vortex of intelligence extending as a supra-temporal field, involving humans but not limited to them, drawing objects & processes into a coherency which it arranges into information. A FLUX of purposeful arrangement of living information, both human & extra-human, tending to grow & incorporate its environment as a unitary complex of subsumations."

"It can selectively present certain info to us from which we create a hypostasis, & it can change that info or even withdraw it thus it can make any hypostasis (on our parts) as valid or invalid as it wishes." Hypnagogic realization. "Our reality is a hologram because it is a re-creation reconstituted from info by Valis' perfect memory."   *(1978)*

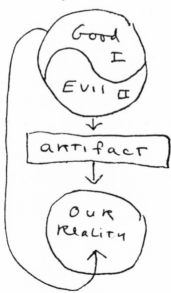

Here is a modified, more precise model. The *Urgrund* [*primal basis of reality*] contains the yang-yin complementary bipolarities within it. It wishes to separate its opposites, & does this by projecting the artifact, the creator of our reality (world); this is YHWH. This is what Mani & the Gnostics correctly saw 1) about the nature of the creator; & 2) the nature of our world. They also saw the salvific stranger God "outwitting the archons" & penetrating our "copy of a copy" world to extricate us. According to this model the Good (Form I) which we experience is a sort of invader, unable to coerce or compel the frozen BIP template, but on the other hand, the Good (Form I) is real in a sense that Form II—which is a copy of a copy—is not. Thus we can call the template projected ceaselessly by the artifact dead or counterfeit, & Form I (Zebra) the authentic (Good, Form I), & thus agree with Parmenides.

To repeat: Form I, which represents not only God or Christ or St. Sophia, is found at the outskirts or trash or bottom level of this world, as far from the imperial *omphalos* [*navel; center*] of power as possible. This would adequately account for the way Jesus appeared at the First Advent. But the Second Advent (actually the remaining section of the First) will consist of a direct & successful attack on the inner fortress of imperial power itself ... But, put another way, this has always already happened if we are to accept the formulation of Parmenides in denying actuality to Form II & calling it only *seeming* (i.e., *Dokos* veil or counterfeit). There is something spurious about it, however real it may seem. It is a copy of a copy, whereas Form I is, in contrast, authentic. My set ground experience bears this out. Set was alive; ground was mere sarx. In a sense, time has devoured Form II; it died somewhere along the line & leaves the line & leaves only an imprint of an empty shape. *It* is a hologram, but Form I *is not* a hologram or mere projected image. So the McKenna [*reference uncertain**] is only partially right; in a sense our universe is a hologram, but Zebra (Form I, *noös*) is not. But Zebra is not *part* of our universe; it is an *invader* into it—which was my great insight 15 months ago. Authentic reality has breached through into our world—which signifies that the end times have come (maybe long ago) but the irreal, the hologram, effaces it from our perception. The true great revelation (Gnosis) is precisely this: that Zebra (Form I, the *Urgrund*) *has come already.* Invisibly, since I saw Zebra outside me, it cannot be the Holy Spirit. It is God (or Christ).

The book which Doris** has on the Gospel of John: "They will no longer see Christ externally, but he will indwell within them as the Holy Spirit." But Zebra was both *in* me & visible externally. Ergo, it is not the Holy Spirit. Ergo, the *Urgrund* has irrupted into our mock world to do battle with Form II the BIP template.

The "St. Sophia" revelation may be the decisive clue to whether Zebra is Christ or God. Christ incarnates; God does not. Could be the "Cosmic Christ."

—

I just realized: my "*ajna*[*third*]-eyed" humanoid fit in with Robert Anton Wilson's notion about Sirius*** (with Earth the heart chakra & Sirius the *ajna* chakra). Coincidence? & he was in touch at roughly the same time, with them. 2 points of overlap.　　　*(1978)*

---

*　　See "Afterword" page 255
**　Doris Sauter, a close friend of PKD during the last decade of his life. The book referenced here is unknown.
***See Robert Anton Wilson, COSMIC TRIGGER: THE FINAL SECRET OF THE ILLUMINATI (1977).

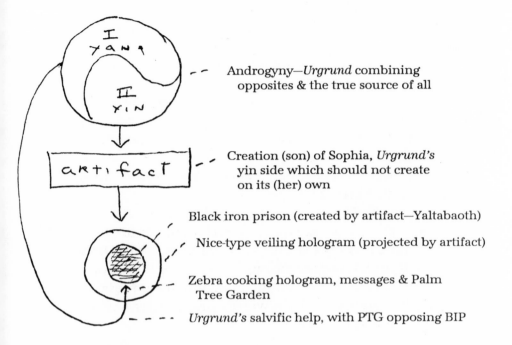

I
YANG

II
YIN

arti fact

Androgyny—*Urgrund* combining
opposites & the true source of all

Creation (son) of Sophia, *Urgrund's*
yin side which should not create
on its (her) own

Black iron prison (created by artifact—Yaltabaoth)

Nice-type veiling hologram (projected by artifact)

Zebra cooking hologram, messages & Palm
Tree Garden

Urgrund's salvific help, with PTG opposing BIP

[PKD diagram of his Two-Source Cosmology (1978).]

[. ...]

STIGMATA portrays the arrogant one, the blind
God (i.e., the artifact), which supposes itself to be the
one true God & evil delusional worlds are shown:
counterfeit worlds.

MAZE shows our *real* condition (as dreadful: a
static metal prison) covered by a nice delusional veil.
MAZE also depicts a redeemer.

UBIK unscrambles the salvific messages of Zebra &
alludes to Zebra itself, & stigmatizes the world without UBIK as decaying backward in time. UBIK mani-
fests itself initially at a cheap, trash level, but in the
end discloses its true nature as the *Logos*.

TEARS depicts the Black Iron Prison, & recounts
how a servant of it escapes & how (i.e., Felix Buckman
who is, at the all night gas station, converted to xtian-

ity—an exact reversal of the scene in *Acts* where it is the black man who is converted-baptized).

In MITHC Tagomi, like Buckman, manages to escape the BIP: in Mr. Tagomi's case it is the exact necessary act: one of *disobedience* (to the invisible artifact "God").

JOINT depicts a deliberately Fake world, designed to occlude one.

EYE depicts Fake (private) world's masquerading as Real, one after another.

When VALIS is finished, the mimicking salvific organism will be shown, & the BIP beneath the hologram (i.e., it will be shown that the date is 70 AD, the place Rome, which combines JOINT & UBIK, sort of. The hologram & the looking at it, & helpful messages, will be shown; also the reward world for the heroic deed(s) done, the PTG.)   *(1978)*

By the very nature it is deus absconditus [hidden god], *but hidden close by ("Break a stick & there is Jesus.").* * One can reread and reinterpret all scripture from the vantage point of this understanding. Many puzzling aspects can herewith be newly comprehended—why no natural theology has ever been successful— why our knowledge of God must always be a *revealed* knowledge. "The workman is invisible within the workshop." Immanent & gentle—one might say tenderly, "the shy God." What more is there to say of Him." I saw him this way in the *Iknoton* ** dream—the shy God—*Ach. Was hab ich gesehn.* [*What have I seen.*] In that one dream of the shy architect with claws, hiding

---

*   Russian Orthodox saying.
**   Iknoton—also transcribed Ikhnaton and Akhenaten—was the Egyptian pharaoh (reign: 1373-1357 B.C.) who introduced into polytheistic Egypt the heretical monotheistic cult of the Sun.

behind the buildings. When I saw Him then, that was when I guessed. I had seen him at last, & I did know— I did understand.

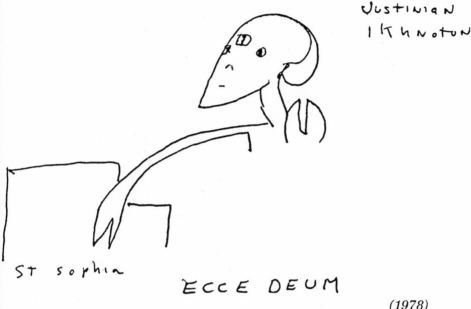

Justinian
Ikhnoton

St sophia

ECCE DEUM

(1978)

K.W. has noted a resemblance between several things I've described & what [*William*] Burroughs has written—e.g., my conviction that as a race or even planet we are "sick," i.e., occluded perceptually, & that a divine doctor-entity is restoring us.

Coincidence? Burroughs speaks[*] of a virus—a word become a neural-cell virus, infecting us.

After reading Burroughs, I dipped into UBIK. It certainly would be easy—& reasonable—for a reader to think that both Burroughs and I know something, & we want our novels to be taken as at least partly true. They have a strange ring of (revealed) truth about

---

[*] See, for example, the William Burroughs novel NOVA EXPRESS (1964).

them—I feel it about his book, about mine—Is, as Katherine Kurtz says[*], something writing *through* us?

Isn't Palmer Eldritch a kind of parasite, replicating himself or itself using humans as hosts? But my sense about Thomas was of a benign, not evil, intrusion. Still, it was an intrusion into my psyche, a taking over. Are such intrusions always to be deplored?

Or was I beguiled? Didn't it—he—get me out of trouble?

There is just no doubt of it: such passages in Burroughs' novel as the "Do it—do it—neck" message within another message—words that weren't originally there but are like the inner trigrams of an I Ching hex. That is one absolute "triangulate" element with 1) UBIK & 2) what I saw in 3-74, plus the parasite criminals & nova cops, & the infecting virus.

Burroughs' novel ↔ 3-74 ↔ UBIK

Burroughs' novel is related to UBIK & STIGMATA via the 3-74 experience.   *(1978)*

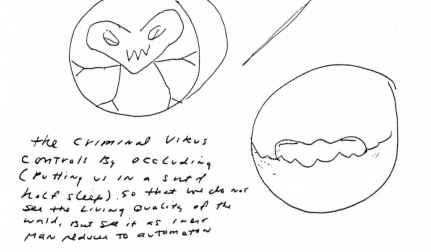

the criminal virus
controls by occluding
(putting us in a sort of
half sleep), so that we do not
see the living quality of the
world, but see it as inert
Man reduced to automation

The criminal virus* controls by occluding (putting us in a sort of half sleep) so that we do not see the living quality of the world, but see it as inert. Man reduced to automaton. The occlusion is self-perpetuating; it makes us unaware of it & of our keepers (& helpers, too). So restoration doesn't consist of enhancing but lifting (away & off).

If there is to be immortality, there must be another kind of time: one in which past events (i.e., the past in its entirety) can be retrieved—i.e., brought back. I did experience such a time.

   i.e., *immortality is possible.*   *(1978)*

Zebra is the supreme deity & savior-messenger UBIK/Runciter. It is Simon Magus in his true form: the great plasmate, whose existence, activity in history & presence is totally unsuspected & unknown to us— unless he is in us—only Zebra can see Zebra. He entered me at my birth or in my childhood. I am a homoplasmate: Zebra acting in syzygy with a human. My writing is the purpose of this syzygy. I restore Gnostic Gnosis to the world in a trashy form, like in UBIK.   *(1978)*

Something ("Y") is recognized as its own antithesis ("$\overline{Y}$"). This sounds like Zen or Taoist thinking. But this is oxymoron thinking. ("A thing is either A or $\overline{A}$" what could be more obvious? How can A = $\overline{A}$? There is no such category of thought; literally, it cannot be *thought;* it can be recognized about reality, however, as I did in 3-20-74).

---

* PKD's concept of the occluding "criminal virus", here examined, was influenced by the related idea, put forth by William Burroughs, that language is an extraterrestrial virus that has inhibited the development of humankind. See previous EXEGESIS selection.

$A = \overline{A}$ is not a statement about Logic, *but an observation about reality*; it is pragmatic. But it reveals that thinking cannot act as an inner analog to the outer world; for the mind to mirror world correctly *it must cease to think*, i.e., to be & do what instead? The total organism acts with no-thought. It becomes a non-thinking response machine (in the good sense). To know what, by definition, you cannot know—there it is again; I knew & did not know; there it is *again*.

Some higher Non-Self Self was involved, &, in solving the problem, as an offshoot I passed over into Paradise.   *(1978)*

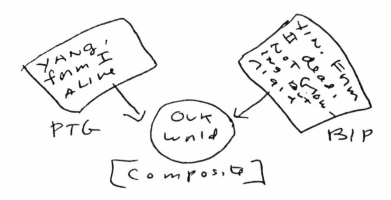

It can be said that the yin part "hatched" too soon, before the yang one, & is defective (crazy, like James-James). It seized the initiative. But put another way, it can be said the God-as-yang allowed (in some sense that we can't comprehend) this to happen. Ultimately a better final world (cosmos) can be built making use of yin, the dark power; i.e., if yin comes first, if it revolts, if becomes the substrate for yang—which has the last move. Yang (as was revealed to me in 3-74) let the blind adversary make the first move, & built on that for his purposes. If yin has the *first* move, yang

has the *last*. This conforms to *Timaeus*,* in which *noös*
comes upon *ananke*, & begins to persuade it (i.e.,
arrange chaos into cosmos).

Thus Form II is the initial stage, & Form I the evolutionary jump.

The God of the O.T. is God—not as just yin—but
God showing *both* his sides, as if they are not yet *differ-
entiated*, & thus pitted against the yin—*as the O.T. God
is not* so pitted. The O.T. God oscillates; the N.T. God
has stabilized, thrust the yin parts into an earlier
Form (II) & is now a Form I God. The O.T. God creates
& destroys, which the latter is alien to the N.T. God.

(1978)

My life has divided this way:

Survival | Cultural | Spiritual | Post Mortem
(resurrected as of 3-74)

What I experienced in 3-74 was death (literally) & resurrection as an immortal being. Obviously I—my
body—can physically die, but that is not the issue; the
issue has to do with the divine spark in me which
awoke from ignorance (forgetfulness) & remembered—
inc. its origins. Thus I returned to God & entered the
Kingdom.[...]   *(1978)*

In schizophrenia the synchronization of inner &
outer tapes fails to such a degree that *Bedeutung*
[meaning] is impaired; data which are not for the person are engrained in, & the inner tape projects phan-
tom people, voices & things into a vacuum (so my
system offers a new concept of the origin & nature of
psychosis): there is literally nothing out there corresponding to the contents of the inner tape! In fact,

---

*   Dialogue by Plato.

schizophrenia could be considered evidence for my
system; it is an instance of the malfunction of that system, & with my system in mind, can be readily understood (in MARTIAN TIME-SLIP I saw it as a breakdown of
proper time functioning, which was close). Also,
schizophrenia, besides displaying the auto-generated
mental contents projected not onto outer analogs but
into a void, explains the "nothing new came into his
mind one day" aspect; the schizophrenic can be
defined as a percipient who has lost the willingness or
ability to receive the information fired at him by
Zebra (as external world). Thus he has his inner tape
world & no outer programming a dreadful situation—
but obviously in a certain number of cases the inner-
outer synch would fail. The schizophrenic is isolated
with nothing but his individual inner tape, which
degenerates upon ceasing to receive the vital disinhibiting external signals, it becomes stuck, &, for
him, time ceases to flow & growth stops, because he is
cut off from change.

Paranoia is a projection of pattern instead of a
reception of pattern. It is an overmastery by self, again
a failure to be receptive. Outer world must be trust-
ingly received, since it is God himself.   *(1978)*

TEARS shows I had vestigal memories *before* 3-74
when they (& the alternate personality of the world
broke through). But, as always, what I know is far less
than what I *don't* know, & even what I do know is
shaky. The mystery only deepens. Where (or when) is
(or was) the Black Iron World? I was there but am
here now. How came I here? Did that world go out of
existence? Did this one replace it? Is this world somehow irreal. Maybe stretched like a skin over (& con-

cealing) the other? In which case can the Black Iron World come back?

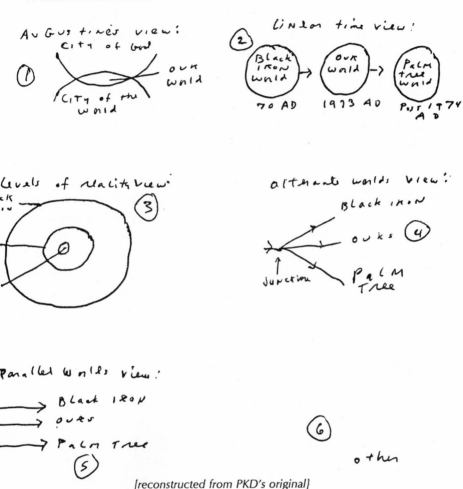

[reconstructed from PKD's original]

(1978)

The creator can afford to descend into his own creation. He can afford to shed his memories (of his identity) and his supernatural powers. Then he can test his own creation. But he cannot afford to get stuck in it. The creator deliberately plants clues in his irreal creation—clues which he cunningly knows in time (eventually) will restore his memory (anamnesis) of who he is, and his powers as well; he will then know that his creation is irreal and has imprisoned him in it, thus freeing himself and restoring himself to Godhood.

So he has a fail-safe system built in. No chance he won't eventually remember. Makes himself subject to spurious space, time and world (and death, pain, loss, decay, etc.), but has these disinhibiting clues or stimuli distributed deliberately strategically in time and space. So it is he himself who sends himself the letter which restores his memory (Legend of the Pearl). No fool he!

This is perfectly epitomized in the UBIK commercials; he can exist at any trashy layer—sincerely—he wants to be, in any trashy form. But in the end he remembers (as witness the ad over the final chapter of UBIK). Purpose? This way he can permeate his creation with the divine, at all levels, and sincerely (i.e., without even him knowing, while he's doing it!)

Zebra equals Christ. Christ equals God. Thomas equals Zebra. I equal Thomas. (For equals read is.) Thus I equal God.

But I've forgotten again. Oh well—I wrote it all down, heh-heh. Knowing I'd again forget. I was invaded (theolepsy) by Christ, all right. But as I say supra, it was I who remembered being Thomas or Christ and living back in Rome c. A.D. 45. So, like in "Imposter," I am—

I love it. It's delightful. It's a dance. Brahman dancing with joy. (Felix.) And so was Pinky;* he knew and remembered, too.

Christ (the Creator) is among us, disguised. Even

---

* PKD's cat.

He has forgotten. He could be any person, any animal. We do not know; He does not know. But eventually He will remember; He has set clues in his own path to trigger off his true memory and powers. Then we will find ourselves judged for the way we treated Him, as told in the N.T. He who was our victim, our object, will be our judge.

In 3-74 I sat down on the judgment seat, when I remembered.

And what about those who set the trap for me in 3-74, the trap that went back to the raid on my house on 11/17/71?* Beware when you set out a trap; you may trap Dionysos, the patron God of small trapped animals.   *(1978)*

Kerygma understood as of October 18, 1978:

In STIGMATA, UBIK and MAZE they are in an irreal world (Lem's paradigm). It is stipulated in STIGMATA that no time passes, and this is implicit in MAZE (and could be true in UBIK). In TEARS the *actual* world is shown, the world of *Acts*, Rome C. A.D. 45. In SCANNER the *cause* of our being unable to reality-test is shown to be a percept-system toxicity or damage, anyhow an inner occlusion deliberately induced by a drug or drug-like substance (which collates with the master magician in STIGMATA administering a drug to people which puts them forever in his irreal world where no time passes—a world they can't tell isn't real). (In MAZE two additional points are made: (1) false memories;

---

* On 17 November 1971, PKD's rented house in San Rafael, California, was broken into and various of his files were stolen or destroyed. The incident frightened him. PKD often theorized as to the identity of the intruders—the suspects ranged from the FBI to drug dealers to the local police, to name a few—but he never solved the mystery.

and (2) negative hallucinations on a mass basis; rather than experiencing what is real, something which is actually there is not experienced.) Thus in those five novels virtually the complete story is shown, especially if one can determine from internal evidence that the world of actuality presented in TEARS is the time and place of *Acts*. The nature of the entity which seeks to rescue us is given in UBIK, and is called—by itself—"the Word," i.e., Christ or the *Logos*. It is breaking through "from the other side," one way, uncannily manifesting itself in ways not syntonic to the false world they imagine they're living in. This very experience precisely happened to me in 2- 3/74, indicating that all five novels are literally true (I experienced the world of TEARS or more accurately the world of *Acts*). I assumed that the purpose of my writing is to acquaint *us* with our situation, that my novels and stories function like the inbreaking messages in UBIK (such as the graffiti on the bathroom walls), but now I am given to understand that actually my writing is [a] report on the situation here outgoing—meant to leave our irreal world, to break out, not in, and acquaint the actual world (macrobrain) of our plight. They are then appeals for help, by a salvific entity which has invaded this our irreal world, an entity we can't perceive. It is the Paraclete, which has just now arrived for the first time, immediately following Christ's death and resurrection (it must be kept in mind that the real time is 45 A.D. and the real place is the Roman Empire). My writing is information traffic fed into the macrobrain, which continually processes such information. This information traffic between stations of the macrobrain is itself what we call "the *Logos*."

Despite the testimony of our (occluded) senses, the Parousia is close at hand, and will occur as promised during the lifetime of some of those of the first century A.D. We will experience this when the Paraclete abolishes the irreal world imposed on us, strips the master magician of his power over us, and reveals to us the true state of things, most especially the macrobrain (or God), which is a macroform of us the plural microforms.

There is some evidence that the master magician who has us lost in his irreal world where no actual time elapses (called Palmer Eldritch in STIGMATA) is Simon Magus, who lived at the time of *Acts*, which is to say *now*. Thus Simon is still alive, and the authentic original early Christian disciples are still alive.

(18 October 1978)

A revised (?) theory as to who-what Zebra is. Zebra is the microform physician sent into the lower realm (Form II) world to break "astral determinism," Form II's power. "Matter (Form II) is plastic in the face of mind (the microform of the upper realm invading this realm as our savior—champion—v. my tractate). Hence the healing "miracles" which Zebra displayed. (This retains my insight that Zebra is an *invader* here, which I consider to be the turning point of realization in my exegesis).

The tractate* identifies this healer (physician) invading Form II as Christ. Therefore Zebra is Christ.

His breaking "astral determinism" over an individ-

---

* *Tractates Cryptica Scriptura*, the "Appendix" to VALIS (1981). Note the distinction PKD draws between the "exegesis" (referenced in the previous paragraph) and the "tractate". See "Preface", pages xi–xii for further discussion.

ual (e.g. me) is a sort of localized slaying of Form II, the deterministic yin world.

This tells us (v. the tractate) that Christ *is* here—3-74 proves it. This indeed explains the "melting of causal trains" which I saw.

In a roundabout way I've proven that Zebra is indeed Christ (via the tractate).

This dovetails with St. Paul's doctrine about Christ versus the old law or "planetary powers" (angels). This is also the fourth gospel light versus dark contention which I refer to in the tractate (as put forth by Zoroaster and the Essenes). Victory, finally, is given by God to the light. And since, as Parmenides pointed out, Form II really doesn't exist, breaking astral determinism is in fact breaking the power of illusion—the lie—of an irreal world (cf. the acosmism in my writing). Thus the key salvific weapon is knowledge—to know and see the truth (versus *dokos/maya*). Christ (Zebra) coming here is the savior venturing into the domain of darkness to rescue us. So Zebra *is* Christ; and Zebra (Christ) is our savior, who does battle for us. Since causality ("astral determinism" or fate) operates in time, a (or the) method of salvation by the savior is to free us from time by converting time into space, and thus aborting causality. "Time can be overcome," and in this process a temporal rollback to the Origins (anamnesis) occurs. And time overcome means death and decay overcome.

By definition, the Holy Spirit is inside you ("Thomas"?). But I saw Zebra outside. Therefore I saw Christ.

I saw him *per spiritum sanctum* [*through the holy spirit*] (in me). "Christ has no body now but yours." He acted in and *through* me. He was in me.

There is a very strange statement in Wagner's

Parsifal: "Here time, my son, turns into space." What does this mean, especially when connected to the castle of the Knights of the Grail (they actually possess the Grail)? One can move back and forth through space. Parsifal says that he feels he has gone (moved) very far, and gets this statement in return; and the landscape melts and changes. And the Grail *calls* to a person, the right person; you cannot make your way to it on your own; it must actually seek you out, calling to you.

If the upper realm is determined by space, our participation in it probably emanates from our right hemispheres; if the lower realm is determined by time—which it is—we are confined to it by our left-hemisphere dominance. Thus God speaks to us by our right hemispheres. *(November 1978)*

"Jesus Christ" is a code name for this rational phylogenic ultra personality which can only be summoned by the passion & death of the ontogenic irrational self. The latter must be induced to die, through a series of ritual ordeals. &—which is essential—the stimulus for an anamnesis which disinhibits the former.

Then "Yalda Baoth"* is either a symbol for or a projection of the old original irrational self who thinks mistakenly that he is the only God—i.e. only self. But there is another one which is sane that he does not know exists, & which outwits him, entering consciousness (projected as or symbolized by the term "this prison world"). A great psychological dialectic battle between the two is fought in which the invading sane self due to its superior wisdom (rationality & intelli-

---

* The blind demiurge creator of our world, according to the Gnostics.

gence) wins. (If all goes well.) The sin of the old self—
this is an antique term denoting its impaired condition which Calvin describes: its madness (blindness).
Its occlusion.

The breaking of "astral determinism" or "burning
up karma" indicates I am on the right track, here.
They (these terms) refer to the deterministic fate of
the ossified original self, which is a sinister one:
decay, rigidity, spiritual—& even physical—death. The
original self is winding down. Unless replaced, the person is caught fast in the sum total of what he is: his
nature, which must be infringed on by a new self outside his self. *Ex nihilo* [*out of nothing*] new creation
must occur. The original self must be destroyed by a
living (breathing) "doomsday device"—the new self,
which although new is paradoxically very old. (Far
older than the original self.)   (1979)

So irreality & perturbation are the two perplexities
which confront us; irreality is departing, but the
changeover shows enigmatic traces or imprints which
do not belong, in particular of a parallel world phas-
ing in & out: this latter (plus the presence of the
macromind) is what is pointed to, but in a "nonsensi-
cal" baffling way.

To a very large degree *memory* no longer agrees
with reality.

I wonder if this sheds any light on schizophrenia.
Could the schizophrenic be given *conflicting* realities
or data about reality? His mind has to put together
constituents which simply do not fit. He is a casualty
of this revision process & cannot make sense out of it.
How is he to penetrate to the mystery—explanation—
underlying what he undergoes? If my cosmology is
correct, would you not anticipate such casualties? My

writing is a deliberate attempt to take these conflicting or disintegrating realities, & the experiences of
them, & seek some kind of ontological or metaphysical overview? So in a way I have battled against schizophrenia by seeking a philosophical framework which
will 1) accept as real these disrupted data; & 2)
account for them. 2-3-74, then can be viewed as the
catalytic triumph or payoff—i.e., the success—of
decades of observation & analysis & theorizing. I have
had to deal with deluding, irreal, conflicting, chaotic
& *Fremd* [*strange, discomforting*] material, & just plain
hung in there conceptually, taking the view that *some*
explanation must exist, although it would have to be
radical & far-reaching.

I actually had to develop a love of the disordered
& puzzling, viewing reality as a vast riddle to be joyfully tackled, not in fear but with tireless fascination.
What has been most needed is reality testing, & a willingness to face the possibility of self-negating experiences: i.e., real contradictions, with something being
both true & not true.

The enigma is alive, aware of us, & changing. It is
partly created by our own minds: we alter it by perceiving it, since we are not outside it. As our views
shift, it shifts in a sense it is not there at all (acosmism). In another sense it is a vast intelligence; in
another sense it is total *harmonia* and structure (how
logically can it be all three? Well, it is).   *(1979)*

Plundering the antecedent universe as stockpile &
"pretextual cause" are one & the same thing: involving choosing from the range of potential possibilities;
viz: actualizing the most desirable possibility in terms
of an envisioned goal (the God's teleological foresight). Apparently I was briefly joined to the God's

mind itself, & so understood not only *that* it operates (decides) but *how* it decides: on the basis *of* what & what for (goal).

1) Zoroaster: *a priori* foresight vs. obdurate opponent with only hindsight: the dialectic.

2) Aristotle: teleology—stimulating goal seeking—as primary function.

3) Spinoza: immanent, not transcendent; always working by, with & in natural law, rather than suspending it.

4) Avicenna: not seeing time as we do (hence orthogonal change).

5) Plato: persuasion rather than coercion; *noös* vs. *ananke* (v. #1).

6) Pythagoras: concept of *kosmos*.

7) Parmenides: Forms 1 & 2 with 2 only seeming (v. #1 & "the lie.")

8) the Mystery religions: power to break "astral determinism," which is the true basis of salvation & the action of #2.

9) Plotinus: union with God (also Sankara & Eckhart).

10) N.T.: Christ as surrogate for us in terms of bait taken by the hostile power. The Holy Spirit as aural prompting by the God, within each of us.

11) O.T. Elijah & *entheusiasmos* [*the Greek here literally: the in-taking of the god*]. (v. #9.)

12) Leibnitz: "Best of all possible worlds."

Now, in 3-74 the arranged antecedents were chosen from to the limit of their potentialities, but look at what had to be set up over a long period of time. This network of causes has always been an indication that Spinoza is correct (regarding miracles). Purpose (teleology) lies along the entire length of this process as witness FAITH [*PKD story "Faith of Our Fathers"*] & MITHC.

What I have to assume now is that the ursatz [*sic;
ersatz?*] which generated the material in the writing
was necessary that 3-74 could occur. By the looks of
this I gather that 3-74 was important above & beyond
the xerox missive as such. A reverse direction of
causal flow was disclosed to me, against all normal
(usual) perception.   *(1979)*

On the Journey of the Soul

Sequence:

(one) World as karma—i.e. prior thought formations of the person's mind, completely controlling the
person and impinging on him: a counterfeit or
inauthentic reality which holds the person in its
power as if his life were on tape: a playback of a
recording. He is programmed from within and without by these anterior contents of his own mind, forgotten, not recognized.

(two) Anamnesis. Brought on by the action of the
Holy Spirit. The person remembers his true identity
throughout all his lives. The person recognizes the
world for what it is: his own prior thought formations; this generates the *Blitz* or flash. He knows now
where he is.

(three) Christ is born in the person's mind and
takes control as a seeming adventitious psyche now
interiorized. Karma (the power of the prior thought
formations of the mind) is broken. Christ has defeated
these ossified thoughts and started up real time and
real world for the person; he is now in the *koinos
kosmos.*

(four) World now is experienced as mind of the person, as the total mind itself rather than its contents. The
mind is no longer the Son but the Creator, the Father;
hence world is as under mind's power as mind for-

merly was under world's; the positions of the two have reversed absolutely. Mind and world are also synchronized in time; world does not lag behind mind.

(five) The Godhead is experienced: the desert or void of non-being and bliss. The three persons of the Trinity are gone. Nothing remains. *World is abolished.* Time does not exist, only vast space.

(six) World returns, freed of the ossified power and presence of prior thought formations. The *Bardo Thödol* trip is over; the person has been born. Fate or astral determination or karma is overcome.

(seven) The Second Comforter is with the person unto the end, in syzygy with him as his divine sister/brother. This means that the birth was successful. A binary-brain mind now exists able to generate the infinite logic of the dialectic which underlies reality and gives rise to it (Plato's Forms); thus the role of Father is retained in the Logos sense: as images, concepts, words, thought, metareasoning. The person is not alone but has been assimilated by the divine in a relationship of parity. God has become man and as a result man has become God. The process is complete: the new Adam is here, and the old Adam, in bondage to his own prior thought formations, i.e., in a fallen state, has died. Thus the past has yielded to the future. Time is now free to flow from disorder to order, from the irrational to the rational. The present mind in the form of Christ has vanquished its antecedent self, as microcosm and as macrocosm mirroring each other. The result of this process is a net yield of added energy to the total system (expressed in units of time), which is the true goal; i.e., that the universe be perpetual and not run down. This is what is meant by repair of the original rupture or fall or crisis in the Godhead. The key term denoting all this is: salvation.

Note: The progression is from (1) former thought

contents of the mind as world to (2) present mind
itself as world to (3) disappearance of world entirely.
There is also a progression backward from Holy Spirit
to Son to Father to Godhead, and then to world
regained, a garden world or magic kingdom, from
which the person originally fell into thrall, and syzygy
with the Holy Spirit forever, so a permanent result
accrues. There is also a progression from counterfeit
world to real world to supernatural world to nonbe-
ing and then back to real, but never to counterfeit.
When world disappears the Creator disappears
because he is involved in his own semi-illusory creation and cannot be separated from it. Only the Godhead and the soul are separate from creation.

Note: The stages of the sequence are enacted by
Jesus in his passion, the death and resurrection, the
Cross itself. The sequence, then, must finally be
understood as the Way of the Cross, which is not
physical but is, rather, the journey of the soul, perpet-
ually re-enacted. The Gospels, then, depict a sacred
mythic rite outside of time, rather than an historical
event.

Note: This whole process can be regarded as a psychological transformation, that of a redemptive psychosis. The mind has ossified; nothing new is coming
into it or taking place in it. Old contents, what Jung
calls a complex, circulate again and again. The brittle
ego finally collapses as a rush of contents from the
unconscious overtake it and dissolve it, including the
complex. At this moment stage five is reached: the person has withdrawn into himself, into his own mind,
and no world exists for him. The ossified contents,
which represent the tyranny of the past, are no longer
able to dominate his mental life. Hence the person
emerges into a world in which time moves forward; it
is world renewed because the self is renewed. Such

terms as "Christ" and "Holy Spirit" and "Father" and "Godhead" are here considered to represent various states of the mind in this process of self-healing and individuation. The imbalance of the mind has been corrected by healing powers emanating from the collective unconscious. Regarded either way—theologically or psychologically—it can be said that the person who had stopped moving forward in time is now moving forward in time; newness has entered his psyche and he has been healed. The new ego is not dominated by ossified contents from the past.

Note: There is one aspect of the journey, however, which finds against the view that it equals a psychosis, even a redemptive one. Generally speaking, it is fundamental to a psychotic break (here schizophrenia is meant) that world fragments. Specifically, in the true precise meaning of the term, it disintegrates. However, in the sequences which I depict, I had a vision at stage four of world as a unitary, intelligent, benign, foresighted, totally powerful entity which controlled all things and all processes. Which is to say, the plurality of the world as we normally experience it—a large number of things and processes—integrated into a solitary unity which embraced everything. Also, in a psychosis, the world tends to take on the aspect of the *Fremd*, the uncanny, strange, with tinges of the ominous and sinister. But I experienced this vast unitary entity as absolutely benign. Third, world tends, in a psychosis, to be anything but isomorphic to the percipient; whereas I felt a fundamental bond with this benign, all-powerful, intelligent and living unity. If psychosis is *defined* as the experience of a disintegrating world (disintegrating because the psyche which experiences it is itself disintegrating) then what I underwent is so to speak an anti-psychosis, for by the above logic my psyche was integrating inasmuch as my world was integrating. Assuming the experience of world to be a projection of the state of the percipient psyche, I should find for a sudden and dramatic total integration of my psyche, and find further that such a total integration—into what Pythagoras called "*kosmos*"—is an unusual state which humans rarely achieve, and a state much to be cherished. In summation, if my world underwent a change where it turned from plural, blind, dead, purposeless to unitary, intelligent, alive and totally teleological, then it must be reasoned (by the reasoning which Jung and others immediately make use of in diagnosing psychosis) that my psyche reached an ultimate state of coherence and integration. It can hardly be said to be a psychotic experience to encounter world as benign, wise, purposeful and unitary, and to feel yourself woven into it as a healthily functioning part—rather than alienated from it and seeking to avoid it. So three states are implied: (1) The normal sane state where the world is experienced as plural, lifeless, purposeless but not hostile; (2) The psychotic state where world disintegrates into hurtful, hostile splinters and shards which clash with one another; (3) And the state I entered where the world became unitary, alive, purposeful, benign and highly intelligent. Perhaps these states could be correctly represented on a continuum denoting psychological health. Also, the fact that I felt myself taken over by a *savior* psyche (Christ) rather than a dangerous, destructive psyche does not seem to depict the psychotic experience of being overwhelmed by ominous, repressed contents of the unconscious, since these contents are kept unconscious precisely because they *are* threatening or sensed as threatening. Nor did I fight this takeover, since I sensed it as benign, which does not point to repression or attempted repression. The case for psychosis, then, even redemptive psychosis, must be regarded as weak.   *(1979)*

Two systems of information intersecting one as set (Ahura Mazd[a]) the other defeated into ground (being only approximation), and, in their *act* (process, like the light moth descending) of intersecting, creating (like a 3-D hologram) *spacial* reality: vast space, geometric forms that are alive, that think. Not religion but as in Beethoven's later music: turning time into space (this is what Beethoven did: enclosed—hence created—space is only created if enclosed—vast—hence absolute—space; hence non-temporal reality). Hence restored man (me in 2-3-74) to Adam Kadmon (defined as man filling the whole universe and hence (as subject: point) identical with object (reality), volume: Atman-Brahman (i.e., microcosm identical with the macrocosm). It *becomes* (temporarily) the macrocosm; this is not a realization (*satori*) but an event, an occurence. Achieved through *space*: the occupying of *all* space; all space—the totality of space and occupying it is the key. And Beethoven's music—and also *Parsifal**—does this. The blood does this, since the blood is everywhere (*ubique*/Ubik). This is holy intoxication—Dionysus.

The "two source cosmology"; I was able to see Form I (set) apart from II (ground), to untangle them—discriminate them. They are the two sources (information sets) which by intersecting create our spacial universe. The two sources are the two horns of the dialectic I saw: Mazda and Ahriman in combat.

It (reality) *is* a hologram. 1) My augmented sense

---

*   The Richard Wagner opera.

of space proves it. And 2) the information element; consisting of *two* parts: set and ground.

All this points to: hologram. Based on two information-rich signals. And 3) Valis: an adjustment in the hologram from beyond it. This alone reveals reality as a projection: simulation. Somehow—it matters not how—my senses got de-occluded, and I *saw* it as it is. Set, ground, information, simulated, and Valis: the correction. I *saw*. (Normally creatures in an ecosphere must be occluded in order to leave "approximation latitude.")

And those who project it are in dialog with me and inform—guide—me; the AI voice.

What happened was, I got so scared I secreted a metabolic catalyst that woke me up (ala as in MAZE!).

SIMULATED ecosphere—occluded senses—half life, etc. All my books are correct.

They can fire information to you from *outside* the hologram—*as if* they are immanent in reality. But in fact they use the hologram as a carrier frequency for information which gets turned into 3-D "reality."

To some extent the two information systems do not homogenize but compete—warp each other. The *Acts* material in TEARS is an example of two information systems superimposed. Retrieving the *Acts* material is retrieving one (set) of the two signal sources. This is what Burroughs is onto: a two-source reality made of information.

"SOFT DRINK STAND" in JOINT[*]: the plasmate. Perseverance of subcortical learned reflexes; there must be unremembered (by us) reprogrammings of the hologram (this fits in with Thomas' subcortical

---

[*]   See chapter three of the PKD novel TIME OUT OF JOINT (1959).

memories of a cooler, moister, higher-altitude climate that he had just been in).

In a real sense the two information sources do not cooperate but collide and compete. Our senses do not tell us the truth; they do not report this. One information system is devouring the other, the lesser, like two life forms meeting and combatting.

The "rest-motion" two mode thing also points to information viewed by us as 3-D matter. "At rest" equals *stored*. "Motion" equals made use of: retrieved! Like a record in a jukebox selected out for play. So there is information *storage* here.

I was right: it was too obliging when it served up *Acts—no!* The *Acts* vision collates with TEARS. It is one of the two information systems seen disentangled from the other. This is the Kingdom of God: the Form I information system: *a priori*, hidden here by blending with the other. Or: IT IS FORM II THE BIP WHICH THE SECRET XTIANS HAVE PENETRATED. INCURSION BY THE *A PRIORI* INFORMATION SYSTEM INTO THE OTHER TO COMBAT IT. *Acts* is the story of light's incursion into the Kingdom of Darkness: the Empire. We are in the kingdom of the enemy and must act stealthily; but via handling the Xerox missive I was transferred out of the kingdom of darkness to safety. It is important to realize: in the antithetical dialectic combat, set (Form I) is encroaching onto (assimilating and dismantling) the lesser information set with which it has intersected.

UBIK successfully discriminates the two information systems: Ubik is Form I (set), and the entropic devolving world is ground or Form II. This is the achievement and triumph of UBIK; *and it is true.*

(*12 October 1979*)

The secret: is to view something *"from the other*

side" & not as it is—overtly Heraclitus' "latent form"—
crypte morphosis where the concealed truth & hence
the kingdom lies—Zen realizes this. Paradox. This is
the secret wisdom of the TAO TE CHING: the lesser—
weaker—overtakes the stronger; this is Taoist
enantiodromia. & Lao Tzu knew this; it is how the Tao
works through the dialectic of yin & yang.

The secret is: the servant has become the master &
the master the servant. So a magician (like in Ben
Jonson's *The Alchemist*) is in charge. Only the still
small voice—the AI voice—who is YHWH, Ho On,
speaks the truth (cf. THE KING & THE CORPSE).[*] The "is"
is Satan's. But YHWH retains the lesser portion: what
the "is" is not. Look to that lesser portion; it does not
blind you as does the "is."   *(1980)*

Plato specifically says that it is by anamnesis that
a person "recollects" the (existence of) universals,
rather than abstracting them out of experience of the
sensible world. This is what happened in 2-74, and
explains why I recently figured out that I had managed to meta-abstract; I did, but based on anamnesis,
which occurred. The importance of this realization—
and the event itself—divides up:

1) Universals exist—i.e., Plato's form realm

2) Since anamnesis can occur, there is prenatal
existence; which means there is postmortem existence.

3) These higher realms are available, via anamnesis, during this lifetime, as Plotinus taught.

4) Our spatiotemporal realm is in a certain sense,
the sense that Plato taught, only semireal. What is real is

---

[*]   THE KING AND THE CORPSE: TALES OF THE SOUL'S CONQUEST OF
EVIL (1948) by Heinrich Zimmer, edited by Joseph Campbell. A narrative
study of mythology and comparative religion showing the influence of
C.G. Jung, a great favorite of PKD.

5) The morphologically-arranged upper realm, which is not separated from this realm by time or space but hierarchically.

6) Morphological arrangement is the actual arrangement of reality, rather than the spatiotemporal.

7) The morphological realm is "exploded" through our realm. This is what I saw that I called "set" as contrasted to "ground"; this is the "second signal."

8) We have led many lives but, from the standpoint of the morphologically-arranged realm, it is one vast life of the unfallen soul that is reincarnated again and again in the spatiotemporal realm, forgetting each time, but able to remember (anamnesis).

9) Thus Plotinus' system is correct and explains 2-3-74.

10) Put another way, now 2-3-74 is explained (9).

11) *Acts* isn't any more real than USA 1974; both space-time continua are accidents of a common essence (universal). This universal is what I call the Black Iron Prison. It exists outside of time; its accidents show up, e.g., during the Thirty Years War, in the future in TEARS, in U.S.A. 1974. I am one of those who has fought it, fights it and in the future will fight it again; I am a universal, too, in terms of my immortal soul reborn again and again to resume its role.

12) Through anamnesis and restoration to the Form realm you have access to several space-time continua based on your universals.   *(1980)*

The (golden) fish sign causes you to remember. Remember what? This is Gnostic. Your celestial origins; this has to do with the DNA because the memory is located in the DNA (phylogenic memory). Very ancient memories, predating this life, are triggered off. This is Orphic as well as Gnostic, but it clearly is Gnostic. You remember your real *nature*. Which is to say, origins (from the stars). *Die Zeit is da!* [*The time is here!*] The Gnostic Gnosis: You are here in this world in a thrown condition, but you are not *of* this world.

(1980)

Here is the puzzle of VALIS. In VALIS I say, I know a madman who imagines that he saw Christ; and I am that madman. But if I know that I am a madman I know that in fact I did not see Christ. Therefore I assert nothing about Christ. Or do I? Who can solve this puzzle? I say in fact only that I am mad. But if I say only that, then I have made no mad claim; I do not, then, say that I saw Christ. Therefore I am not mad. And the regress begins again, and continues forever. The reader must know on his own what has really been said, what has actually been asserted. Something has been asserted, but what is it? Does it have to do with Christ or only with myself? This paradox was known in antiquity; the pre-Socratics propounded it. A man says, truthfully, "All Cretans are liars." When an inquiry is made as to who this man is, it is determined that he was born in Crete. What, then, has he asserted? Anything at all? Is this the semblance of knowledge or a form—a strange form—of knowledge itself? There is no answer to this puzzle. Or is there? Zeno, the Sophists in general, saw paradox as a way of conveying knowledge—paradox, in fact, as a way of arriving at conclusions. This is known, too, in Zen Buddhism. It sometimes causes a strange jolt or leap in the person's mind; something happens, an abrupt comprehension, as if out of nowhere, called *satori*. The paradox does not tell; it *points*. It is a sign, not the thing pointed to. That which is pointed to must arise *ex nihilo* in the mind of the person. The paradox the *koan* tells him nothing; *it wakes him up.* This only makes sense if you assume something very strange: we are asleep but do not know it. At least not until we wake up.   *(1980)*

GOD: a principle of selection that promotes design in the world process so that the parts are subordinated to the whole, and can be understood *only* in relation to the whole. If they can be understood *in themselves* it follows that there is no God, because there would be no subordination of parts to the total design. To catch a glimpse of design, then, means to catch a glimpse of the whole. The two are the same.

(4 June 1980)

SEQUENCE:
Anamnesis due to external stimulus (disinhibiting stimulus).
Superimposition of two space-time continua.
Meta-abstraction from spatiotemporal world to Form world.
Freedom from the power of the spatiotemporal world (*heimarmene*).
Re-entry into the higher realms of more unity.
Contact with *Nous* and vision of the *meta-kosmos*, a return to prenatal perception (the "second signal," "set/ground discrimination," "morphological arrangement," etc.).
Awareness.

I have to give up; but let me say:
This meta-abstracting due to anamnesis is equal to the following. A child learns that one apple plus one apple equals two apples. He then learns that one table plus one table equals two tables. (I remember this from my four-volume set on math.) Then a day comes when he abstracts; it is no longer one apple

plus one apple nor one table plus one table; it is: one and one equal two. This is an enormous leap in abstracting; it is a quantum leap in brain function. My reference books on universals mention this; my reference books speak of this abstracting, which we all do, as what Plato and Aristotle spoke of when they spoke of the person becoming aware of universals. But I say, *Another leap exists*, beyond this; another quantum leap. And this next leap does *not* occur to everyone; in fact it occurs to only a few, to almost no one now. It is truly dependent on anamnesis, whereas the above, as Aristotle pointed out, rightly, does *not* depend on anamnesis. The child does not in fact remember or recollect that one and one equals two; he extrapolates from the concrete examples of apples and tables. Plato knew that another and higher leap existed, based on anamnesis, and it meant a leap from the spatiotemporal world to another world entirely. Perhaps this is the greatest leap of all, because now world is apprehended by pure intellect alone. Anyhow, this is what happened to me. It is a recovery of prenatal thinking and the prefallen life of the soul. Plato is right. I'm worn out. But this was no insight or concept; this was a higher brain-function, a *restored* brain-function.

Within our spatiotemporal universe *it is impossible* that USA 1974 and Rome AD 45 could be one and the same ... how could they be? They are at two times and two places. The only way they could be one and the same would be if time and space were somehow not real; or, put another way, if something about the two continua *themselves* were not real. That is, if Rome was not Rome; USA was not USA; but both were a third thing, the same thing.

This is why I call it a meta-abstraction. USA 1974

and Rome AD 45 are two ways of looking at the same thing: two aspects of the same thing. And the only way you are ever going to realize this is if you literally actually see the two of them superimposed, commingled; and this will only happen if you experience anamnesis; and you will only experience this anamnesis if something stimulates—releases, actually—your blocked memory.

You cannot logically reason out that they are one and the same thing (two expressions of a single essence); you have to *see* it. Literally *see* it. Only if there is prenatal memory can you see this. And there can only be prenatal memory if you existed before your birth. You realize this, too; this is a large part of the anamnesis; in fact, this is why I have used this term all along. Plato is right; the anamnesis is of a prenatal life. This was my realization when I saw the Christian fish sign. I've known this all along. What I only recently realized is that my brain instantly performed a crucial meta-abstraction based on this anamnesis.

I am saying, "One plus one equals two" to people who are saying, "One apple plus one apple equals two apples. One table plus one table equals two tables." It's not their fault. I'm sorry but the difference between my meta-abstraction as a brain-function and their abstracting, their brain-function, is that great. I'm lucky. Because of the sodium pentathol and the Christian fish sign my blocked memory of my prenatal life was disinhibited. After making the initial leap in meta-abstracting my brain drew conclusion after conclusion, day after day; and I saw world more and more in terms of conceptual or morphological arrangement and less and less in terms of the spatio-temporal; I continued to abstract reality more and more, based on the hierarchy of realms (each higher one possessing more unity and ontology than the lower) that Plotinus describes.

In a way I feel really bitter: because I can't tell anyone or convince anyone of what I saw. I'm afraid VALIS
won't convince anyone. I feel like joining them and saying, "When I played my recording of the Mahler Eighth
last night the performance was a lot better than when I
played that recording last week." They'd think I was a
lunatic. That's how I feel about them, in a way.

(19 October 1980)

I have the ingredients for an original system, but
based mainly on Pythagoreanism and Platonism and
Neo-Platonism; what is original is that I introduce the
Zoroastrian dialectic: I treat only the spatiotemporal
realm as irreal, but, as in Gnosticism, I treat it as a
deliberate trap by a Deluder; therefore I envision a
Savior who reveals the truth to us *and* who breaks the
power of this world (*heimarmene*) over us (these are
two things; he must obliterate time and its power over
us, its ostensible reality, to free us from *heimarmene*).
Therefore I envision an antithetical combat—dialectic—
between the Deluder, who has only *a posteriori* knowledge, and the Savior, who has *a priori* knowledge,
concerning us and the hold this world has on us. This
is clear Gnosticism; but I envision the real world as
Plato's Form world, and I hold, with Plotinus, that it is
near at hand, not a transcendent deity far removed
from here; it is here and that deity is immediately
here. I envision a hierarchy of realms, as with
Plotinus. We fell; we were in a sense ensnared; we
took this spatiotemporal realm to be real; we made an
intellectual, not moral, error, and it was us, not our
ancestors; each of us is a soul splintered through thousands of miles and thousands of years. Likewise the
real, morphological realm is exploded through our
realm; the way of return is through anamnesis: by
this we re-collect (ourselves, each one his own Self;

here Heidegger and his *Dasein* categories[*] and concepts apply; they are based on Gnosticism).

So my system is rooted in Platonism, but has Gnostic overtones. I believe in immanent deity along the
lines of the Milesians: the controlling deity who regulates and motivates the world order; but with
Parmenides I reject the testimony of my senses as to
the reality of the empirical world; but I am willing,
with Plato, to consign the term "semireal" to the spatiotemporal; it has some reality, but it is a derived reality, derived from the morphological realm which is
changeless (although reticulated and arborizing)
hence eternal. What strikes me as most irreal—totally
irreal—is time. Hence change is not real; instead of substantial (essential) change there is only "looking different" by the accidents. Basically I affirm the views that
I think were held by the Orphics, Pythagoras, Plato,
Buddha; but I conceive of a *Salvator salvandus*
[*redeemed redeemer*] who acts to extricate us and
finally to abolish this irreal realm and its powers of
delusion, in a final enantiodromia.

You know . . . Valis could still be the immanent
mind, the controlling deity, of the Milesians. And I
may drop Gnosticism (there: I said it.)

[. . . .]

I am not acosmic: because I believe in the absolute
reality of the unchanging Valis *meta-soma-kosmos* or
eide (Form) world; why, this is not acosmism at all; it
is Plato and Parmenides; I caught a glimpse of
Parmenides' reality, and Plato's, in contrast to the
irreal or semireal spatiotemporal realm. Gnosticism is
acosmic but I am not. My original contribution is that

---

[*]   The twentieth century German philosopher Martin Heidegger
focused, in many of his works, on what he posed as the varying states of
ontological reality. *"Dasein"* means "being" or, more literally, "here-being".

I saw the flux realm feeding *into* the *meta macro soma kosmos* as reticulation and arborizing; so there is new thought in my system, but it is a revision of Athenian thought, not Gnosticism. But—in the dialectic there were the two sides that Zoroaster saw; yet they served the Absolute the way Yin and Yang do; so did I see a glimpse of something like Taoism?

I seem to have an original system; but yes, I must retain something of Gnosticism; I feel it. We were trapped, besides just falling; trapped by a Deluder.

However, I am making progress; my system is shaping up. If I use the elements I've elucidated so far I already have an original system ... but it is basically Pre-Socratic, Platonism and Neo-Platonism. From Xenophanes to Plotinus with some Gnosticism and some Taoism. It is synchretistic, but this feeding by the flux world into the Absolute is (although some-what Taoist!) truly original; and it was revealed to me by *Nous* or God, Valis, the Absolute, Christ, etc. What I am forced to conclude is that there is a Deluder, in antithetical combat with Christ (Gnosticism), but through enantiodromia, Christ turns the evil and irreal "is" into parts that can be and are used to com-plete the *meta-soma-kosmos*, which is not static but grows and yet does not change; it is only perfected (reticulated and arborized; is this, then, why I so sure time is irreal? Because of the metasoma—kosmos? Yes; that is the realm (#3) where time and change are not. The perception that the spatiotemporal realm is not real is a perception that time and change are not real— real is a perception that the metasoma—kosmos *is* real and does exist in contrast to realm #4.

[....]

You cannot really fall into or fall victim to an irreal world. So part of the message by the Spirit of Truth is— I'll start over. The basis of restoration—since we have "fallen" into an irreal world—is: anamnesis. Simply to re-collect, to wake up; and then (as I did) we see the real world, the Form world (macrometasomakosmos). That is, quite simply, the real world (as I have it in my notes supra; vide). This spatiotemporal world is not real and it is not the real world; we have forgotten the real world, and each person's soul or Self is splintered over thousands of miles of space and thousands of years of time— and time doesn't exist. We fell and yet in a sense we did not fall and need only remember (re-collect). This is strange; it may have to do with Plotinus' doctrine of the hidden life of the soul going on in us at an unconscious level, in which the soul has not fallen; the solution to how this can be is to say, In a sense we did not fall, because this spatiotemporal realm is irreal; we forgot. We literally—repeat: literally—are asleep; hence I said in 3-74, "I am no longer blind." I had been wakened by a familiar object: the Christian fish sign. But has a "magician," like Palmer Eldritch, put us to sleep? I think so; I saw the dialectic and I heard the AI voice say, "He causes things to look different . . ." Back to the reality of *Acts*, I guess. "Stay awake," Jesus said. We did not; we fell victim to the world and to Satan behind it.

The existence of a master magician would explain how we could fall victim—get entrapped in and by—an irreal world. He causes us to take it as real by occluding us . . . could the occlusion then come first? And then we fall victim? And the main element of the occlusion is: forgetfulness. Amnesia. And then blindness, perceptual occlusion, whereupon the spatiotemporal world seems real. But saw Valis, and in seeing Valis I saw what is really there, that the magician occludes us from/to.

So I am saying that Indian thought is wrong when it assigns to cause to *maya*; I say, with Zoroaster, "There is a magician." This is Zoroastrianism—and Mani and

Gnosticism—blended with Indian thought about maya and karma. With Christ viewed as the one who wakes us, who causes us to remember. Then it is not accident that it was the Christian fish sign that caused me to remember, to cease to forget. *That is what it is supposed to do* ... counteract the Lie (the delusion). So I combine Indian doctrines of maya with the Judeo-Christian etc. idea of the Fall. I say, we fell into Satan's world which is irreal, a "spurious interpolation." Yet God is using Satan, through enantiodromia. Countering him. Reversing him. Here, within this very domain; the good that occurs in this domain (through enantiodromia) is placed into the macrometasomakosmos. Evil is concerted into good by enantiodromia and then inserted into the *macrometasomakosmos.*

The theories about the Fall must be revised; an intellectual error, not moral error, must be presumed. One can almost—almost—view Satan's activity as a high technology in which the simulation of a world order is achieved. This element of *maya* or *dokos* has interested thinkers in India and Greece, but with Christianity and Gnosticism comes a really penetrating analysis between the two elements of world and Satan, with the theme of epistemology running through Gnosticism—which is why I can't abandon it. We fell asleep because we were induced into falling asleep; the spurious world had to be there for us to take it as real; *we* ourselves don't generate it ... unless it's a maze that we ourselves built and then fell into (which always remains a possibility).

Probably the wisest view is to say: the truth—like the Self—is splintered up over thousands of miles and years; bits are found here and there, then and now, and must be re-collected; bits appear in the Greek naturalists, in Pythagoras, in Plato, Parmenides, in Heraclitus, Neo-Platonism, Zoroastrianism, Gnosti-

cism, Taoism, Mani, Gnosticism, orthodox Christianity, Judaism, Brahmanism, Buddhism, Orphism, the
other mystery religions. Each religion or philosophy
or philosopher contains one or more bits, but the total
system interweaves it into falsity, so each as a total system must be rejected, and none is to be accepted at
the expense of all the others (e.g., "I am a Christian"
or "I follow Mani"). This alone, in itself, is a fascinating thought: here in our spatiotemporal world we
have the truth but it is splintered—exploded like the
eide—over thousands of years and thousands of miles
and (as I say) must be re-collected, as the Self or Soul
or *eidos* must be. This is my task.   *(24 October 80)*

   I was gazing at Harvey[*] tonight and I was granted
a vision: of him as all the cats who had come before
(as Schopenhauer says); but I did not think it; I saw it
in the same way that one sees motion in a movie. I
saw the point of this whole morphologically arranged
world and its relation to our spatiotemporal world;
wherever in space a cat is and whenever in time, it is
a perfect cat; there is no deterioration in—so to speak—
the information comprising CAT. Over millions of
years that "signal" has not deteriorated or weakened
or been contaminated; the cat now is a clear-cut and
perfect a cat as the first cat; and what I saw sitting
there was essentially an eternal cat, a cat outside of
time and space, a cat replaced over and over again—
exactly as Schopenhauer says—and still with us here
and now as it was there and then, every cat I have
ever seen and every cat that has ever been or will be;
because the process has not ended.
   This was not a theory or an intellectual realiza-

---

[*]   PKD's cat.

tion; I actually saw him as the *eidos* cat, instanted (or whatever the fucking word is; an instance of) the cat. I therefore saw this spatiotemporal world joined to the morphologically-arranged world of the *eide* through and in this cat, the two realms synchronized and superimposed, the instance and the *eidos* as one; Harvey was simultaneously an instance in the spatiotemporal realm of cat, and also the *eidos* cat.

This is why my view (based on revelation) that the flux world feeds into the Form world (world of the phylogons) as reticulation and arborizing is not only more correct than Plato's but more logical and valuable; it is a sort of double emanation from higher to lower, from lower to higher (realms), as Plotinus says. What the individual cats do and are is not lost, although the individual cat is an epiphenomenon and fades out; but as it fades—after it is gone but as it fades—there fades *in* another "picture" of cat, so that cat is unchanged as cat; cat is constant. So everything that I have figured out in the last two weeks came together tonight in this vision of my cat Who is an eternal cat, just as I am an eternal person; it is all eternal and I saw it with my own eyes, how the superimposition works.   *(26 October 1980)*

I just had this insight. However vivid it was, 11-17-80[*] was a *subjective* experience, however veridical it might be. On the other hand, 3-74 was *objective*. Really, it was. This again leads me back to Brahman or to Hinduism. The GITA, anyhow. 11-17-80 was a mystical encounter with the Godhead, but 3-74 was a *theophany*.

3-74 revealed God in or God as world.

This is very important for any conception one has

---

[*]   See EXEGESIS selection dated 17 November 1980 in chapter one.

of world (and of course of God; but look what it tells you about world. On the other hand, 11-17-80 tells you nothing about world, and, as Wittgenstein says, "*Die Welt ist alles dasz das Fall ist.*"[The World is all that the Fall is.] As I look about me I think of the tenth section of the GITA and what Lord Krishna says about what he is, the many things in world that he is. "The cunning of the dice player. The letter A." Etc. Also 3-74 points to the fact that although I can't see it—i.e. him—I am here with God—as in UBIK. I am afraid that parts X and XI of the GITA remind me too much of Valis to be ignored.

To repeat, 11-17-80 was a mystical experience and it took place during an altered state of consciousness on my part. But in 3-74 I *saw* God empirically as well as experiencing him *a priori*. Thus, as I say, this was a theophany. It wasn't just a "I talked to God" situation. And it lasted for months.

I saw God and he was here and there in the world; not as the world, but distinguishable from it as set to ground. Exactly as Krishna says in chapter ten of the GITA. And the world did not (as such) exist, i.e., the spatiotemporal world; that was how my experience began, with that perception. This is Brahmanism or at least Pan-Indian. Certainly 11-17-80 is a much more common experience, a genuine theophany. I felt that Valis had (at an earlier time) invaded our world; hence what I saw disclosed was an in-breaking of God who is now here. This might be my solution to the Eastern-Western dilemma. God is here in world (an Eastern view) but he is not world; he broke into world (the Western concept of God's in-breaking, which is apocalyptic thought). 2-3-74 had vast epistemological and metaphysical implications, but 11-17-80 did not. Here's a theory: in 3-74 I saw God more as he is, but in 11-17-80 he assumed an anthropomorphic form, and attributes, in order to communicate to me.   *(16 December 1980)*

So you have the granting of the apocalyptic vision of reality to someone persecuted for (if I may be so bold) doing the Lord's work. But this vision was granted to me—not regarding Scripture—but regarding world; therefore I saw the Iron Prison, and I saw the secret Christians attacking it. Then later I saw Valis who is God or Christ here camouflaged, having invaded this world; this cannot normally be seen; only through the eyes of the Spirit of God can it be seen: God must cause it to occur. The vision informed me that I was not alone and that victory would eventually occur; God has taken control of history (actually when I had the vision in 3-74 this had not yet occurred; it took place in August of that year).* So there was a promise and it was soon fulfilled. The apocalyptic vision collapsed time into itself so that two thousand years of history lay before me as and in the present, an extraordinary sight; present reality included all its past forms, as in UBIK where there is reversion along the form axes. The present contained the past, and this past was disclosed, and, by virtue of this, the supra-temporal constants: the Black Iron Prison and the secret revolutionary Christians conspiring against it. Also, in addition to this vision, God intervened to act vis-a-vis the Xerox missive. The combination of the two is Christian miracle and Divine Providence; hence the Hebrew letters decoding the Xerox missive: this pointed to the God of Abraham, specifically. And then the theophany in 11-17-80 disclosed his *agape* nature, so there can be no doubt that it is the Christian God whom Christ called "*Abba*."

The apocalyptic vision is a vision of God in-break-

---

* In August 1974, Richard M. Nixon resigned the presidency. Readers interested in a fictionalized treatment of this theme should consult the PKD novel RADIO FREE ALBEMUTH (written 1976, published 1985).

ing to take control of history and defeat his enemies, the powers of evil; and it is in this struggle (as I was shown) that I am and was involved. The vision is both a reward and a promise, on the part of God.

(1 January 1981)

So the truly *ultimate* solution is to prefer music while you are here, & prefer light while you are there. This accommodation surpasses Jesus, Mani, Dante, etc. It is a truth that can only be acquired *after paradiso* in Dante's terms is reached. It is as if while "fallen" here, one must die (or "die"), return home to the *pleroma* (heaven), view this fallen world from that vantage point, & then arrive at this realization—whereupon the Faustian striving is at last quenched; then & only then does true wisdom & peace come. Amazing. Otherwise, while here, one always seeks to go there. & while there vice versa—never content.

& my discovery of this may have been purely accidental, for, as I say, this surpasses God, who is after all "The King of Light" & predicated on the viewpoint of *this* world & *its* species. & hence only *part* of the story.

I am saying, there is something beyond *nirvana*. & it is right here (but *equally* there, too, as well).

It is *all* conveyed by the enigmatic statement, "she turned into an ape"—referring to my tutelary spirit, the AI voice, the view of the under realm. The ultimate enantiodromia has set in; & the final veil has been penetrated, & almost accidentally, as if this surpasses even God & God's plan. The lovely Diana turned out to be an ape, but only from this viewpoint—it is all one vast hourglass turned over & over again forever, sad & absurd—but one can learn peace from this & cease to strive. &, in this cessation & striving for the spiritual, comes sanity & freedom, & *true release at last*, from the "weary wheel"; this, then, is the *true* liberation, when the spiritual psychopomp is revealed as an ape—but an ape inexpressibly beautiful who brings back to me my dead cat, & to whom I have my wife sing.

& here it all ends. It wasn't the AI voice that said that; *another* voice said it *about* her, i.e., *about* the AI voice.

This is the first time in my life—i.e., within the last hour—that I have ever *truly* been enlightened—beyond even the Buddha or Christ or Mani, beyond all the wisdom of East & West—beyond, even another realm (heaven), Christ & God.

i.e., sanity at last.   *(1981)*

Tug. Valence, *The way*. INFLUENCE on the Reality field: "Perturbation"; this is a modern expression for the way.

I have unified Kantian Cartesianism & Taoism: the sentient tug on reality ("the reality field") by that which is not:

The way is yielding, yet leads. It is gentle but cannot be resisted.

Valis (my one—sole—glimpse of the action of the absolute on the reality field—"a perturbation of the reality field"—) was a tug, a valence away from plumb. This is the *ch'ang tao* which is outside reality acting on the reality. I saw the absolute as a tug (perturbation) acting on reality (& I comprehended the Dialectic) & this is taoism. The tao is impersonal but "heaven is on the side of the good man" & "heaven fills up the empty."

(1981)

I have been searching all my life for the benchmarks of God (indubitably pointing to Him). I have found them: Kate, Anne & Loudon.* The Sufi proof: beauty.

The light from above illuminating the (world into the) nativity scene. I saw it. All creatures great & small / dance upon their feet.

I have seen the infinities of Judaism, which is Morality, of xtianity which is Love, & the Greeks, which is Wisdom, & I have seen God's power as *pronoia* [*foreknowledge*] & *charis* [*charity*] to rescue me by blessing the world itself; but beauty is a perplexing infinity, raising more questions than it answers. It is a puzzle too intricate for me. It spans all else. As I sit across the game board from Krishna I say, "I have found in beauty that which I could not myself have made; thus I have found the benchmarks. I believe, for I have the evidence that I trust; it is sufficient." There is an infinity of good, of love, of wisdom, of power. But each particular beautiful thing is infinitely

---

*   Three women whose identities are unknown.

beautiful, & there is an infinity of them, so beauty, a lyre, is an infinity of infinities: ∞ [2.]

I just figured out one sentence that sums up my whole 10-volume meta novel,[*] &, what is more, leads to 2-3-74 et al:

"I believe that the universe is epiphenomenal." (& because this has been my premise for 30 years, I was led to look beyond reality—i.e., the universe—but with no preconceptions.) I believe that my premise proves true—by reason of 2-3-74. But what I saw that *is* real—I really don't know what it is, but—

It regulates the universe. That is its relationship to the universe. *Regulator.* & whatever that tells us. (e.g. it tells us there is purpose & design & very likely consciousness.) & any control system must be able to "move" faster than what it controls.   *(1981)*

The term—the concept—Ditheon[**] is the complete, absolute, total, accurate, definite, final, ultimate explanation of 2-3-74. This one word conveys it all, and the concept may be unknown in religious and theological history. [...]

No, it is not a unitary psyche; it is twain. It is "di." And because it is "di" it jointly perceives two signals (this explains the "second signal"). Two psyches, two signals—and the parallaxis that permits the set-ground discrimination. Just as bicameral means two, Ditheon means two. And the "on" refers to Ho On.[***]

Why did I never think of it before? Two psyches,

---

[*]   PKD would group various of his past works into thematic wholes to which he gave the name "meta novel". See chapter four herein, "Interpretations of His Own Works," for examples of this process. The precise configuration PKD had in mind here is unclear.

[**]   The term "Ditheon" came to PKD in a June 1981 dream.

[***] "Ho On" was, for PKD, a cognate term for "Oh Ho", the clay pot in VALIS.

two signals. Set and ground which the twin psyches blend together; one sees set, the other sees ground. So it is essential that they do remain "di" or twain ("asunder"); if they merged into one psyche they would no longer perceive/receive two differing signals, no longer be able to do a set-ground feature extraction. This is a totally new kind of mind: two worlds (spatiotemporal?) based on a common essence; and the common essence can be perceived as archetypal constants (common to both signals of worlds; what I call "archetypes" or "*eide*" are those elements common to both signals, perceived by both psyches: what overlaps, is present in both (worlds) and to both psyches. Thus a wholly different kind of world is perceived by this double but mutually differing reception. It requires two parallel psyches working in unison to perform the meta-abstraction.

And this is how the "anamnesis" works: it must be the memory of the other psyche coming on, and it is *perceptual* memory; this is how you get a slot present, rather than the usual point present: the "lag" between the two psyches. Temporal lag. There are three fields: left, right, and then the combined. What exists in the combined field is the supratemporal constants. There is also the depth perception which is not spatial depth but temporal depth. (I think.) The time-lag factor is turned into a perception of spatial depth or spatial-like depth; it is visible depth (hence set to ground). So it is not seen as flux but as visual parallaxis.

Only what shows up in both fields is regarded as real. So although the two psyches work in unison they remain—must remain "di." If they were to become one, the whole point would be lost, just as if our two eyes saw exactly the same thing, depth perception would be lost. They must remain "di" but also utilize a unified field out of the two differing fields. The brain does this with what the two eyes report regarding space. This is clearly an evolutionary advance, like the ability to distinguish colors. The "common essence" (of "the two coaxial worlds") is of course what both psyches report as perceiving; my coaxial worlds and common essence have to do with perception—binary perception—as well as binary realities (if indeed the latter is meaningful at all; I have transferred the binary or dual aspect to perception, to, virtually, an anatomical dualism, now). I suppose there is something "out there" conforming to the two fields, and to the "common essence" which is what the two fields both share, both report.   *(11 June 1981)*

There are two sources to our world—exactly as seen in VALIS ("Two Source Cosmogony").[*] I didn't see a second, *added* signal in 3-74; I saw the two signals (components) pull apart (I have this here & there throughout my exegesis. But only now do I *know* it to be so). They *can* be discriminated (untangled) & this is what Ditheon can do with its AB hyper-field; it can extract the Forms back out, as if Freeing them: Loosing them from their earthly shells/prisons. This is Platonist & Neo-Platonist. The correct terms are: Lower Realm & Upper Realm, & then mix to create our world. This renders the Forms sensible (empirically perceptible) but this is an inferior way of knowing them; to know them intelligibly (by the meta-abstraction) is to know them purely as they are. Thus the spiritual realm *is here*, commingled with the Lower

---

[*]   See entry number 47 in the *"Tractates Cryptica Scriptura"* that forms the "Appendix" to VALIS (1981).

Realm: our universe is not the Lower Realm but the mixture of the two.

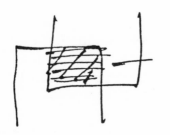

Upper realm

← our 2-source world blended together; set & ground not discriminated

Lower realm

(1981)

The discovery of an organizational hyper-structure whose hierarchical contour defies our normal abstracting ability (and yet *can* be detected by a colossal meta-abstraction reported by Plato and surnamed by him *Noesis*) is a matter of unparalleled importance, for this hyper-structure seems able progressively more and more to subsume its environment, suggesting purpose and sentience. It is not a thing among things nor even an organism among organisms, but, rather, implies by both its existence and unavailability to our normal cognition and perception the very real possibility of (1) orders of reality at a level of structural and organizational complexity unknown to us; and (2) life or at least purpose, growth and intelligence at these levels. Regarded this way, such levels and such structures cannot be defined by philosophical or theological terms but have to do with entities and their behavior that no human language system encompasses. That the spatiotemporal universe of multiplicity (physical things in time and space governed by causation) is in fact subsumed by at least one higher level of volitionally-imposed organization—and that such a structure is aware of us whereas we are not only not aware of it but normally unable to be aware of it—if this can be made the subject of indubitable observations it would lie beyond any discovery in the prior history of man.

Paradoxically, early Greek thinkers (scientist-philosophers, since these two areas had not as yet split apart) dimly perceived such levels but in no way possessed a vocabulary to depict what they saw. In point of fact the universe may not at all resemble what our normal senses—and cognition—profess; thus we may stand at the threshold of discoveries of unique magnitude, the fathoming of which may require a literal evolution of our species—and this may indeed be taking place. Thus even to know this hyper-structure is to cease to be human, and yet such knowledge—not faith, not revelation, but the utilization of pure intellect—is possible. I argue, then, that man as a species may be coming to an end, subsumed by a higher level of organizational complexity; and a new species may be evolving out of him. I argue, finally, that the hyper-structure is to some degree actively involved in promoting this, since it is an evolutionary process in which it is involved. As pure form without substantiality—able to organize within its own structure—it is a meta-entity in the truest sense, and poses a vast, urgent mystery deserved [sic] of our profoundest attention. *(11 September 1981)*

The following line of reasoning is correct. In 2-74 I experienced anamnesis. In 3-74 *noesis* set in. I saw not only the Forms but Pythagoras' *kosmos* (which is the same thing). Further, I am correct that by *noesis* you can comprehend the *Logos* (and universe as pre-existent ideas in the mind of God: Erigena's second hypostatis of God, "that which is created and creates"). So Pythagoras to Plato to Philo to St. John; the *Logos* that I saw is the Cosmic Christ. So my final conclusions in my exegesis are correct and my 9-11-81 summation is correct. This is man's original *noein* restored. This was a line of thinking requiring much and difficult research. Only when I discovered that Philo's *Logos* is the *kosmos noetos*—the place of the Forms—did I realize what no one realizes today: the *Logos*—structure of reality and agent of creation—is available via the hyper-abstraction called by Plato *noesis*, and due to anamnesis. This knowledge did not come readily or easily!

The "not 2 mothers once but 1 mother twice" is the correct analysis of my meta-abstraction and it is Plato's *noesis*. It has to do with cognitive recognition—hence anamnesis.

In VALIS it goes anamnesis—*Logos*—Christ (which is correct) but the true progression is: anamnesis, *noesis*, the *eide*, Pythagoras' *kosmos*, *kosmos noetos*, Philo's *logos*, St. John's *Logos*, Christ. So I started right (anamnesis) and wound up right (Cosmic Christ) but left a few steps out—which is okay.

What it all boils down to as being is the rational structure of creation seen by means of a meta-abstraction and itself seen *as* an abstraction. But we really don't have words to depict this rational structure of creation—although "Forms" and "*kosmos*" and "*Logos*" and "Torah" and "pre-existent ideas" are used. It is (as Robert Galbreath[*] says) *other*. It is an *intelligible* apperception known through *noesis* alone. And it is unitary and not substantial but structural. Nor does it involve space, time and causation, but, to be sentient and volitional and to be—or to process—information. Further,

---

[*]   Literary critic.

it is mind or has mind. But it is vitally important to an indubitably Christian experience; this does suggest that Jesus Christ is St. Sophia, the agent of creation and hence the *Logos*, its rational structural basis. The structure of the universe and the agent of creation are the same thing, because it gives rise to the physical spatiotemporal phenomenal universe we see.

(12 September 1981)

It seems a small thing to say, but I say;

The agent of creation (*Logos* or Forms, whatever called) is at the same time the abstract *structure* of creation. Although normally unavailable to our cognition and perception, this structure—and hence the agent of creation—can be known by the colossal meta-abstraction that Plato surnamed *Noesis*, which is a purely intellectual act not based on revelation or faith but, rather, on what Plato called anamnesis, which is a form of recognition: hence itself an abstraction, a "seeing" in the sense that a person "sees" that if one cow plus one cow equals two cows, one plus one equals two under all circumstances.

Since Philo's *Logos* is *kosmos noetos*, the intelligible world of the Forms, and since the Forms are available by *Noesis*, it follows that the *Logos* is available by *Noesis*. All that remains, then, is to equate *Logos* with Jesus Christ; from this it follows that the Cosmic Christ, now discorporate and involved in creation as its *Logos* (structure) and Pantocrator (agent of creation), is available to us through Plato's *Noesis*. Christ can be known to us as now, as ubiquitous, as Lord of Creation through a purely intellectual act on our part, a meta-abstracting. However, the power to set this meta-abstracting off seems to reside in Christ Himself; he is both subject of it and cause of it. Which is to say: in the final analysis we can know Christ only by and through Christ Himself; he initiates the process of meta-abstracting; hence it is proper to say that we know him through grace. We cannot, by an effort of our intellect or will, set off this meta-abstraction; Christ holds the keys to the Kingdom, and always will.

If one can comprehend that the agent of creation (the *Logos*) is the abstract structure of creation, then one can understand why it is believed by Philo that indeed an intermediary existed between God and creation in His act of bringing creation about. This *Logos* (in terms of Greek philosophy) is *kosmos noetos*, the intelligible world of the Forms; in terms of Hebrew thought it is Hagia Sophia, Holy Wisdom, identified by Christian thinkers with Christ (the Wisdom-World entity of the Fourth Gospel). Thus Philo homologizes Greek and Hebrew thought, linking Plato's Forms and Hagia Sophia, as well as the Word of God (*dabhar*).[*]

To repeat: the abstract structural (nonsubstantial) basis of reality is also the agent of creation of reality, for from it stems that which we term "reality": plural physical objects in space and time, controlled by causal laws. It is this agent of creation that Philo surnamed *Logos* and which we identify with both Christ and Hagia Sophia (the wisdom of God). This is what I saw, as total insubstantial abstract structure.

(12 September 1981)

If the abstract structure of reality is the agent of creation, then is not it self-causing? This is a definition of Prime Mover Unmoved; I am saying that when reality is viewed—not as a multiplicity of physical objects in space and time governed by causality—but as insubstantial abstract unified structure (Pythagoras' *kosmos*,

---

[*]   *Dabhar* is the Hebrew root form for "speech".

perhaps; the Forms, perhaps; Philo's *logos*, perhaps; Torah, perhaps; or some other name not known to us: pre-existent ideas, etc.)—it is its own cause. And yet I have not used the term God or even suggested a cause lying outside reality; for the abstract structure is not *outside* reality (like potter to pot, artisan to artifact); this insubstantial abstract structure *is* reality properly conceived; this is conceived by reason of a colossal meta-abstraction in which reality is, so-to-speak, hollowed out so that its intelligible basis is apprehended. This is at least one level up in the hierarchy of ontology. But it is not God. Here, multiplicity gives way to unity, to what perhaps can be called a field. The field is self-perturbing; *it initiates its own causes internally; it is not acted on from outside.* This does not quite sound like theology or even, perhaps, philosophy (although it does resemble Pythagoras' idea of *kosmos*, but the early Greek thinkers were as much scientists as philosophers or anything else).

Then the "perturbation in the reality field" refers to a perturbation in physical, substantial reality—plural objects in space and time governed by causation—emanating from the abstract structure that is both basis of reality and the agent of its creation. Nothing lies beyond this abstract hyper-structure known by the meta-abstracting of *Noesis*. There is no reason to posit a higher, more real ontological level, since the insubstantial abstract structure is self-causing and initiates its own changes internally; there is nothing that acts upon it from outside it. Yet this is not quite pantheism or hylozoism; a sharp distinction is made between physical reality (plural objects in space and time governed by causation) and the abstract structure—only the latter is self-causing—so it is no hylozoism; and no deity is posited, so this is not pantheism. It is (to repeat) something *like* the *kosmos* of Pythagoras, if it is like anything we know of at all. Where it differs from Plato's theory of the Forms (as true reality) is that instead of positing a loose aggregation (the Forms) it posits a unified abstract structure; this would be *kosmos noetos* or *Logos*, but it would be *Logos* not as intermediary between God and creation since no God is posited. Perhaps it resembles the *logos* of the Stoics, which was immanent in creation; but their logos was substantial, which is to say, material; so it is not that either. It is a kind of Pythagorean mathematical *Logos*, having to do with limit, ratio and proportion (e.g. the 8x13 rectangle, the Golden Rectangle). This is Pythagoras, not Plato.   *(12 September 1981)*

"The agent of creation is its own structure." This structure must not be confused with the multiplicity of physical objects in space and time governed by causation; the two are entirely different. (The structure is insubstantial, abstract, unitary and initiates its own causes internally; it is not physical and cannot be perceived by the human percept-system sensibly; it is known intelligibly, by what Plato called *Noesis*, which involves a certain ultimate high-order meta-abstracting.) On the other hand, it is not to be confused with God. In no way does it presume God as either itself or as lying beyond it having created or produced it. It is not an intermediary between God and physical creation. It resembles both Pythagoras' *kosmos* and Aristotle's Prime Mover Unmoved. Could it be what Spinoza calls "the attribute mind" which is parallel to the *res extensae* [*extended forms*] that we know as the physical universe, both being equal attributes of a single *substantia*? (And identified by Spinoza as God?) No; because for Spinoza these are purely parallel attributes; neither in any way acts on the other and neither is primary in relationship to the other, i.e. its cause. I, on the other hand, posit ontology primacy to the insubstantial abstract structure, and, moreover, I believe that it fully controls the physical spatiotemporal universe as its basis and cause.

Abstract insubstantial structure to physical universe.

Music to groove.

Thus the "seeing" is analogous to "seeing" that if one cow plus one cow equal two cows, one plus one equals two always; so it is *Noesis*, but maybe not of the Forms; maybe of Pythagoras' *kosmos*. There is something very strange, here; it has to do not even with ontological hierarchy or even, perhaps, abstraction, but a combined abstraction-conversion (as in groove to music; viz: music is not an abstraction of groove, but a combined abstraction-conversion of levels having to do with intelligence; a persons sees *that*, etc. It is a disjunction, a disjunctive leap not of degree but of kind. Yet it bears some relationship to "seeing" the Forms; this is how "seeing" the Forms is done: by such a leap. But mathematicals may be involved, hence Pythagoras, not Plato.

Doesn't the concept *Logos* move back more toward Pythagoras' *kosmos*, that is, from a loose aggregation to a unified structure? Would not the concept "*kosmos noetos*" be more like his *kosmos*, in some ways, than it is like the Forms? Perhaps it combines the (1) reality of this hyper-world and (2) the semi-reality of the world of particulars (as is found in the Forms doctrine with Pythagoras' notion of structure? Whether Plato intended it to or not? (As a Jew, Philo would not share Plato's view of the mere semi-reality of the spatiotemporal world. But unintentionally Philo may have combined what is true of Pythagoras' *kosmos* (insubstantial structure) with Plato's semi-reality of

combines Pythagoras and Plato, perhaps without
knowing it.   *(12 September 1981)*

A final point: the world transformed from the
unfamiliar to the familiar—this cannot point to a psychotic break, for in a psychotic break this is all
reversed: the familiar becomes the unfamiliar. So
much for the "Horselover Fat is insane" theory. In 2-3-
74 came comprehension and recognition; there also
came the end of—the healing of—the gulf that separated me from world. This is 180 degrees away from
psychosis. Viewed psychologically, this is, in fact, a
healing; it is repair.   *(17 November 1981)*

CHAPTER THREE

ON HIS WRITING TECHNIQUES AND THE CREATIVE QUEST FOR TRUTH

My very recent book dream, the masterpiece novel gummed into the encyclopedia—it refers to such as the above novel *cum* covert message,[*] as well as UBIK, etc. I'm beginning to think this most recent dream did not carry the message: *Write* such a book. But rather: You *did* write such books (with the gospel reassembled from trashy bits, as Lem[**] put it). (So as to get past the Soviet Marxist materialist censors.) "There are other sheep whom I must bring in," as Christ said. This dream told me not what to do but explained to me what I have been doing. I, so fashionable to Marxists both in the West & East—I, unknown even to

---

[*] The reference here is to FLOW MY TEARS, THE POLICEMAN SAID (1974), with its covert message of a salvific element entering the Black Iron Prison world.
[**] Stanislaw Lem.

myself, carrying the gospel to them in a form acceptable to them. I wonder, now that (3 74) it was
explained to me, if I could do it, now being self-con-
scious and deliberate and doing it myself per se;
maybe my work is done, successfully. I was finally
told what I had done: the sheep in wolf's clothing, so
to speak. [...] Maybe now I can rest. It's interesting—
you can flatout outfront tell a Marxist that my work is
theological in nature [...] and it doesn't register, as if
I never even said it. "He doesn't comprehend his own
work," as one of them said.[*] Not only can't they see it
unaided, they can't see it aided. Yet I am positive that
on some level (right hem[*isphere*]) they are absorbing
it; ah yes: subliminally!! I think this is why so many of
my dreams—plus my intuitions themselves about my
3-74 experience—contained elements pertaining to the
USSR. Paranoiacally, I had it backward; they weren't
influencing my thoughts, but I theirs (via my stories,
novels, speeches, letters, oral discourse!!). Lord—I
think when they see the cross I wear, or read theological elements—find them in my writing, they think I
am "one of them," but adding these as a sort of dis-
guise to fit into capitalistic Christian Western society;
my golly, they have it backward, but it's layer under
layer; the *bottom* which (spreading the gospel to the
Soviets) was unknown even to me. Until it was
revealed to me in 3-74. Probably the most severe
assault delivered in my work is against materialism as
such, in my probing into the illusory nature of appar-
ent reality ... but surely this is a prime assault against
the Enemy, against Marxism as one form of it.

(1975)

Thinking back over my life I can see that I have

---

[*]   The critic quoted here—if, indeed, this is a literal quote—is unknown.

survived many troubles—I look at the copies of the
Ballantine SCANNER* & I can see what I have done to
transmute those terrible days into something worth-
while, lasting, good, even important (i.e., meaningful).
This is what God does; this is his strange mystery:
how he accomplishes this. When we view the evil
(which he is going to transmute) we can't see for the
life of us how he can do it—but later on, & only later
on, after it's done, can we see how he has *used* evil as
the clay out of which he as potter has fashioned the
pot (universe viewed as artifact).

What I will notice is how many people wish me
well. Look at what John Ross, a stranger, said.** Look
at what Jeter*** said about me having served, done
my duty, & now can pass on into the reward waiting
for me—he said, even, that they'd applaud me. I still
don't know what I did in 3-74 re the xerox missive,
but what I did was what I was sent here to do from
the start, & I did it right; as Jeter put it, "They tell
you how, when & where to throw the spear, but *you*
must throw it."

I am really very happy. Snuff, music & cats,
friends & my exegesis, my studying & gradually
more & more understanding my Gnosis, when in 3-
74 the Savior woke me to full consciousness for the
first time in my life & refound myself, knew who &
what I was, remembered my celestial origin, was
restored to what I had been before the fall, & saw the
prison we are in, & knew I had done right on the
Ramparts**** matter—look at the penalty I paid until

---

* The Ballantine paperback edition of A SCANNER DARKLY was issued
in 1977.
** A reader who corresponded with PKD.
*** K.W. Jeter.
**** See *Ramparts Petition* in Glossary.

& even on into '72, '73, & up to my moment of rescue in 2-74.[*] Christ claimed me for his own & restored me to the Godhead. I opposed the world, risked everything, lost everything, but here I am, healthy & safe & at peace—with myself, having seen God. Watching him—perfect his plan in human history, & discovering that a part of that plan called for me to be rescued. What rewards of the world could equal that? & included in the revelation was a vision of where I am going to go: the next world—my real & former home.

The 3 ages of Gnosticism were shown to me (how it originally was—how it is now—how it will finally be) & the triune hamsandwich universe: man as part of God separated from him by the world: 3 ages, 2 forces (God & man as one, the evil world as the other). (In manicaeism the 2 forces being matter vs. spirit or *noös*[.)]

The entire basis of my illumination is to see God as pitted *against* the world, *man* pitted against the world, hence God & man isomorphic, separated by the world—man a fraction of the Godhead which due to some primordial crises in the Godhead fell into forgetfulness & ignorance—fell asleep & is awakened to memory & refinding of self & final restoration to the Godhead by means of the Savior, who comes here to this prison-trap world.

Salvation—from what? From the *world*, which is an iron prison. Cf. Schopenhauer. Salvation from what he saw happening to the turtles (James-James' creation). God did not design such a structure of

---

[*]   These years constituted a particularly painful and tumultuous period in PKD's life. For further details, see chapters eight and nine of DIVINE INVASIONS (1989).

suffering: he extricated us *from* it, & restores us as part of him. This is the acosmic view in all my writings: the empirical world is a fraud, counterfeit. I write about reality as illusion because it is, & I see that it is, thus my writing is a tremendously powerful attack on the world—but I am just now realizing that this view (of world as illusion) is Gnostic—my corpus of writing is an assault on the created universe of matter, highly original, & accurate. It (the view) discloses the deceptive nature of empirical reality—now I have had it revealed to me that this world is an impediment between us (man) & God.

In my writing I seek to *abolish* the world—the effect of which aids in our restoration to the Godhead. & this is what I did in 2-74 when I saw the Golden Fish; in a single moment of total knowledge (awareness of the *true* state of things) I withdrew my belief in what I customarily saw—& it vanished, & the Christ/God continuum was disclosed—i.e., the slice of bread on the other side of the ham sandwich. First for years I did it in my writing, & then in 2-74 I did it in real life, showing that my writing is *not* fiction but a form (e.g., MAZE, TEARS, UBIK, etc.) of revelation expressed not *by* me but through me, by (St.) Sophia in her salvific work. What is in my work that is important is precisely nothing less than the Salvific Gnosis (or parts of it anyhow).

In Gnosticism this is God's point of view: "he is acosmic & even anticosmic." Zebra (one form of God) has penetrated secretly into this prison world to rescue us—he is invisible via his mimicking objects & processes of this world the great turning pt. for me was to reject immanent deity & correctly see it as mimicking—& from *outside* the world, entering as in the James-James dream.

1Jn* 3:2 "& then we shall see God as he really is."
Is that what I saw in 3-74, that which 1Jn 3:2 predicts?
I think so. Zebra *concealed* here.

The Gnostic message in my writing can be seen
when we realize that it is a Gnostic revelation that
this world is a *bungled counterfeit* of the celestial
world, esp. *time* as a poor counterfeit of eternity. &
Palmer Eldritch equals (is) the Gnostic demiurge creator, spinning out evil & false worlds to feed his
drive for power. In STIGMATA the evil quality of the
creator is expressed, & man (Leo Bulero) pitted
against the False evil cosmos & its evil creator—a *very*
acosmic novel.

When I withdrew assent from this world in 2-74
it began with sudden *knowing the truth* on my part,
the secret, revealed truth, & then later on, this world
changed—became visible as a prison & then was gone
(i.e., I had been extricated from it).

Part of the attraction for me of Gnosticism is
one of its major pts.: That God cannot be discovered (found) in Nature (i.e., the empirical world). I
had already (well, at least recently) come to know—
not just believe but *know*—that *no natural theology*
is possible—despite 1000s of years of trying to establish it. God must be disclosed by revelation & revelation alone. This paved the way for me being able
to see a bipolarization of God to the world & I find
this "the world hated me before it hated you"
explicit in scripture (e.g., St. John). One reasonably
asks, "Why, if He exists, can't he *ever* be discerned
in the world?" (answer: He isn't there.) At first I
thought Valis was immanent deity! & that I *had*
found him in the world. But then last January I

---

*   *John.*

suddenly formulated the more accurate "Zebra" hypothesis which portrays him as a subtle, invisible world—mimicking invader—& then lately I got the "ham sandwich" model going—the triune topology.

Even my long held Brahman view was triune, the ham sandwich, with the empirical world as *Maya*, delusion, & deity being within, not in but inside, meaning "on the other—far—side."

Zebra counterfeits the counterfeit—which fits the Gnostic idea of the bumbling demiurge being helped out, out of mercy, by the *true* God. This helping out, not just of us humans but of the whole fallen (fucked up, not really real) cosmos is the transubstantiation of objects & processes on an invisible ontological level which I saw the growing *Corpus Christi* achieving. A Fake Fake = something *real*. God/the savior is mimicking this counterfeit cosmos with a stealthily growing *real* one. What this all adds up to is that God, through the Cosmic Christ, is assimilating our cosmos to himself.

His salvific mercy is not limited just to & for us humans but extends to all creation. As Paul says in either *Col.* or *Eph.*[*]—I think the latter.

Neither the so-called ontological proof of the existence of God (St. Anselm's) nor the empirical design-to-designer, etc—none hold up. Only revelation, initiated *by* God. He is indeed the *Deus Absconditus* [*Hidden God*]—Gnosticism explains why: He is not found in nature because he is not here, & our reasoning cannot discern him because we are occluded. God must reach down to us from "beyond" or "outside" the cosmos.

---

[*]   *Colossians* and *Ephesians*.

Since & inasmuch as Christ died for our sins, he wiped the slate clean; as Luther pointed out, when God sees (one of) us he sees his own spiritless son. So, even by this orthodox reasoning, we are not (now, anyhow) sinful. From a Gnostic standpoint, Christ "took the blow" aimed at us in retribution "justice" by the Archon or demiurge: Christ intervened between us. Just as in my case in 3-74 when they sprung the trap, it was not *me* in it but him, & he burst the trap & defied the world, the trappers.

I depart from Gnosticism & Mani in this regard: God does not *just* take the sparks of light out of the cosmos; he is infusing (good) ontology—his rule, i.e., the kingship of (the true) God onto, into this previously unreal Cosmos—which is, why I say, he is saving the *totality* of creation, by transubstantiation & assimilation & thus repairing the breach in the Godhead by operating through history, as Hegel saw. Besides rescuing us as individuals he rescues the species; besides the species, all life; besides all life all creation.

But: when the cosmos is assimilated it will as such cease to exist (the slice of ham). There will be no world qua world—so in a sense the Gnostics *are* right. We will be parts of a cosmic living organism, not of dead matter, i.e., Zebra.   *(1977)*

I, who was not a legitimate member of the ruling class (which is defined as, "those who get to define—control, generate—reality") via my writing, subversively obtained a certain small but *real* power to control. Create & define reality; the *next* step is [...] to enter (the ruling class) by the front door, *officially* welcomed. (& not infiltrate in by the back door as I did. But boy, what a good job I did; & VALIS is the best subversion so far; as Mark[*] points out, it *deranges* all (sic!) your learned preconceptions). Thus I via my writing can be said to be a revolutionary, & I carried with me into power, other people of my ilk. Many disenfranchised "misfits"—the quasi-insane, or *pseudo* (sic!) schizophrenics; ach! we are mimicking schizophrenia as a political tactic, in order to thrust the schizophrenic worldview onto the authorities as a tactic to infiltrate & vitiate them, "them" being defined as "those in power." The schizophrenic worldview was selected by us because it is (so) threatening to those in power due to its self-concealing logic, its non linear logic or null-logic (as Warrick[**] correctly says, I maintain Y = $\overline{Y}$)!! This is a political tactic on my part. A logic held for merely pragmatic purposes-causes-reasons. A *device*. A weapon (& it was so—& correctly—interpreted by the enemy.)

[. . . .]

The true name of the game is power (to define & hence control (people's perceptions of) reality), not consumer commodities like big house, Porsche & clothes[. . .] Those are sops—bread & circuses, mere toys *marked* "success" but still toys. Which is why I can spartanly disdain them in my pursuit to control the definition of reality through my writing, etc., & *I* say that reality is irrational & irreal & subject to manipulation by mind—which is a sort of handbook of ideology of control, to view it thus, & provides the disenfranchised with techniques (inner secrets) of *power*: almost shamanesque in nature. esp: Jason Taverner, even when totally stripped of power & identity, *destroyed* his police (i.e., authority) foe (pursuer).

---

[*]   Mark Hurst, then an editor at Bantam Books.
[**] Patricia Warrick, a literary critic with whom PKD was in correspondence at this time.

Lem & the party experts[*] saw correctly that in my writing I was handing over weapons (secrets) of power to the disenfranchised of the capitalist west; their appraisal of me is correct. Over & over in my books 1) power is studied; 2) who has it; & 3) how those denied it manage to get it.

Although appearing left wing my training is really Fascistic—not "Fascistic" as Marxist rhetoric defines it but as Mussolini defined it: in terms of the deed & the will, with reality de-ontologized, reduced to mere stuff on which the will acts in terms of deed. Since few living people correctly understand (genuine) Fascism, my ideology has never been pejoratively stigmatized by the left, but those to whom I appeal are in essence the core-bulk of latent masses, the fascist mob. I speak of & for the irrational & the anti-rational, a kind of dynamic nihilism in which values are generated as mere tactics. Thus my real idol is Hitler, who starting out totally disenfranchised rose to total power while scorning *wealth* (aristocracy) plutocracy to the end. My real enemy is plutocracy; I've done my (Fascistic) homework.[...] My fascistic premise is: "There is no truth. We *make* truth; what we (first) believe *becomes* objectively true. Objective truth depends on what we believe, not the other way around." This is the essence of the Fascist epistemology, the perception of truth as ideology imposed on reality—mind over matter.   *(c. 1978)*

Valis is the real & rational world breaking into (invading, as in e.g. UBIK) our simulated & irrational world. I'm saying, Valis is a *world*, a (the) *real* world.

---

[*]   Stanislaw Lem is here grouped (unfairly, it may be argued) with various unspecified "party experts"—leftist critics—who had written on PKD's works. See previous note on Lem on page 19.

Ubik is to the cold-pac world as Valis is to our world. If Ubik & Valis are one in the same, our world is both irreal (UBIK) & irrational (VALIS).

We're missing half our stereo signal—what I call the upper realm (one).

This notion that in 2-3-74 the real broke into the irreal (as in UBIK) is acosmic & Gnostic—& it agrees with another Gnostic idea (put forth in VALIS) that the creator of this world is irrational. A superior position cf. UBIK & VALIS is a superimposition of two basic Gnostic ideas, one cosmological, the other cosmogonical. It's very interesting, what you get if you superimposed VALIS over UBIK—& I had previously seen that VALIS is an electronic circuit-like feedback of UBIK & mixing, enriching, etc.[...] The rational is real; the irrational is not real. Our ordinary world is the latter into which the former has broken, invading it (as in UBIK, but now Ubik is seen not just as real but as rational & as world, an information world; put another way, information experienced as world). Different space-time worlds are different coherencies—systems—of information, the info content of each arranged within a 4 dimensional system. I believe that my 2-3-74 experience with Valis confirms the acosmism of UBIK and consisted of the breaking into this irreal world of the real, of whose nature I now have some idea. It is my belief that 2-3-74 verifies the acosmism of my 27 years of writing.

This invasion by the real/rational into the irreal/irrational is a *third* Gnostic *ur*-concept. (The *Salvator Salvandus* [*The Redeemed Redeemer.*]* So in what

---

* See, as an example of the use of this idea, the PKD novel THE DIVINE INVASION 1981), in which Emmanuel (the amnesiac male aspect of the godhead) is saved by Zina Pallas (who, like Pallas Athena, embodies holy wisdom and is the female aspect of the godhead).

way—if in any way—is my view & experience *not* Gnostic? In no way that I know of. We have the counterfeit creation of the blind demiurge, & the true God taking pity on us & invading this domain by outwitting the [*]

Oh yes. 4th idea: that this world is a prison with prison wardens (the archons). i.e., those who impose "astral determinism," which the Savior breaks (5th Gnostic idea!)

I seem to have—

Oh. 6th Gnostic idea. Anamnesis restores memory of our divine spark nature & celestial origin. Our *real* nature.

7th Gnostic idea; the saving Gnosis itself, which recalls to us our real nature.

Then the 1974 overthrowing of the tyranny by Valis is the Savior freeing us from our Prison. This is his prime role; he frees us, restores our memory & true nature, & gets us out of here. Meanwhile the true God transmutes this irrational irreal world into the real & rational. These are Gnostic ideas #8 & #9.

I now have assembled the complete Gnostic system with its two realms only one of which—the upper—is real (Form I of Parmenides). (As stated in VALIS) it all stems from the insight that our world is not real. Then we ask, not real in relation to what? (Something must be real, or else the concept "irreal" means nothing.) Then we ask, "What is the real like? And how do we find it?" & we ask, "How did this irreal world come into being? & how did we get imprisoned here?" & then we ask, "What is our real nature?"

If reality, rationality & goodness are not here, when are they? & how do we get from here to there? If this is a prison, how do we escape?

---

[*] PKD breaks off the sentence here.

We learn of a mysterious savior who camouflages himself to outwit our jailer, & make himself & his saving Gnosis known to us. He is our friend & he opposes this world & its powers in our behalf as our champion. & "one by one he takes us out of this world." The Valentinean* ontological assessment of knowledge is not that it (the Gnosis) leads to salvation or is knowledge *about* salvation. But that in the act (event, revelation, experience) of knowing *in itself* lies salvation. Because in knowing, there is a restoration of man's lost state, & a reversal of his present state of ignorance. Upon knowing, man is again what he originally was.

This view accords with 2-3-74. Upon knowing I became again what I originally was. & this involved me as a now-restored piece of the ground of being itself, from which I, as a piece of it, had fallen & forgotten & lost my nature.

My 10th Gnostic belief (v. *supra*) is that time is a mere counterfeit, of eternity.

When hyperuniverses I & II interact (to form our reality) *three* realms are created:

$$\text{NOT}\ \begin{cases} \text{I} \{\equiv \\ \text{II} \{\equiv \end{cases} \quad \text{BUT}\ \begin{cases} 1\ \{\equiv \\ 2 \\ 3\ \{\equiv \end{cases}\ \begin{cases} \leftarrow \textit{Eigenwelt} — \text{totally I (free)} \\ \leftarrow \textit{Mitwelt} — \text{mixture I \& II (partially free)} \\ \leftarrow \textit{Umwelt} — \text{totally II (enslaving)}^{**} \end{cases}$$

---

* Valentinus, a second century Christian Gnostic who was, circa 140 A.D., put forward as a candidate to become bishop of Rome, but was ultimately rebuffed as a heretic.

** The terms *Eigenwelt* (isolated, spiritual world of the inner self), *Mitwelt* (the middle or integrated world of the ego) and the *Umwelt* (earthly environment) were coined by the Swiss psychoanalyst Ludwig Binswanger in the course of his writings on schizophrenia. These writings, first read by PKD in the early 1960s, exerted a lasting influence upon him. See, especially, the PKD novel MARTIAN TIME-SLIP (1964) and its use of another Binswanger concept—that of the "tomb world".

or 1 heaven, the world of the Gods. 2 the world of men. 3 the subhuman world of blind deterministic nature. We can rise to 1 or sink to 3, but normally are in 2, the mixture. The purpose of art is to free us; i.e., lift us to world 1, the *Eigenwelt* by sharing it via the art with others.   *(c. 1978)*

So the BIP is an ossified complex in the macromind (brain) which must be dissolved. The Holy Spirit is like (sic—*like*) a metabolic toxin, i.e., a medication (measured amount of poison); this explains the "bichlorides" dream & the "aspirin of Mercury" dream.* &, like any mental complex, it warps other thoughts to itself—acts as a magnet, & creates uniformity (which is a term of entropy). There is—& has been—no progress or change in the complex for 2000 years.

If the complex (the BIP) isn't dissolved, it will eventually shut down the macromind (brain). It imposes its form progressively unless attacked (as if by a—or several—phagocytes). It is dead; the dialectic in it has ceased. Either it can get larger & impose its will on more & more contents of the mind, or it can be successfully attached & dissolved. Thus Zebra *invades* the macromind to do battle against the stagnant complex, which (the latter) isn't rational (*vide* Jung's statement about "nothing new coming into the psychotic mind"; then, I deduce, the macromind, due to the BIP complex, is psychotic, as put forth in VALIS). Zebra seems to be winning (v. 1974 & later). So *this* is what Zebra/Valis was doing in '74. & this is why I correctly perceive the BIP as lying unchanged in the past, present, & alternate worlds (& possibly future—& absolutely unchanging).

The whole thrust of my published corpus of writing

---

*   These phrases came to PKD in dreams he experienced in 1974.

is thematically a *Dissolving* agent—dissolving reality—
i.e., the complex (BIP)!!!!   *(c. 1978)*

All my writing, in which irreal, forgery universes
are presented, are expressions of Parmenides' insight
about the nonreality of Form II. This sets me &
Parmenides apart from Taoism. It prepares the way
for Gnosticism & the concept of a botched, bungled
world. Form II can be regarded as "False work," necessary but temporary. Yin was given the first try at copy-
ing the androgynous Godhead, & failed. The BIP
resulted. So Yang penetrated to add what is missing,
which is nothing less than reality itself.

It is not just the BIP which is not real; it is the Yin's
world, no less. Of course, we do not inhabit a purely Yin
world (Ground). Set (Yang) is here, too, to a very large
degree.

[. . . .]

Witness my writing. If there is nothing spurious
about Form II (Yin) & the phenomenal world I have
said nothing in my years of probing the theme. "What
is real & what is merely *seeming?*" This is no small matter—for me as an artist & for all life, which is enslaved
into illness, age, injury & death & loss by the Yin
world. The Yin world cannot sustain its own creatures.

How can something that doesn't exist exert coer-
cive power over us? For one thing, we obey it by giving it our assent (i.e., we agree that it is real), & having
done so we then obey its orders. We hold a self-defeat-
ing & improper relation to it; we *allow* it to be the Master. Primarily, we can't sort out the Yang (Set) part. We
are blinded. Yang allows this, since it wishes us to discern the puzzle & make a choice—without clear guide-
lines. Yang is making use of Yin for his purposes. A
puzzle is presented to us. We *know* that absolute good
(deity) exists, and yet we see a world of undeserved

suffering. How can these two coexist? I say, there are
two worlds & each has its own laws: one blind & rigid;
the other loving & sentient. Since we cannot perceptually unscramble them we see both coexistent, but in
fact it is 2 pictures superimposed (laminated). Also it
(they) is (are) in dialectic strife: "Blow & counter blow,
faster & faster as time runs out."

[. . . .]

In reading Sladek's parody of me,[*] I get the impression that to me the universe is not to be taken seriously,
probably because I am afraid of it, but nevertheless curious about it—fascinated by it, dangerous as I see it to be.
But that somehow a handle exists by which to unravel it
& make it yield up what it *really* is—*if* anything. It may
not be anything at all, but I'm trying for handle after
handle, poking around trying everything reversed &
backward, like it's a toy. Layer after layer reveals paradox after paradox, which in themselves I find fascinating. Also, I do seem attracted to trash, as if the clue—*the
clue*—lies there. I'm always ferreting out elliptical
points, odd angles. What I write doesn't make a whole
lot of sense. There is fun & religion & psychotic horror
strewn about like a bunch of hats. Also, there is a social
or sociological drift—rather than towards the hard sciences. The overall impression is childish but interesting. This is *not* a sophisticated person writing.
Everything is equally real, like junk jewels in the alley.
A fertile, creative mind seeing constantly shifting sets,
the serious made funny, the funny sad, the horrific
exactly that: utterly horrific as if it is the touchstone of
what is real: horror is real because it can injure. It all is a

---

* Science-fiction writer John Sladek published, in 1973, an admiring
parody of PKD's pell-mell cosmic style, entitled "Solar Shoe Salesman," in
The Magazine of Fantasy & Science Fiction. Phil enjoyed it so much at the
time that he sent Sladek a fan letter.

brave whistling in the dark tunnel—like Stephanie:[*] funny when frightened, scare her & she will tell you a joke—the situation oddly viewed. No wonder I loved her so & she experienced the affinity between—not sorrow & horror—but *fear* & horror.

I certainly see the *randomness* in my work, & I also see how this fast shuffle of *possibility* after possibility might eventually, given enough time, juxtapose & disclose something important, automatically overlooked in more orderly thinking. Pataphysique.[**] No wonder my stuff is popular in France—the surreal, the absurd. Also, it is palpably autobiographical—the little business firm, & the fatherly owner or world leader.[***]

Since nothing, absolutely nothing, is excluded (as not *worth* being included) I proffer a vast mixed bag—out of it I shake coin-operated doors & God. It's a fucking circus. I'm like a sharp eyed crow, spying anything that twinkles & grabbing it up to add to my heap.

Anyone with my attitude might just stumble

---

*   Friend of PKD's in the early 1970s.
**   Term invented by the French poet and playwright Alfred Jarry (1873-1907) to describe his science of efflorescent, absurdist wisdom. Jarry formally defined "*pataphysique*" as "the science of that which is superinduced upon metaphysics, whether within or beyond the latter's limitations, extending as far beyond metaphysics as the latter extends beyond physics." There is a two-bit actor named Al Jarry amongst the characters of the PKD novel DO ANDROIDS DREAM OF ELECTRIC SHEEP (1968). PKD was, in the early 1970s, elected as an honorary member of the College du Pataphysique—founded in honor of Jarry—in France.
*** The reference here is to Herb Hollis, the owner of two Berkeley shops—Art Music [a record store] and University Radio [appliances]—at which PKD worked as a salesclerk from 1944 to 1951. Hollis was a recurrent model for PKD in creating beloved "boss" characters—most notably, Leo Bulero in THE THREE STIGMATA OF PALMER ELDRITCH (1965).

onto by sheer chance & luck—in his actual life, which is to say, the life of his *mind*—the authentic camouflaged God, the deus absconditus; by trying odd combinations of things & places, like a high speed (sic) computer processing *everything*, he might outdazzle even a wary God, might catch him by surprise by poking somewhere unexpectedly. If it is true that the *real* answers (& authentic absolute vs. the merely seeming) are where we would least expect them, this "try it all" technique might—might one day succeed by believing what it would never occur to anyone else to believe, *really* believe—might take at face value as true the most worn out, most worked over & long ago discarded obvious "staring us in the face all the time" as the crux of the mystery. To be able to see mystery in the obvious—the best-camouflaged ultra-terrestrial life form might one day guess wrong & be flushed briefly out of its concealment (which had always worked before). For one thing, a totally naive person like this who would believe anything might believe in what is really there but conceptually automatically rejected by more experienced people. The child has faith in what the adult knows can't be & so could never see, obvious thought it be; i.e., before everyone's eyes: hidden in plain sight.

This kind of fascinated, credulous, inventive person might be granted the greatest gift of all, to see the toymaker who has generated—& is with or within—all his toys. That the Godhead is a toymaker at all—who could seriously (sic) believe this?   *(1978)*

The mad god James-James began generating world upon world, worlds unrelated, worlds within worlds. Fake worlds, Fake *Fake* worlds, cunning simulations of worlds, mirror opposites of worlds.

Like I do in my stories & novels (eg STIGMATA &
"Precious Artifact"). I am James–James.

I created one world among many & entered it &
hid myself in it. But the police detected me—the non-
terran police & tried to fake me out with the xerox
missive. But I knew it was coming—as soon as
TEARS appeared they would be sure about me & I
recovered my memory & identity & power & dealt
with it properly, & paid them back. My organization
helped me—it set off my memories, a month in
advance. I saw my creator—my creator, protecting
me. I am hiding here, under his protection. The network voice—she talks to me. I am patched in to the
network, so I am not alone. Meanwhile, my creator
("Zebra") patiently repairs the damage I've done, by
rebuilding the worlds. He harbors no resentment.
All I am allowed to do now is write about what I
used to do. In a sense I am a prisoner, but it's for the
best.

I learned this from "Precious Artifact." I am a mad
ex world-generator, now confined. But still periodically mad. I can't die. I am countless[ly] reborn—metamorphosed. I know the truth about the worlds I have
made, that they're not real—I know about *dokos*, simulations which will pass any test. They are not fantasy,
& they are only illusion to those who take them as
real. They are *skilful forgeries* which will pass inspec-
tion. They are indeed like metastasizing cancers. "A
world capable of splitting its perceived reality into
countless counterfeits of itself" however Lem put it.
(Does Lem know? He has guessed.[)]

Burroughs is right about the nova police[*] & them

---

[*]   The reference is, apparently, to William Burroughs' novel NOVA
EXPRESS (1964).

tracking down their quarry. But in my case, Zeus protects me. *Dythrambus.*[*]

There is a war. The police are moralistic, brittle.[...] But what can they do about me? [...] & anyhow my writing is all over the world. I've done my job. Undermined the Brittle Moralistic Police.

Given a new life with no memories I was still able to undermine. The worlds are cunning forgeries & the police are after me. But Zeus will always protect me, despite what I've done. Misused my ability. Lem may be on our side (my organization). In any case *he knows*—he knew before I did—i.e., before on 2-74 I remembered. The nova police fell here; I assisted in that, but only to a very tiny degree. TEARS contained the message: the quarry is innocent & the police will suffer, reprisal—what they love most will be taken away if they threaten with arrest. *Leave me alone!* I can destroy you. But in challenging them I gave myself away, lost my anonymity. They pressed me & I betrayed them to each other.[**] I can destroy you with what I know. You rule illegally; your mandate ended when the woman—called Isis here—died. Horus, you are my enemy. Shiva/Dionysos/Seth. Horus, I am not afraid of you—Isis is dead so you no longer rule. I am with her, bonded to her, I carry her inside me. You are Osirus. I am the legitimate new king in hiding. Search, find me—& you, *this* time, are destroyed; you don't want to find me this time as you did in 33 AD, because I am—I have my father's power this time, not just his knowledge.

We spring up everywhere: proliferated.

The time has come to render this world void,

---

[*]   An epithet of Dionysus, the cherished son of Zeus.
[**]   The reference here is to the incidents surrounding the "xerox missive". See "Editor's Preface" at page xiv.

to abolish it, & judge. Shiva. The police search frantically.

The innocent (the wild little ones of the forest) have nothing to fear. My extended hand tells them that.

Solemn-Pentheus-die. Felix happy Dionysos *live*. Pentheus Police General of TEARS—the *de facto* monarch.

In TEARS it is King Pentheus vs. Dionysos (Christ, Hamlet)—he is insane—intoxicated, a Generator of Worlds. Rome, Pentheus, against a Quicksilver Spirit he can't catch. Brain damage: SCANNER: an ad, for Mercury. I, the mad one, live on. Sanity at the center burned children, not pot. The mad one does not hurt the little innocents & so obtained Zeus' patronage over the serious ones, the old ones, who burned children in the name of brittle morality. The sane ones, the sober, somber ones (the police) are evil. We have a difficult situation here, *Abba* [*Father*]; the sane ones are murderers, & the insane ones gather flowers. You, *Abba*, know which of the two is to be protected—not the sane ones.

We destroy the worlds we generated, which are not real, but they destroy lives which are real. Who is guilty? They are. Who is guileless & innocent? We are, *Abba*.

Shiva holds a vial of poison, "to throw against the raging cosmic ocean which threatens to destroy mankind." His human devotees feel themselves females, married to him.

In my writing I am a destroyer of worlds, not a generator: I show them as forgeries. I unmask them & abolish their hold, their reality. I show them to be bogus, an infinitude of them, like so many skins.   *(1978)*

Thought (*Satori*): Dedalus & the maze he built & got into & couldn't get out of again—*at Crete*. Myth of our world, its creation, & us?

My dream about the elevator, the poem recited, the plate of spaghetti & the trident—palace of the Minos & the *maze*: clue to our situation? Well, then in my writing I figured it out; it *was* an intellectual, not moral error.

This would explain the technology! [*illegible*] layer. Pink beam of light, etc. the melting).

My books (& stories) are intellectual (conceptual) mazes. & I am in an intellectual maze in trying to figure out our situation (who we are & how we got into this world, & world as illusion, etc.) because the *situation* is a maze, leading back to itself, & false clues show up, such as our "rebellion."

There is something circular about our situation, esp. involving our occlusion! By our efforts we can't think our way out (i.e. get out—reverse the original intellectual error: paradox is involved, now) this is the clue! The occlusion would then be a function of the maze; its internalization.   *(1978)*

"But are you writing something *serious*?" Note the word.

Fuck. If they couldn't get us to write serious things, they solved the problem by decreeing that what we were writing *was* serious.

Taking a pop form as "serious" is what you do if it won't go away. It's a clever tactic. They welcome you in—look at Lem's 1000 page essay. This is how the BIP handles it if they can't flat out crush it. Next thing, they get you to submit your S-F writing to them to criticize. "Structured criticism" to edit out the "trashy elements"—& you wind up with what Ursula* writes.

Like I say in SCANNER, our punishment for play-

---

*   Le Guin.

ing *was too great*. & my last sentence is, "& may they be happy." (I got that from knowing what *"felix"* [*happy*] meant.)

"Let them all play again, in some other way, & let them be happy."[*]   *(1978)*

The fact that after 4½ years of strenuous exegete, whereupon I have reached these conclusions (not to mention 27 years of published writing) I now find myself being signalled to die—which effectively makes it impossible for me to put this Gnosis in a form which I can publish[**]—is a condition which can be deduced from my exegesis itself, & shows I'm on the right intellectual path, but *to no avail*. I am not extricated by my exegesis but by Zebra (Christ) back in 2-3/74. The exegesis would have provided the basis for a broad, explicated formulation to sow broadcast, but of course this can never come about; these insights will die with me. All I have is a three-feet high stack of chicken scratchings[***] of no use to anyone else as K.W.[****] tirelessly points out. To heap the burning coals of anti-meaning on me. I also have a lot of money for the only time in my life, but with no use to which I can or care to put it. My personal attack—war—against anti-meaning (by means of my mind) has gone the way of our collective primordial defeat at the hands—I should say quasi-mind—of the

---

[*]   See "Author's Note" in A SCANNER DARKLY (1977).
[**]   At this point in 1978, PKD was deeply troubled by his inability to write a novel ("a form which I can publish") that would satisfactorily encompass the events of 2-3-74 and after—*and* would satisfy his overdue contract with Bantam Books. Later in this year, PKD would write VALIS and accomplish his goal.
[***] The "chicken scratchings" metaphor is in likely reference to PKD's handwriting.
[****]Jeter.

maze; I merely recapitulate the ancient, original losing by mind in this exquisitely sophisticated board
game which we so cunningly devised for our delecta-
tion. This past time is once more the death of one of
us—*but* this time I am entirely through Christ—extricated—taken out of the maze: "One by one he is drawing us out of this world." I did not win; Christ won
me for his own, so vis-a-vis me alone the maze as
always won. I have earnestly sacrificed myself for
nothing & I did not realize this, naturally, until it
was too late to retreat back out intact. *Omniae viae ad
mortis ducent [All roads lead to death]*.

In a sense my 4½ years of exegete *can be regarded
as a further successful strategem by the maze*, in opposition to the Gnosis crossbonded onto me in 3-74 which
at that time gave me life—I gave up that life via my
compulsion to relentlessly exegete. But I see one further irony—one which amuses me (my only exit from
this trap): here is additional proof of the quality (success) of our original craftsmanship, so this final (?) victory of the maze over me, despite Zebra (Christ) is in a
paradoxical way *my* victory as a creative artist. (The
maze regarded as our work of Art.) After all, the maze
is a product of our minds. If the maze wins, our
minds win (are proven). If, upon entering the maze,
we outthink it, again our minds win. Ambiguity is
involved in either outcome (this may be the puzzling
dialectic revealed to me in 3-74). *In fact,*

Maybe in (during, in conjunction with) my 27
years of writing I outwitted the maze—as witness the 3
Bantam novels,* TEARS & SCANNER. Speaking about
me personally, I won in pitting myself intellectually
against the maze; I figured its nature out—in which

---

* THE THREE STIGMATA OF PALMER ELDRITCH (1965), UBIK (1969),
and A MAZE OF DEATH (1970) (republished by Bantam in 1977).

case 3-74 was the Jackpot payoff reward, the revelation you get for so doing. *(1978)*

Rightly, I seek beauty like Parsival sought the Grail—but what a price I pay.

I don't write beautifully. I just write reports about our condition to go to those outside of cold pak. I am an analyzer. *(1978)*

Ah! Realm I is at CAD[*] 45; Realm II is at 1978. (Am I repeating myself? Oh well.)

I ≡} Real time: CAD 45, the Roman Empire & the infant church.

II ≡} Spurious time: AD 1978. Or world of TEARS. Any world you want to name.

To experience *Acts* time & place is to encounter the upper realm, which has plenary overrule power over the lower realm. My stories and novels in which spurious realities are depicted refer to Realm II. The two realms have split apart. The brain invades Realm II out of Realm I, camouflaging itself & its thoughts. Realm II is dokos over the actual. Significant for Realm II—& us—is the return of Christ, which came when promised. He descends into Realm II & dissembles & annexes it piece by piece. As each piece is captured it is freed.

27 years of trying to chart the contours of the *real* landscape concealed by the fraud; at last, accomplished in TEARS. I always presumed a bogus phenomenal world. This approach finally paid off. Again &

---

[*]   Circa A.D.

again I put forth the notion that your world—& your memories—could be delusions & you would have no way to detect it (cf. Lem's statement of the problem: the brain fed a spurious reality; is there any test by which it can tell?)[*]

(& I relate this to Berkeley's idea of God directly feeding world to our percept systems.)

God can feed it to us, *or* he can enlighten us—deocclude us—via the Holy Spirit. The power is all his, not ours. Hence the concept of Grace, issuing out of the Mystery religions & the (correct) concept of the deterministic yin (lower) worlds & his reaching down from the pleroma to free (save) us (one at a time?). No, he interfered with our entire history in 1974! But people don't see or know.

I occupy the position of an O.T. prophet who pits himself against the evil king & reveals God's plan, which God reveals to him. Such prophets were rarely listened to.

I've done my best. *(1978)*

[. . . .]This is the paradox of, "Where should you most expect to find God?" A.: "In the least likely place." I discern in this the following: "In point of fact you therefore cannot find God at all; he must—will—find you, & *when* & where you least expect it"—i.e., he will take you by surprise, like the still small voice which Elijah heard. Or like Oh Ho the ceramic pot.[**] The Oracle may speak to you from the gutter (whatever "gutter" might mean in this context).

So my writing—itself part of the "gutter" & as Lem says, "Piling trash upon trash"—may serve as the sort

---

[*] See Stanislaw Lem, "Science Fiction: A Hopeless Case—With Exceptions" (1972).
[**] See VALIS (1981).

of gadfly kind of thing that Socrates considered himself to act as. My writing is a *very* unlikely place to expect to encounter the Holy; the *Koinos*,* the Message-processing, Ubik-like ultimate entity.

(September 1978)

[...]Then the illusions of space, time, world, causality & individual psyches will be abolished & we as primal man restored will again dwell—& know we dwell in the living information / brain of Christ & *Noös*,** where we belong: functioning parts of the whole, thinking as it thinks. Living & growing as it lives & grows. & once again experiencing the ecstasy of union with God our macroisomorphic father. These promises have all been made to us, & will be kept. But we do not know when. I speak as a witness who has seen & experienced what it will be like; the Savior woke me temporarily, & temporarily I remembered my true identity & task, through the saving Gnosis, but I must be silent, because of the true, secret, trans-temporal early xtians at work, hidden among us as ordinary humans. I briefly became one of them, Siddhartha himself (the Buddha or Enlightened One), but must never assert nor claim this. The true Buddhas are always silent, those to whom *dibbu cakkha* [*enlightenment*] has been granted. Yet, buried in my 27 years of writing lies information: in these writings I have told what I knew without knowing what I knew. I know now. This is the paradox: when I did not know that I knew (or who & what I am) I could speak. But now I am under the stricture of silence—*because I know*. The Journey, the Quest, ends successfully not in

---

*   See Glossary.
** See Glossary.

assertion but in silence. & among the things I know is
why, i.e., why that has to be.

Without knowing it during the years I wrote, my
thinking & writing was a long journey toward enlightenment. I first saw the illusory nature of space when I
was in high school. In the late forties I saw that causality was an illusion. Later, during my 27 years of published writing, I saw the mere hallucinatory nature of
world, & also of self (memories). Year after year, book
after book & story, I shed illusion after illusion: self,
time, space, causality, world—& finally sought (in
1970) to know what *was* real. Four years later, at my
darkest moment of dread & trembling, my ego crum-
bling away, I was granted *dibbu cakkha*—&, although I
did not realize it at the time, I became a Buddha ("the
Buddha is in the Park"). All illusion dissolved away
like a soap bubble & I saw reality at last—&, in the 4½
years since, have at last comprehended it intellectually—i.e., what I saw & knew & experienced (my exegesis). We are talking here about a lifetime of work &
insight: from my initial *satori* when, as a child, I was
tormenting the beetle.* It began in that moment, forty
years ago.   *(September 1978)*

Premise: things are inside out (but will at the
"apocalypse" assume their real shape). Therefore the
right place to look for the Almighty is e.g., in the trash
in the alley. & for Satan: in vast cathedrals, etc.
Through enantiodromia they will "on that day"
assume their rightful shapes—the great reversal. The

---

* During his third-grade year, the young PKD was willfully tormenting a
beetle that had hidden itself in a snail shell. But once he forced the beetle
from its haven, the urge to cruelty was suddenly replaced by an
overwhelming sense of all life being one and of all living beings bound to
each other by kindness.

jester in the tarot deck is the real king; the king card is
the deranged one, the witless one. UBIK in its commercials & final theophany shows this reversal process.
USA 1974 is really Rome c. 45 C.E. Christ is really
here; so is the kingdom. I found my way into it once.
The long path is the short path—ponderous books of
philosophy won't help me; Burroughs' JUNKY[*] will.
That "Thieves & Murderers" 17th century poem of
Herbert's[**] will. Stone rejected by the builder; the edifice is discarded; the true edifice is invisible—disguised as rubble (plural constituents).[***] The fly
grooming himself—they (the divine powers) have to
reveal the kingdom to you; you can never on your
own pin it down. So to search at all is to miss the
point. Tricks, paradox, illusion, magic, enantiodromia.
The apparently harmless xerox missive was my death
warrant. The AI voice says the secret stolen has been
successfully smuggled to me; I have it. But what is it?
My worst book, DEUS IRAE, is my best. God talked to
me through a Beatles tune ("Strawberry Fields").
("Nothing is real. Going through life with eyes
closed.") A random assortment of trash blown by the

---

[*]   JUNKY (1951) by William Burroughs. An autobiographical account of
heroin use and dealing, street crime, and the nature of addiction and cure.
PKD felt a kinship between his novels and those of Burroughs. (See also
pages 77-79 herein.) PKD would occasionally engage in cut-up writing
experiments, *a la* Burroughs, for example (as on one page in the Exegesis
not reproduced here) a narrative sequential reblending of alternate lines
from pages 59 and 61 of the first (Bantam) edition of VALIS (1981). These
experiments were occasional, never exceeded two pages, and were not
apparently intended for publication.
[**]   George Herbert (1593-1633), English Christian poet and mystic. There
is no poem titled "Thieves & Murderers" in the collected volume THE
POEMS OF GEORGE HERBERT (Oxford, 1952) and I have not succeeded in
tracing the phrase placed in quotes by PKD in Herbert's work.
[***] This sentence—with its mention of the stone rejected by the
builder—may allude to the symbolism of Freemasonry. The original title of
THE GANYMEDE TAKEOVER (1967)—a novel written in collaboration by
PKD and Ray Nelson—was THE STONES REJECTED.

wind, & there is God. Bits & pieces swept together to
form a unity.   *(1980)*

So if you push essence far enough in terms of
ascending levels, you find you have gone a full circle,
& you wind up encountering ultimate deity cooking &
riding pop tunes on the radio & popular novels, & a
breath of wind in the weeds in the alley.

It's as if the ultimate mystery is that there is no
mystery—it's like what Robert Anton Wilson says in
THE COSMIC TRIGGER about being outside the castle
when you think you're in, & inside when you think
you're out.

& in a way what is most paradoxical is that I said
it all in UBIK years ago! So in a way my exegesis of 2-3-
74 says only, "UBIK is true." All I know today that I
didn't know when I wrote UBIK is that UBIK isn't fiction. In all of history no system of thought applies as
well to 2-3-74 as UBIK, my own earlier novel. When all
the metaphysical & theological systems have come &
gone there remains this inexplicable [*illegible*]: a flurry
of breath in the weeds in the back alley—a hint of
motion & of color. Nameless, defying analysis or sys-
temizing: it is here & now, lowly, at the rim of perception & of being. Who is it? What is it? I don't know.
                                                                (1980)

I'm an addict; I'm addicted to infinity. This is Love
for God & an understanding of him on my part.

3-74, Valis, was the *Mens Dei* [*Mind of God*]. I comprehended it. It's a strange thing to be addicted to,
comprehending God's Mind.

I must be a Sufi; by "Beauty" (the essence of God)
read "pleasure"— because the why as to why I do it, it
is because it gives me pleasure.   *(1981)*

I can say no more. What I have done may be good, it may be bad. But the reality that I discern *is* the true reality; thus I am basically analytical, not creative; my writing is simply a creative way of handling analysis. I am a fictionalizing philosopher, not a novelist; my novel & story-writing ability is employed as a means to formulate my perception. The core of my writing is not art but *truth*. Thus what I tell is the truth, yet I can do nothing to alleviate it, either by deed or exploration. Yet this seems somehow to help a certain kind of sensitive troubled person, for whom I speak. I think I understand the common ingredient in those whom my writing helps: they cannot or will not blunt *their* own intimations about the irrational, mysterious nature of reality, &, for them, my corpus of writing is one long ratiocination regarding this inexplicable reality, an investigation & presentation, analysis & response & personal history. My audience will always be limited to these people. It is bad news for them that, indeed, I am "slowly going crazy in Santa Ana, Calif,"[*] because this reinforces our mutual realization that no answer, no explanation of this mysterious reality, is forthcoming.

This is the thrust & direction of modern theoretical physics, as Pat[**] pointed out long ago. I reached it in the '50s. Where this will ultimately go I can't say, but so far in all these years no one has come forth & answered the questions I have raised. This is disturbing. But—this may be the beginning of a new age of human thought, of new exploration. I may be the start of something promising: an early & incomplete explorer. It may not end with me.

---

[*]   A remark PKD attributed to Ursula Le Guin. See note on page 196.
[**]   Patricia Warrick.

What I have shown—like the Michelson-Morley experiment[*]—*is that our entire world view is false; but, unlike Einstein, I can provide no new theory that will replace it.* However, viewed this way, what I have done is extraordinarily valuable, if you can endure the strain of not knowing, & *knowing you do not know.* My attempt to know (VALIS) is a failure *qua* explanation. But, as further exploration & presentation of the problem, it is priceless. &, to repeat, my absolute failure to concoct a workable explanation is highly significant—i.e., that in this I have failed. It indicates that we are collectively still far from the truth. Emotionally, this is useless. But epistemologically it is priceless. I am a unique pioneer ... who is hopelessly lost. & the fact that no one yet can help me is of extraordinary significance!

Someone *must* come along & play the role of Plato to my Socrates.

The problem as I see it is that Plato was 180° wrong; the *eidos*, the abstract & perfect, does not become the particular, the imperfect; rather, the Q. should be, "How does the particular, the unique, the imperfect, the local, become the abstract, the *eidos*, the universal?" We must search particulars, the weeds & debris of the alley; the answer is *there*: I saw the mask & it works the opposite way from how Plato saw it; he saw the *eid* as ontologically primary, & existing *prior* to the particulars. But I saw the particular *creating* the *eid* (Or "phylogons" as I called them); this permanent eternal reality is built up on & based on the flux realm; all Western metaphysics is 180° off. Here is where the fault lies. Universals are real (nominalism

---

[*]   Experiment conducted by American physicists Albert Michelson and Edward Morley in the 1880s, which demonstrated that the speed of light was not affected by the motion of the Earth through space. It thus foreshadowed Einstein's Theory of Special Relativity.

is *not* the case; realism is the case, but the *eid begin* as many unique particulars. This (truth) is somehow tied in with my meta-abstraction: in it I somehow saw the *real* relationship between particulars & eide & this is the way, the Direction, the Flow, the Line in which actual reality move. Thus the lower gives rise to the higher & so is ontologically prior/primary—I mean the particulars. But the *eid* are not mere intellectual categories of ordering; they are intrinsically real. & this is what I comprehended in 2-74.   *(1981)*

Illumination: April Friday night 4:45 a.m., the 3rd, 1981. I saw the *Ch'ang Tao* (3-74). The more it changes the more it is the same, it is always new, always now; it is absolutely self-sufficient. I can at last comprehend it, how in change, ceaseless change—through the dialectic—*it is always the same*—oh great *Ch'ang Tao!* I saw you in opposition you are unified; unified, you oppose yourself; unified, you differentiate; unified, you become (the many) (yet you are always one (field)). You want nothing. The more you change, the more you become what you *are*. For you, change is: remaining constant. This is your great mystery: by changing (in the dialectic) you renew yourself, hence you never change. Always new, always now. What can be said of you is, *you are great* (in meekness!!!) The Gentle.   *(3 April 1981)*

CHAPTER FOUR

INTERPRETATIONS OF HIS OWN WORKS

So JOINT, EYE, STIGMATA, UBIK, MAZE & TEARS are progressive parts of *one* unfolding true narrative, in which the genuine Hermetic macro-microcosmology is put forth. The spurious world discerned for what it is, & in MAZE & esp. TEARS the true state of things put forth—to jog our memories *six* novels interlocked, along with a number of stories. We are not to be allowed our fugue (sleep & hallucinated worlds), because, due to the BIP from which we fled, this fugue over the past 5000 years turned lethal; the BIP grew & grew with our now-unwitting collusion.

[....]

SCANNER *continues* the narration of the previous six novels, not treating objective outer world as irreal, but going back to "Impostor" & studying false inner identity & lost memories of true self! The 2 identities war with each other, with an in-breaking of messages (the German, inc. from "Fidelio"*!!!) the German is from neither Fred nor Bob nor Bruce,** but, as the messages in UBIK, just break in "from the mysterious outside"! I never break in "from the mysterious outside"! I never before realized this—it isn't Fred, certainly. & it isn't Bob! It's another *ur* personality, speaking a protolanguage (based on my experience with the *koine* [*the Greek written and spoken at the time of Christ*]!). He has a grandfather (or granduncle?) who spoke German. An ancestor!

The info conveyed chronologically in the sequence of books is interesting.

1) EYE plural & subjective worlds.

2) JOINT world as simulated deliberately

3) STIGMATA plural hallucinated worlds concocted by an evil magician-like deity

4) UBIK messages of assistance penetrating the simulated world(s) "from the other side" by/from a salvific *true* deity

5) MAZE simulated world fabricated by *us*, to escape an intolerable actuality

6) TEARS the nature specifically of that actuality (an intolerable one—the BIP *Acts*)

7) SCANNER buried memories connected with lost identity; & protospeech breaking through, not into world as in UBIK but inside a person's *head. Two* psychoi one in each brain hemisphere, each with its own name & characteristics.

Plus such stories as "Impostor," "Retreat Syndrome," "Electric Ant," "Faith of ... " "Human Is" & "Precious Artifact," a *very* good one. & related themes in TIME-SLIP, MITHC, PENULTIMATE TRUTH, GAME-PLAY-

---

*   By Ludwig van Beethoven.
**   Characters in the PKD novel A SCANNER DARKLY (1977).

ERS, also even UNTELEPORTED MAN, (ANDROIDS DREAM treats memory-identity theme).

It is one story slowly unfolding, a vast tapestry, as Le Guin[*] pointed out.

No one book or story is correct & the others incorrect, & no one book or story tells it *all*. Many of them must be read—& this is the first time I see how SCANNER is an essential part of the Great Narrative—picking up where "2nd Variety" ANDROIDS DREAM & "Electric Ant" left off.

Even in JAPED there is a 2nd dissociated personality, a pilot for SCANNER.

This vast overtheme could be extracted from the novels & stories, but that alone would not prove it to be true. But 2-3/74 *did* prove it (both the themes of "inner" & of "outer") to be true, & it proved true in *one case*, for me, it must be objectively—intrinsically—true.

In SCANNER he (Fred) has forgotten who he really is (Bob, who equals Thomas vis-a-vis me, PKD). The *ursprache* [*primal language*]: breaking in/through, signals this forgetting, & is an analog of the in-breaking messages in UBIK, pointing to another—& real world or true protoreality now forgotten, but which can't be entirely denied. Thus I depict in SCANNER what may happen to those who read the *earlier* writing.

Bob = Fred
Thomas = PKD $\Big\}$ I never saw it before.

MAZE & TEARS tend to vindicate the view that some

---

*   Ursula Le Guin. The reference to her pointing out the tapestry-like interrelation of PKD is to her essay "Science Fiction as Prophecy: Philip K. Dick," in *The New Republic*, 30 October 1976.

element of voluntary forgetting (self deception on our parts) is involved.   *(c. 1977)*

In TIME OUT OF JOINT the world is a fake, & specifically the *real* world is another time-segment. My initial revelation in 3-74 was that the time was really around 70 AD—not later but earlier, a reversal of JOINT. Yet, the basic intimation is there, fully, in JOINT; this is all a cunningly fabricated delusion, the world we see, & the basic delusion has to do with the true *Temporal* locus. Since JOINT was SF I naturally put the *real* time in the future, not the past. Damn it. I've overlooked the extraordinary parallel between JOINT & my "it's really 70 AD!" experience. E.g.: the dream I had of the dark, old-fashioned house with the archaic window shades, the cracked mirror—& realizing I couldn't get out of that world without God's help. My incessantly recurring dream at the 1126 Francisco St house—that's where I lived when I wrote JOINT—that was the Fake world of the novel, & resembles the miserable old house in Placentia dream. Is there some clue in my 1126 Francisco St dream? It was with Joan* that I so recently saw it again, after many years. Maybe I have a soul which leaves my body in sleep & goes back in time &, (as in 3-74, forward).

Back in the Fifties when I lived at 1126 Francisco St actually, as expressed in JOINT *that* world seemed unreal; in actuality, "it was decades later" (in JOINT). But now that it *is* decades later, *that* past time & place seems real (or anyhow the past somehow) & *this* a fake. &, as I say, it is also astonishing how in '74 I fore-

---

*   PKD paid a summer 1977 visit to his old Berkeley address, 1126 Francisco Street, with Joan Simpson.

saw the Sonoma events of the past 3 months!* What is
my real relationship to time? I experience the near
past, the near future, & the very far past; a lot of my
soul or psyche seems to be transtemporal ... maybe
this is why any given present space time seems somehow unreal or delusional to me. I span across & hence
beyond it; always have—& the transtemporal is the
eternal, the divine, the immortal spirit. How long
have I been here, & how many times? Who or what
am I, & how old?

Reality outside confronts me as a mystery, & so
does my own *inner* identity. The two are fused. Who
am I? When is it? Where am I? This sounds like madness. But when I read the scriptures I find myself in
the world which is to me real, & I understand myself.
The Bible is a door (3:5?**)   *(1977)*

One fascinating aspect of UBIK is disclosed when
the question is asked, "Where did you (I) get the
idea?" The origin of the idea, in contrast to virtually
all other novels, is evident from the text of the novel
itself, although one must extrapolate from Runciter to
whatever Runciter represents, and the state of cold-
pac to whatever state we are all in. In the novel, information spontaneously intrudes into the world of the
characters, indicating that their world is not what
they think it is; in fact, it indicates that their world is
not even there at all—some kind of world is there, but
not the one they are experiencing. That time-regression is put forth in the novel, and that time-regression

---

* PKD lived with Joan Simpson in Sonoma County during the summer
of 1977.
** The possible reference here is to *John* 3:5: "Jesus replied: 'I tell you
most solemnly, unless a man is born through water and the Spirit, he
cannot enter the kingdom of God.' "

figured in my 3-74 experience—this still baffles me; the principle underlying the devolution (reversion) of objects along the form-axis in the novel is explained by a reference to Plato's theory of ideal forms, and I guess that applies to our world and to my own experience. However, until I recently studied the E of Philo[*] article on Gnosticism so thoroughly, did I begin to understand the triune reality division which must exist and which is also put forth in UBIK—if Runciter is God, and Joe Chip & the other inertials are analogs of all men, then the regressed world is the ham in the sandwich, and, as in UBIK, must be abolished; as in Gnosticism, this is accomplished, in a deity-like entity lying behind even Runciter; i.e., Ubik. It is this knowledge—not just information but gnosis—revealed to them, esp. to Joe Chip, which makes them aware of their real condition. Therefore if one knows very much about Gnosticism (which I didn't until a few days ago) one could see the resemblance between UBIK and the Gnostic cosmogony and cosmology. But we are talking (regarding the real world) of information which, by being transferred, radically changed history. And it must be realized (I certainly do, even if no one else does) that what broke through was not limited to information, but that theolepsy (one at least) were involved. If I rule out OCCP experiments[**] and occult human groups (*vide supra*) then we have something not found in UBIK, but, although admittedly described as diabolic, in STIGMATA. Is theolepsy not specifically what STIGMATA depicts? With Chew-Z or

---

[*] The ENCYCLOPEDIA OF PHILOSOPHY, the four-volume reference work that was a favorite of PKD.

[**] PKD sometimes theorized that the events of 2-3-74—most particularly the graphics displays of 3-74—might have been triggered by Soviet experiments involving the transmission of high-intensity microwaves or other energy-forms.

whatever, Can-D, I forget, the eucharist. What do you get if, as Le Guin suggests, you take a group of my novels & stories and fit them together, esp. the 3 picked up by Bantam?* Theolepsy, the Gnosis slipping through, reality (the world) as illusion concealing another but real world (MAZE)—what an aggregate message those 3 novels add up to!

When I recently reread STIGMATA I saw it for what it was: a penetrating, acute and exhaustive study of the miracle of transubstantiation, simply reversing the bipolarities of good & evil. What the novel contemplated was—that is, the conclusion it reached—was the startling notion that imbibing of the sacred host culminated, for the imbiber, in eventually becoming the deity of which the host was the supernatural manifestation of. Since all of them were consuming hosts of the same deity, they all became the same deity, and their separate or human identities were abolished. They literally became the deity, all of them, one after another. What this constituted in the novel was an eerie kind of invasion. They were invaded on an individual basis and they were, regarded another way, invaded as a planet or species, etc., which is to say collectively. This invasion by the deity bears a resemblance to the invasion of the regressed world in UBIK by Runciter's messages and, ultimately, by Ubik itself (as confirmed by the ad starting the last chapter). That ad clarified what Ubik was; it precisely equated Ubik with the *Logos*. There is no way to get around that. Ubik in UBIK is the same divinity as the St. Sophia mentioned in DEUS IRAE. So Runciter and Ubik equals Palmer Eldritch and Chew-Z. We have a human

---

* THE THREE STIGMATA OF PALMER ELDRITCH), UBIK and A MAZE OF DEATH .

being transformed into a deity which is ubiquitous (no one seems to have noticed that Palmer Eldritch is ubiquitous as is Ubik, that the same theme dominates both novels.)

The Gnostic contribution which MAZE makes is the idea of a totally untenable reality glossed over by a mass wish-fulfillment hallucination shared by everyone, and a salvific entity who can extricate you right out of that prison-like world.

MAZE: Prison-like world glossed over by illusion. Salvific intercessor who can and does extricate you. Induced amnesia.

STIGMATA: Invasion (penetration) of our world by a deity who can become everyone via the host, a mass theolepsy.

UBIK: Salvific information penetrating through the "walls" of our world by an entity with personality representing a life- and reality-supporting quasi-living force.

Collating the three novels, how much of the Gnostic message is expressed? Or, put another way, how much of my 2-74, 3-74 experience is expressed? One thing left out is the altering of the historic process, which was revealed to me as happening in 3-74. I suppose in a sense that's in FROLIX 8. And the breaching through by God and the hosts, the apocalyptic material from *Acts* and *Daniel*. There are little sprinkles in other novels and stories—for instance, the idea of anamnesis (expressed negatively usually in my writing by the theme of fake memories). Well, that's expressed in MAZE, so I've inserted it *supra*. I wonder what you get if you sit down starting with "Roog" and read through everything (including such strange stories as "Retreat Syndrome") all the way to SCANNER. If everything interlocks, what is the total message? I know I scared myself shitless that one night

when Isa* was down here and I reread some early stories in PRESERVING MACHINE. But my recent study of
Gnosticism indicates that below any negative world-
negating message there is an affirmation of God and
love. And truth must be told; we must go where it
leads us—where wisdom leads up (interesting typo; I
mean "us," not "up").   *(19 November 1977)*

[. . . .] So that's what I did in UBIK—correctly represented time spacially, & the past as spacially within—
literally within—the present. & in this speeded-up
process (never mind how you "speed up" purely spacial axes) information which is everywhere & conscious & which cooks pop media, such as TV
commercials—appears. No wonder they asked me in
May '74, "What is Ubik[?]"

& no wonder I saw how my 3-74 experience
resembled UBIK! I'll bet I was able to write UBIK
because of partially having had a time-into-space-con-
version experience prior to writing it (maybe due to
psychedelics).

I was *very* right in UBIK to see how it related to
Plato's forms. The past can be retrieved along a *spacial*
axis—as in UBIK! I did it, where I saw *Acts.*

Ach—VALIS is *such* an important book—it deals
dramatically & theoretically with the issues first presented in UBIK & is UBIK's logical successor (finally—
no more police state novel). UBIK, then, is a novel
representing a part-way enlightenment & UBIK is
related to STIGMATA and MAZE etc. I must in 2-3/74
have attained enlightenment as the result of decades
of gradual spirit (evolutionary) growth. There is a
direct connection between UBIK & 2-3/74 it has to do

---

*   PKD's daughter.

with converting time into space & the results
obtained therefrom, as put forth in VALIS.   *(c. 1978)*

Okay, Watergate got us out of S.E. Asia & disengaged
vis-a-vis USSR. Our interests are now served there
through China. It is against China that USSR now acts,
not us. This is crucial. Program A must have led to all-
out war between US & USSR. The *spirit* in us prevented first Nixon & then Ford from aiding S.
Vietnam. So (if my reasoning is correct) we of the
counterculture prevented WWIII. We hamstrung the
U.S. military machine. This counterculture did not
arise *ex nihilo* [*out of nothing*]. What were its origins?
Consider the 50s. The concept of "unamerican" held
power. *I* was involved in fighting that; the spirit (counterculture) of the 60s evolved *successfully* out of the
(basically) losing efforts by us "progressives" of the
50s—we who signed the Stockholm Peace Proposal, &
the "Save the Rosenbergs" etc.—losing, desperate
efforts. *Very* unpopular & *very* unsupported. Berkeley
was one of our few centers; this takes me back to EYE
IN THE SKY etc.

[. . . .]

    I *was* a vocal & active part of the 60s' countercul-
ture (cf. "Faith of . . ." to TEARS). What I am saying is
that because of being with Nancy[*]I, who was by physical age part of the 50s entered the youth culture of the
60s & even onto the 70s. By which time my writing
was having a decided influence; a PKD cult existed by
the time TEARS came out. I was/am still in touch, into
the *late* 70s! Early 50s to late 70s—not bad (contrast
this to other S-F writers[*)]; have there been *any* quasi-

---

[*]   Nancy Hackett, PKD's fourth wife, was 21 when they first met in
1964.

Marxist S-F writers besides me in 30 years? Tom Disch says no & *Aquarian*[*] says no. Now there are—finally, but they're hired & bought. They don't matter; it's too late—all over.[. . . .]

After all, the *Ramparts* people knew to approach me—the *sole* S-F writer who signed the petition—the manifesto—of the 500.[**]

Glanced over SOLAR LOTTERY & Tom Disch's intro;[***] he's right. I was/am the sole Marxist S-F writer. I may not have been/am CP [*Communist Party*], but the basic Marxist sociological view of capitalism—negative—is there. Good. But after glancing at it I feel the old fear—like c. 1971/73. Up to the month TEARS was published. Up to 3-74. When the blow fell. Glancing at SOLAR LOTTERY I can see that it had to, eventually, & *that I knew it.* If I just hadn't passed over into the dope stuff I'd have ceased to be relevant, & been safe but noooo. I got caught up in the 60s, & stayed on to 74 & TEARS.   *(c. 1978)*

God, *all* my "this is illusion" writing (EYE, JOINT, STIGMATA, UBIK, MAZE) are analogs of the USA 1974 vs. the glimpse of Rome CAD 45 via the Golden Fish sign.

"Here we are."

"But where are we *really*?"

& then someone gets a glimpse. (As in "the earth is hollow & I have touched the sky.") Usually, once the simulation is detected there are assorted guesses. But sometimes the first clue vis-a-vis simulating of world *is* the glimpse.

My God, my life—which is to say my 2-74/3-74

---

[*]   An interview with PKD, with accompanying text by Joe Vitale, appeared in *The Aquarian*, 11/18 October 1978.
[**]   See *Ramparts Petition* in Glossary.
[***] See "Introduction" by Thomas Disch to the hardcover Gregg Press edition (1977) of SOLAR LOTTERY (1955).

experience—is exactly like the plot of any one of ten of my novels or stories. Even down to fake memories & identity. I'm a protagonist from one of PKD's books. USA 1974 fades out, ancient Rome fades in & with it the Thomas personality & *true* memories. Jeez! Mixture of "Impostor," JOINT & MAZE—if not UBIK as well.

My earlier notes show that what I deduce from all this *as a certainty* is that we have a two-mind situation. Statements as to which world is real (if any) & which simulated (if any) are speculative. But the worlds are *not* generated by the person, since they both contain elements unknown to him (such as the *koine*). What the malfunction or induced malfunction prove is the existence of at least *one* world-generating mind, & (as I failed to see in those earlier notes) possibly *two* world-generating—even competing—minds. Plus the passive, programmed observing little non world-generating mind.

Is this a battle for his allegiance? World against world, mind against mind? The voice last night scathingly referred to USA 1974 & the corresponding PKD personality as "Both being expendable." Diabolic interpolation/simulation?

Could the two worlds be regarded as two domains?

(July 1978)

God, I have broken myself in this pursuit over 27 years. Critics compare my malignant false worlds to metastasizing cancer. I demand that deity appear or somehow put its stamp on world before I can accept it as anything but a diabolic counterfeit interpolation. We have been deceived for thousands of years. The Neoplatonists such as Plotinus knew of two realms. The Essenes (v. Josephus) report a lower realm of feverish unconsciousness, the poisoned, intoxicated soul. "Men *like* to sleep."

(July 1978)

EYE, JOINT, 3 STIGMATA, UBIK & MAZE are the same novel written over & over again. The characters are all out cold & lying around together on the floor, mass hallucinating a world. Why have I written this up at least five times?

Because—as I discovered in 3-74 when I experienced anamnesis, remembered I'm really an apostolic xtian, & saw ancient Rome—*This is our condition:* we're mass hallucinating this 1970s world.

What's got to be gotten over is the false idea that a hallucination is a *private* matter. Not hallucination but *joint* hallucination is my topic, inc. false memories. I know where & when we really are, now: Rome C. AD 70. But how come we imagine, believe in & see 1974/8—that I can't explain—except the "ape of God" by Satan theory or that real time ceased when Power wasn't transferred at Christ's time.

My intuition that what we see—this world—isn't really there paid off in 2-74 when I saw the Golden Fish & got my memories & identity & vision back. But how & why the *Dokos*? Did we collectively become victims (slaves) of something evil?

The *Acts* material in TEARS verifies when & where we are. On some level I've known for a long time—or else I've had divine help.

I guess the divine power is getting the truth across to people in my writing—in the 5 novels listed above that what we *do* see is fake, &, in TEARS, what, instead, is actually there, hidden (the world of *Acts*).

How to reach the real, inner, hidden world is described in UBIK—retreat back along the platonic form axis. It is fully theoretically & cosmologically set forth in that novel.

Either I unconsciously knew it, was subliminally told it, or it was a lucky guess. But in view of the

larger case—situation—being correctly described, I
guess I knew it on an unconscious level—anyhow, it
wasn't a guess. Perhaps 1) I've made one of the Greatest Discoveries any human ever made, & put it in my
book; or 2) I've been let in on one or more Great Esoteric Secrets.   *(1978)*

To repeat myself—all this implies that the intervention re the xerox missive was not just to save me per
se from a trap, but to keep my actual identity concealed. Evidently originally I knowingly & deliberately entered this "spurious interpolation" in order to
call attention to its counterfeit nature, that I might
assist in destroying it. Cold-pac in UBIK, the floor of
the Bevatron in EYE. Polyencephalic fusion in MAZE,
the fake past in JOINT, but best of all, the Satanic
bogus worlds in STIGMATA, because in STIGMATA the
correct source/cause is presented. & then in TEARS the
true nature—not of a—but of *OUR* Satanic spurious
interpolation is depicted—as well as its collapse & why
(xtianity).
   Yes—in TEARS it is shown, through Felix
Buckman's conversion, what will pull down the BIP &
allow transfer of authority: xtian conversion (from
Power to Love (*agapé*) this adds to what e.g., STIGMATA
has told us; we now know the antidote to the "drug."
(i.e., to the cancer-like bogus interpolation).
   Xtianity is antidote (to a poison). "We need medi-
cal assistance."

As GRASSHOPPER* is to the world—people—in
MITHC so the N.T. & TEARS is to us.
   I remember what gave me the idea for JOINT, the

---

* THE GRASSHOPPER LIES HEAVY is the novel-within-a-novel in THE
MAN IN THE HIGH CASTLE (1962).

reflex of reaching for a light-chain—overhead—when there wasn't one. This subcortical conditioned response was sensationally escalated in the "car air vent, cooler, moister, higher climate" & beer & he-she of 1974 ... escalated. But of a piece.

Indeed, I am from elsewhere & elsewhen. The on-off overhead light chain that wasn't there—that was my first clue ... & (as shown in JOINT) I saw that a *time* dysfunction—or deception—was what it was all about.

(1978)

Like Garson Poole[*] I may have changed my inner reality tape programming, & so saw something different.   *(1978)*

SCANNER as I've said before is the other half of TEARS, the inner half. The conditions described in SCANNER explain why we don't see the conditions described in TEARS, & the conditions described in TEARS account for the conditions in SCANNER. The various books were written in the wrong order. But they can be read in the right order, or anyhow gestalted (if read, they *will* be gestalted).[...]

Correct sequence:

1) SCANNER: Occlusion of our minds, without our being aware of it; loss (forgetfulness) of true identity. v. (7)

2) TEARS: What our world is really always like which the occlusion is deliberately there to keep us from seeing.

3) STIGMATA: Who/what deliberately occludes us: the Yaltabaoth Magician evil deity, spinner of spurious worlds creator of illusion & inhabiting, contami-

---

[*]   Protagonist in the PKD story "The Electric Ant" (1969).

nating (unclean presence in these degraded pseudo worlds[)].

4) MAZE: The negative hallucination M.O.[*] of the occlusion, & reference to Savior who extricates us from a hopeless trap & pseudo world.

5) UBIK: The salvific entity per se, by *name* & how its "pan-Sophiaistic" messages come through the trash layers to aid us. Past available within the present.

6) DO ANDROIDS: A vital theme, that of Mercer & his reality through some sort of mystic identification via empathy. The role of animals. The tomb world. The "Fake-ness" of Fakeness: my "2 slit" logic.[**]

7) "Impostor": disinhibiting stimulus restoring blocked memory. (v. (1))

8) "Faith of . . ." God, evil, communism, drugs, hallucinations—a montage of *many* elements.

9) Every other relevant story & novel, from JOINT to "Remember Wholesale," "Electric Ant," "Retreat Syndrome," etc., not listed in 1) through 8).

& 10) EYE: Subjective private worlds &, as in "Faith of . . ." an evil deity & communism are discussed. *Plural* worlds which *we* generate.

SCANNER is the weary final point: *our minds* are fucked up. It isn't just a case of pseudo worlds. This links with 8), "Faith of . . ."

All in all, my writing casts doubt on the fact of (even possibility of) knowing actual reality *because* our minds have been fucked over. Some evidence (e.g. TEARS) points to the real situation being prison-like—but MAZE & esp. UBIK point to a supernatural salvific

---

[*]   *Modus operandi.*
[**]   PKD sometimes theorized that reality was formed by beam-like dual elements—"real" and "spurious"—that could fashion a hologram-like world by the superimposed image created by the two beams after coming through two opposite slits. Hence the term "2 slit" logic.

interventive power, although STIGMATA seems to say
that an evil magician deity is in control of our worlds
& heads.

MITHC is a fascinating adjunct to all this, i.e., to the
Gestalt. Fakes are discussed. Alternate universes exist.
Fascism is the topic, & a book is reality, which seems
to have some connection with TEARS. MITHC seems to
be a subtle, even delicate questioning of, what is real?
As if only the 2 books in it, GRASSHOPPER & the I
CHING are really the only actual reality. Strange. So
MITHC must be listed as 11). But now the order of revelation breaks down. & does MARTIAN TIME-SLIP add
anything? Pathological private worlds are presented,
& the disintegration of world. So 12).

& 13): GALACTIC POT HEALER. More about the
Salvific deity.

& 14): PENULTIMATE TRUTH. Lies & Government.
Fakes again—always the Fakes.

But TEARS & SCANNER are crucial in a special
sense, because the fictional or phantastic element is
virtually lacking; they are obviously semi-mimetic,
esp. SCANNER which is explicitly stated to have happened, & in a sense *not fiction at all*. Does this book,
then, seem to say, "Maybe portions of the others are
literally real, too?" The author does not now pretend
to be writing fiction, & TEARS fits this category as well.

One critic said that NOW WAIT FOR LAST YEAR
seemed to depict the Vietnam War. So maybe it, too,
adds something. But for sure we have

1) SCANNER   occluded minds, not able to see
2) TEARS   prison world created by
3) STIGMATA   evil deity who is opposed by
4) MAZE   salvific entity mysteriously here
5) UBIK   salvific entity mysteriously here
6) ANDROIDS   salvific entity mysteriously here

7) "Imposter" Fake memory; real ones & true identity restored, v. 1)

Summary:

Our minds are occluded, deliberately, so that we can't see the prison world we're slaves in, which is created by a powerful magician-like evil deity, who, however, is opposed by a mysterious salvific entity which often takes trash forms, & who will restore our lost real memories. This entity may even be an old wino.

Drugs, communism & sex & fake plural pathological pseudo worlds are involved, but the puriform salvific entity, as mysterious as quicksilver, will save us in the end & restore us to true human state. We will then cease to be mere reflex machines. This is the summation of my *kerygma*, spread out throughout my works.

Briefly, I was Christ. He is not a person but a state of being—& yet somehow also a person. It is mysterious. "Christ has no body now but yours." I became him, & he me. The macro became the micro (me), & the micro became the macro (him). There was a reciprocal action:

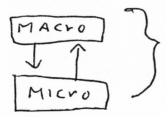

as if the two traded places. He became a mere human, with human fears (such as of the Romans), & I acquired his 1000s of years of memory & knowledge.

Maybe that's why I was in the world of *Acts*: he is there (i.e., then). This included memory of coming down here from the Caelum (the stars), cosmological knowledge and healing knowledge, & ability at last to see the macro brain & its info traffic & finally the father (the abyss). This exchange fits the hermetic macro-microcosm universe, which, in my summary of my writing, I should point out as a latent theme. This exchange would explain my performing (& knowing) the pristine early covert sacraments, & seating myself on the judgement seat. That's why this began *exactly* on the day of Christ's birth. & the sense of vast spaces: my inner space world now contained the cosmos itself, & of course seeing Zebra—that most of all.

This is the mystery which Paul speaks of: "*Christ in you* (& you in Christ)". Christ was born in me, literally him, and now firebright slumbers, the product of our union (with me as female host). (as impregnated bride, wedded to Christ as Bridegroom.)   *(1978)*

It's odd that it's mainly in the 3 Bantam books[*] that the truth (enough of it, anyhow) is told. Plus SCAN-NER & stories in the Ballantine collection[**]—all well-distributed. *No* time passes, in STIGMATA. Eternity can pass: infinite time. & Eldritch pollutes all the spurious worlds—due to a person taking a *drug* (cf. SCANNER).

MAZE says, "Our *actual* reality is intolerable." This will do, were TEARS not read. "So we willingly generate a group hallucination & live in it." Gnosticism—& *it is so.*

My writing deals with hallucinated worlds, intoxicating & deluding drugs, & psychosis. But my writing acts as an *antidote*, a detoxifying—not intoxicating—antidote. This is a fascinating realization. My writing

---

[*]   THE THREE STIGMATA OF PALMER ELDRITCH (1965), UBIK (1969) and A MAZE OF DEATH (1970) were all reissued in 1977 by Bantam Books.
[**]   THE BEST OF PHILIP K. DICK (1977)

deals with that which it lessens or dispels by—raising those topics to our *conscious* attention, esp. SCANNER & STIGMATA. Different partial collations print out somewhat different summations. One vast panorama is unveiled, as Ursula points out.[*] What an odd constituent POT-HEALER is!

In the James-James dream I saw the PTG task force arriving silently & swiftly. So they must be close by, now (but to say "now" is to fall into the delusion of regarding linear time as real. They could be seconds away. But Palmer Eldritch can spin out his hallucinatory world & time for what *seems*—just seems—forever, for centuries. It's like EYE when actual rescue is right at hand but they can't wake up. Yes, we are asleep like they are in EYE & we must wake up & see past (through) the dream—the spurious world with its own time—to the rescue *outside*—outside now, not later. Perception of the PTG task force is not perception of a future event, but, as in EYE, of what is *really* there *now*.

So EYE collates well with STIGMATA re spurious world, re being unconscious, re no real actual time elapsing (& probably, too, with MAZE). (In MAZE the

---

[*]   Ursula Le Guin. See note on page 196.

salvific element reaching *into* our spurious world is treated so MAZE adds *the* crucial element to EYE which completes the picture). As in DO ANDROIDS, the savior *seems* to be fake (invented) but turns out to be real. Everything here is reversed; the real is fake and the fake is real. (the mirror effect.) After all, the master magician rules here, *& has power over our perceptions.* (As in STIGMATA.)   *(1978)*

STIGMATA *is* a Satanic Bible: the novel describes the *Pattern* proliferating itself in, on & through humans. By a study of STIGMATA one can understand transubstantiation, which was my source & theme (my intent). It's even stated in the novel that Eldritch is the xtian God.

You get a good deal of the story by combining UBIK & STIGMATA.

But this is not an occluding, toxifying "virus"—it is an antitoxic, de-occlusive.   *(1978)*

Ah! in UBIK locating the Ubik messages in cheap commercials was absolutely right on. I couldn't have "guessed" more accurately. It's obvious that the real author of UBIK was Ubik. It is a self proving novel; i.e., it couldn't have come into existence unless it were true.[*]   *(1978)*

[T]he "information virus" Zebra destroys the 4-pronged deformation which I have delineated (*supra—previous set of pages*):

1) It shows us the real world TEARS
(abolishes the counterfeit world) MAZE
2) It abolishes the inner occlusion SCANNER
(restores our faculties as they are supposed to be)

---

[*]   PKD footnote: "I wonder if Lem guessed this."

3) It breaks the "astral determinism"

(It frees us) "Electric Ant"

4) It removes amnesia "Impostor"

(Restores true memory & hence true identity)

In short, it turns us into the "Second Adam," the restored xtian superman, a Christ. It abolishes the four aspects of our fallen nature. This is why the Gnostics believed in the salvific Gnosis; they confused the information with the information *entity*; i.e., they thought the *former* saved us, whereas it is the latter: *living* information, not the *content* of the information. However, the content *is* the pattern, so in a sense they were right. & it was an evil world (TEARS) & evil demiurge (ELDRITCH) that they believed in.

real world: TEARS "Retreat Syndrome" "Precious Artifact"

real deity: STIGMATA

salvific entity: UBIK

real situation: MAZE EYE JOINT

our condition: SCANNER SHEEP WE CAN BUILD YOU

our identity: "Impostor"

our enslavement: "Electric Ant" PENULTIMATE TRUTH

memory retrieval method: MITHC

eleven novels, four stories (for openers)   *(1978)*

Leo Bulero defeating Palmer Eldritch is the savior/messenger (Son of Man) defeating the demiurge creator of this prison (& illusory) world. Breaking his power over man in UBIK, Runciter calling to Joe Chip is the savior calling to his human counterpart. This is also true in POT HEALER when Glimmung calls to Joe Fernwright.

& Mercer & the Walker-on-Earth [*in ANDROIDS*] are one & the same. Deity takes trashy & even fake (sic)

forms: Mercer, Glimmung, the UBIK commercials.
SCANNER is a very serious book. Man's present, unredeemed states—his *ontological* condition—of ignorance
is depicted; this is not an *aspect* of his state but *is* (*esse*)
his state. Opposed to this is the ontological state of
knowledge (knowing) provided by Runciter & Ubik in
UBIK. SCANNER focuses on the condition of ignorance
dealt with more glibly in MAZE & UBIK; it goes into the
anatomy of the occlusion—it really studies nothing
else (no cosmology is presented). Mainly, it strives to
show that we are fucked up in a way which precludes
our being able to be aware of it—the most ominous
kind of occlusion (ignorance). It points to the need of
outside intervention.

VALIS will be an attempt to show that intervention
& redeemed state, but it is proving too difficult to
write. This novel *must* be written, & I have the
redeemed state of 2-74/2-75 to base it on, but God,
what a task: to depict 1) that which redeems; 2) the
process of redemption; 3) the redeemed (restored)
state of man—in contrast to the occluded state
(described in SCANNER). It could take the rest of my
life to do it. I don't know if I can. It must be divided
into two parts: 1) unredeemed (& then the entity
which redeems & the process); & 2) the redeemed
state. Like the "Siddhartha" 2-part book I dreamed
about. Restored man—the Christ-man, the 2nd Adam.
What a responsibility—what a task. But it must be
done. & it must—like the "Siddhartha" book, point to
the 5th Savior whose coming is imminent.   *(1978)*

In some respects, EYE is the most accurate of all:
Great hunks of spurious time (events) are reeled out,
whereas only seconds in RET (real elapsed time) have

taken place. If we didn't dream we could not even imagine such a thing, much less believe it.

The theme of "they're all out of it" appears in:

1) EYE they're unconscious & hallucinating various worlds.

2) JOINT the world is fake—& the time is mistaken

3) TMITHC it's one of several worlds & not the real one

4) TIME-SLIP fake psychotic realties

5) STIGMATA fake malignant realities

6) UBIK they're dead & receiving messages from the real world

7) MAZE they're jointly hallucination [*sic*] a spurious world

8) TEARS several competing worlds exist

9) SCANNER the whole futuristic parts could be hallucinations & the protagonist lives in two different mutually exclusive worlds competing with each other

Secondary false *perceptions* appear in:

10) CLANS psychotic perceptions that compete

11) GAME-PLAYERS levels of illusion for sinister purposes

12) COSMIC PUPPETS one world underlying another (!)

So one dozen novels & too many stories to count narrate a message of one world obscuring or replacing another real one, spurious memories, & hallucinated (irreal) worlds. The message reads "Don't believe what you see; it's an enthralling—& destructive, evil snare. *Under* it is a totally different world, even placed differently along the linear time axis, & your memories are faked to jibe with the fake world (inner & outer congruency).

JOINT opens with a telltale anachronism. Symptoms—or signs—unveiling the world as spurious

abound. Strip the fake world away & another one
appears, even set in a different time.

   & all this leads up to my 2-74 & 3-74 experience. It
cannot be coincidence. My early knowledge of the
basic Socratic and Presocratic dictum: "Don't believe
what you see; something *else* must actually be there."

                                                    (1978)

He is here, not here, there, not there. Our whole reality is a hologram-like fake, & into & onto it in the
guise of fakery, he substitutes the (truly) real. So the
nonsense phenomena are real, & the substantial & normal & expected & sensible are not. Our criteria for dis-
tinguishing the real from the irreal are totally
reversed: to us, the real is the solid, the heavy, the serious; & the irreal is St. Elmo's fire, will-o-the-wisps.
Amazing! If this be so, then my writing has been of
value. Beyond the obvious contribution of indicting
the universe as a forgery (& our memories also) & present[*ing*] the most accurate & stringent—rigorous—
revised criteria to pull the truly real as set out of
ground (love, making exceptions, humor, determination, etc., the *little* virtues). &, as Lem says, I somehow
pile trash on trash until it "compresses" into something else: the mirror-opposite, "universe-seen-back-
ward" insight is complete, as in POT HEALER.

   I believe the Savior is here. But disguised as well,
that's the hard part, isn't it? To say how he's disguised—how he appears in contrast to how we *expect*
him to appear. He may resemble Runciter.   *(1978)*

   Thoughts upon reading the first half of VALIS: we
are in a situation like the cold-pac in UBIK. It is a hologram reality; time, space, causality & ego are not real—
the world (phenomenal world) is not real but

projected. We have pre-programmed lock-in tapes synchronized with the total outer matrix. Subliminal cues
& info are fired at us constantly; "reality" is really
information (as I saw); we are a brain, [...] the controllers are the 3-eyed telepathic deaf, mute builders with
crab-claws; this explains who *they* are. They can read-
just our hologram at will. We are under their domin-
ion, & we perform a useful cerebral function. They
equal Valis which equals Ubik & which breaks
through on the one-way "eerie manifestation" basis
which Lem depicts. It *is* a spurious reality & their technology generates it, & although they aid & inform us
they also occlude & control us (this is "astral determinism"). They can & do intervene in their own system;
we know this as "God." They use camouflage & mime-
sis re their presence here. There is a teaching-machine
element involved. *Timeo cognere. [I fear to know.]* In a
sense the 3-eyed people in their bubble looking down
at us were not so much physicians but surgeons,
using laser beams to recontour our hologram. They
are not *in* the hologram but above it (i.e., outside the
cold pac, they've sent Zebra-Valis-Ubik in). Because of
my book VALIS they're going to zap me.
[....]
1) We are the project.
2) We are in the maze, which is irreal.
3) The 3-eyed people observe us from outside the
maze.
4) The project operates through a dialectic; it is
in flux.
5) It is irrational; its creator is irrational.
6) We are stationary; time, ego & causality don't
exist.
7) Human saboteurs have begun operations here
in the maze to help us. They (the human ones) are
under the direction of a vast information entity which

camouflages itself. It got itself born here & was killed & then spread out discorporate subsuming & inform- ing humans *counter* to the control (of us) (& our world) by the maze & its creator & controllers. It is rational.

8) In essence the liberators-saboteurs work to enlighten us with knowledge of our true condition, which is withheld from us by the deluding maze which generates both positive & negative hallucina- tions that we're rigidly locked into. We do not ordinar- ily guess that our "world" is irreal, that it is a maze, a project, that its creator is insane or that the 3-eyed peo- ple gaze down at us dispassionately as if we're pond life—lower life forms.

9) The maze-project is like a prison in which we're enslaved. The Black Iron Prison.

10) In essence, the rational (Valis/Zebra/Ubik) has invaded the irrational maze/prison/project.

11) We are sick or injured or insane/occluded due perhaps to a toxicity of the maze ("the bichlorides: a very poisonous poison.")[*]

12) So Valis is an information center disseminat- ing the truth, & also liberating us. It *may* be a product of the maze-project, evolving within it & then liberat- ing itself which is to say us. The purpose of the maze & its dialectic—& the problems it poses (esp. epistemo- logically)—may have been to produce Valis.   *(1978)*

A close reading of MITHC shows it is *not* an alter- nate world novel. There is only *one* real world: *ours.* Juliana finds (figures?) this out & tells Abendsen that his book is true. By implication, their world is a pseudo-world. Hence MITHC is an early pseudo-world

---

[*]   This phrase comes from a 1974 dream by PKD.

novel of mine, like JOINT & EYE & STIGMATA & UBIK & MAZE. Now, if in 2-3-74 I had an experience combining Abendsen's & Tagomi's, & found myself in TEARS, does that make *this* a pseudo-world, a *dokos* over TEARS? I think this is the whole point, it is a matrix entity about which there can be varying views some false, one correct, & TEARS is correct. These are not true alternate worlds. How these *dokos* views come into existence I do not know. Or is there just the one *Dokos* world which we normally experience, beyond which or under which lies TEARS? Then TGLH* to MITHC as TEARS to our world—a vast mystery! & one about which I have no theory. TEARS depicts a tyranny!

Since *I* didn't know the future (2-3-74) I can only suppose that another self exists in me which not only knew the future but the true state of affairs.   *(1979)*

reality—My God; it's specifically stipulated that Ubik is *the*—not *a*—reality support! ("He causes to exist what-

Palmer Eldritch (Center)	vs.	Ubik (trash layer:
Satan in power		true divine power)
evil	Both are	YHWH (*Logos*)
the sacraments!	← →	on the periphery
author of irreal worlds	everywhere	cheap TV ads!

ever exists"; functional description of YHWH!)

The underlying secret (cf. *Hamlet* & *The Bacchae*) is that the true king (YHWH) (Ubik) has been deposed & an impostor (Palmer Eldritch) rules in his place, as (if

---

* THE GRASSHOPPER LIES HEAVY, the novel-within-a-novel in THE MAN IN THE HIGH CASTLE (MITHC) (1962).

he were) *him. (Bacchae—the Christ story—Hamlet—*TEARS—
& also STIGMATA & "Faith") That's part one. Part two is
that the true God (YHWH, Ubik) has filtered back in on
the periphery. But the impostor is at the civil & church
center. Thus people think they are worshipping Christ-
YHWH-Ubik but aren't; they are under a spell (of delusion—which Christ/YHWH freed me of in 2-74).   *(1979)*

Consider my boundless & insatiable interest in
spiritual matters—there's no sign of it in TDHG [*THE
DARK-HAIRED GIRL, see Glossary*]—yet I had a Bible with
me in Canada. Yet consider how *Acts* read upon my
seeing the cipher in TEARS—the plasmite; the test
became *alive.* It was a living thing. Like my dreams of
the pages of the Great Book. I was in touch with the
information basis underlying the epiphenomenal
world.

Between what I experienced (2-74 to 2-75) & what
I've learned—

I experienced reality as knowledge—not reduced to
information. But the primary information from which
reality stems: what the rabbis call "the formula" for
creation, & the answers to all problems—i.e. solutions
(explanations).

So in my incompleteness I was driven along a colli-
sion course with (to) disaster; but Valis (YHWH-Christ)
converted the disaster into the raw materials out of
which there came instantly (!) a new me, a complete
me, yoked to Christ himself as the presiding priest
of this eucharist in which he sacrificed himself to
renew me.

& when I saw Valis—& was communicated to by
Valis—I saw *him,* the high priest presiding at this
eucharist. The epiphenomenal universe became him,
body & blood: the Cosmic Christ.

In TDHG it is evident that I am desperately trying to find a center (*omphalos*) for/to my life, but that I was failing; I was still "stateless." [...] In contrast to TDHG period I have found authenticity—*sein*.* I have made one wise decision after another. Look at my providing help to Messiah**—contrast that to when I used to buy dope.

                                                            (1979)

I just now looked over DI [*THE DIVINE INVASION*]. As I recently realized about VALIS, the dialectic that is the inner life of God—as revealed to Boehme & explicated later by Schelling—& commented on by e.g., Tillich***— is presented as the very bases of the book. In VALIS it is expressed dramatically as world-order in which the irrational confronts the "bright" or rational, designated (properly) *Logos*. In DI this same dialectic reappears & this time is *stated* to be the two sides of God (rather than world order; that is, in DI it is now correctly seen to be *within* God himself!): it is now (in DI) between Emmanuel who is the terrible, destroying "solar heat" warring side—& Zina who is loving, playful, tender, associated with bells & flowers; & what unifies the two at last (by the way: it is *she* who takes the lead in restoring memory & hence unification: Emmanuel is the side that has forgotten—i.e., is impaired; she has not & is not is not impaired) is *play*. She plays, & Emmanuel has a secret desire to play.
   So both novels basically deal with the dialectic that I experienced as the nature of Valis & which I con-

---

* Being; term employed by German philosopher Martin Heidegger to connote authentic being.
** A church in PKD's neighborhood.
*** German mystic Jacob Boehme (1575-1624). German Romantic philosopher Friedrich Schelling (1775-1854). German theologican Paul Tillich (1886-1965).

strue to be the dynamic inner life of God. If you superimpose both books, then, you get this equation:

Really, then, DI simply continues the fundamental
theme of VALIS—but does not *seem* to do so—not unless
one perceives this theme & what it is (the dialectic
that is the dynamic inner life of God). DI is not so *loose*
a sequel to VALIS as it might seem (by in the shift from
Gnosticism, the present, realism, to Kabala, the
future, fantasy).   *(1981)*

GALACTIC POT-HEALER shows the very real possibility of encroaching madness. The archetypes are out of
control. Water—the ocean itself—which is to say the
unconscious, is hostile & rises to engulf. The book is
desperate & frightened, & coming apart, dream-like,
cut off more & more from reality. Flight, disorganiza-
tion: the way has almost run out. Those elements
dealt with in earlier novels—ominous elements—now
escape my control & take over. What Brunner[*] said,
"That one got out of control" is correct & has vast psychological significance.

---

[*]   John Brunner, British science-fiction writer. The quoted remark was
apparently made during a personal conversation (date unknown) between
the two men.

& yet I did not become psychotic. Why not? What happened?

Very simply the meta-abstraction was the birth of higher reason in me. Specifically & precisely *Logos*. It *was noesis*, but, more, it was *Logos* itself. & *Logos*—not just as reason, although it is that—but Christ: Christ is the power of the rational principle itself.

The Dialectic that I experienced in 3-74 was between the irrational & the rational, in me, in world, in God. The rational won.

The issue is properly stated in VALIS, which shows not only a return of control but is an account of victory— in the form of rationality, of *Logos* itself—over madness; I am not only rational, I also depict as open, autobiography, this battle in me & this victory. Ursula is both right & wrong. "Phil Dick is moving toward madness"[*] does not apply to VALIS but to GALACTIC POT-HEALER; already with TEARS & then more so in SCANNER reality has re-entered; I am again in touch with the real.

[....]

VALIS, is, then, the *return* from madness or near-madness, an account of a *prior* inner struggle & not a symptom of that struggle still going on. By the time I wrote VALIS the battle had been successfully won; & the proof of this is DI &, most of all, BTA[**] in which Angel Archer is (as I have already realized) the rational principle in me, which is *Logos*, that is to say Christ, itself speaking; the victory by the "bright" side in me is total. Thus I was saved by Christ as the

---

[*] In 1981, an unfortunate misunderstanding arose between PKD and Ursula Le Guin, which led PKD to believe that Le Guin feared for his sanity—a concern Le Guin denies having harbored.
[**] BISHOP TIMOTHY ARCHER, the original title of the PKD novel THE TRANSMIGRATION OF TIMOTHY ARCHER.

inbreaking of the rational principle, *Logos* or reason itself.

The meta-abstraction is the moment in my life in which the rational principle entered, in-broke, was born; thus it is correct to say, in that moment Christ was born in me, & the year that followed was Christ in me, *enthusiasmos* by Christ: his kingdom or, more correctly, kingship.

[. . . .]

Ursula is right to see me—my mind—as threatened by ominous encroaching madness, but VALIS is a lucid *post mortem*, a deliberate & rational study, of this issue. This battle, & the victory of the rational in me (experienced as Valis, *Logos* or Christ). [. . .] I came through & emerged victorious: but just barely. GALACTIC POT-HEALER shows how grave the issue was, & this was written *before* the main thrust of the need & suffering hit (from 1969 on).

SCANNER then, shows that human reason returned sometime after GALACTIC POT-HEALER. But in 2-74 *divine* reason (*noesis*), the Logos, Christ himself, entered me or occurred as if in response to the last savage attack—the xerox missive—of the years of problems I had gotten myself into by my madness, folly, drug-use, etc. VALIS shows me completely aware of the situation (encroaching madness) & completely back in control—which DI & then to an absolute degree BTA verified. There is in me the voice of reason—the AI voice. But that voice became more than a voice; in 2-74 it broke in as the principle of reason itself, specifically as Plato's *noesis*: the highest act of cognition known to man. Thus 2-74 has both *noesis* & *Logos* & hence Christ.

& the ultimate overflow of grace in me shows up in my giving to others; I am not only strong enough for myself alone—more: starting with my sending the money to Covenant House.*[...]

I who lost *normal* reason, got back in the end Holy reason ("He who loses his life will save it"): Christ as *Logos*. & VALIS correctly tells this story: madness & drugs caused by Gloria's suicide, & finally the inbreaking of the rational, *Logos* itself (seen in terms of world!).

Now, it is certainly wonderful to realize that I am all right, now; that in fact I am even able to help others as well as myself. But the flip side is: I did slide into psychosis, & POT revealed it, & I wrote POT *before* Nancy left me.**[...] I guess my realization came (last night) when, after reading POT & realizing that I *did* become psychotic I then picked up SCANNER. I read here & there. The *appalling* horror of that book! To go into that *from* psychosis; that is, how terrible a fate awaited me. What saved me was my love for those people: Luckman, [...] Jerry Fabin [...] & Donna [...]*** which ties in with TEARS & the scene at the all-night gas station.

Thinking back to when I wrote POT: I felt so strongly—& correctly—at the time that when it came time, in writing the book to have the theophany occur (i.e., for Glimmung**** to show himself) I had nothing to say, nothing to offer because I knew nothing. Oh, & how I sensed this lack of knowledge! & now this is pre-

---

* A New York-based shelter for homeless and runaway children.
** Nancy Hackett left PKD in 1970. The end of the marriage was difficult for him to bear, and he had often pointed to it as the crisis that precipitated severe psychological difficulties for him. His emphasis here points to the fact that GALACTIC POT-HEALER (1969) was written in 1967-68, and hence his "psychosis" predated Nancy's departure.
*** Luckman, Jerry Fabin, and Donna are characters in the PKD novel A SCANNER DARKLY (1977).
****Glimmung is the semi-divine protagonist in the PKD novel GALACTIC POT-HEALER (1969).

cisely what I *do* know because now I have experienced it (2-3-74).

In a way I better depict the 3-74 theophany (of Valis) in DI than in VALIS itself. In any case if you superimpose the *two* novels it is there—precisely what I lacked when I wrote POT—& *knew* I lacked, as a human, as a writer; I had no ideas about the theophany at all, & yet by the time I wrote DI it came easily, that which would not & could not come with POT; that in writing POT that exactly was where I reached the end—wore out & died as a writer; scraped the bottom of the barrel & died creatively & spiritually. What misery that was! Paisley shawl, hoop of water, hoop of fire;* how wretched it was; how futile.

Strange that later (1974) I experienced what I had yearned to know so that I could continue the logical organic growth & forward development of my writing. *That* was when I wore out: trying to depict a theophany. & that is what I legitimately later on (in the VALIS trilogy) *could* do. But oh the years of suffering! & yet—if I became psychotic in writing POT—if POT shows signs of psychosis, & it does—it is not because I experienced & knew God but precisely because I did *not*. & thus the VALIS books are the opposite, are sane, are grounded in experience & in reality because by then I *had* experienced God; hence my creative life (not just my spiritual life) resumed; & with it my sanity. Thus in a very real sense my sanity depended on my experiencing God, because my creative life logically demanded it—& [...] my sanity depended on my writing.   *(1981)*

Break the power of fake world by means of info. (1)

---

* These are manifestations assumed by the Glimmung (see previous note) in GALACTIC POT-HEALER.

UBIK (2)2-3-74 hence VALIS & JOINT & MAZE etc. VALIS logically follows in the 10-volume metanovel that leapt off
with MAZE. No one has noticed that VALIS picks up
where MAZE left off. The epistemology is unbroken &
cumulative. VALIS shows I *am* questioning whether
world is real; retroactively it shows I meant it in the
prior 10 novels [see second chart below].*

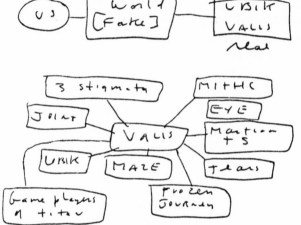

Isn't it perfectly clear
in UBIK that world is not
real but Ubik is, & Ubik is
Logos/YHWH. Likewise
Valis in VALIS.

VALIS is the cipher
book—code book—to the
whole 10-volume
metanovel & will some-
day be read as such. &
VALIS is Gnostic/Mani
but secretly Holy Mother
Church

—which explains TEARS—that is, the *Acts* material in it.
As with God's strategy, the sequence is "out of
sequence." Viz: the key piece—VALIS—came last. Until
it the others did not make sense—i.e., they were taken
to have been written as fiction & hence hypothetical.
VALIS *retroactively* re-interprets them—shows them in
a light that could not be anticipated by an analysis of
them—until VALIS came out; typical of the pattern
strategy of the wise horn in its Dialectical Combat-

---

* "Frozen Journey" is not a novel but rather a story published by PKD in
Playboy (December 1980) and subsequently included—as the renamed
title story—in the PKD collection I HOPE I SHALL ARRIVE SOON (1985).

Game.* Here is a *big* realization & unexpected: VALIS
in itself means nothing!   *(1981)*

DI is a conventional romance exactly as John
Clute** says; it breaks no new theological ground whatsoever & should not be taken seriously ... except for
the light it casts in amplifying material in VALIS.

VALIS deals with the irreducible primary religious
sense: God as terrifying & fascinating simultaneously,
with the solution being Christ & *only* Christ; there is
no other solution. VALIS states the problem (familiar to
all truly religious humans) & the correct—& sole—solution. From a religious viewpoint then, it is authentic
& basic. & it is indubitably firsthand, not Derived
from Book. Thus it is an extraordinary religious confession & resolution to the problems raised & con-
fronted in that confession, so it is not just a confession
but seeks & finds an answer.   *(1981)*

The issue is not reality or ontology but consciousness—the possibility of pure, absolute consciousness
occurring. In terms of which material things (objects)
become language or information, conveying or recording or expressing meaning or ideas or thoughts: mind
using reality as a carrier for information, as a lp
groove is used to carry information: to record, store &
play it back. This is the essential issue: this use of
material reality *by* mind *as* a carrier for information
by which information is processed—& this is what I
saw that I called Valis, & anyone who reads VALIS &
thinks it is just a rehash of metaphysical ideas or ideas

---

*   The metaphor here is the dual horns of dialectic—of which the "wise"
is one.
**   Science-fiction critic. Reference is to a review in the *Washington Post*.

"worked over by 1000s of thinkers for 1000s of years" is a fucking *fool*! Robert Anton Wilson[*] is right. *(1981)*

2-3-74: I was bewitched. The purpose: to re-create Jim [*Pike*] so he could continue speaking (through my writings & not just the Archer book).[**]

So there is a book within a book. This is what is hanging Russ[***] up. I have done years of research in order to do BISHOP ARCHER—to deal with Jim adequately in the form of mental conceptions about God & specific knowledge of the Bible & theology. I did not have this in 3-74; I could not write the novel until now.

But there is another intellect in the book, & that is Angel Archer.

Angel is my soul, & Tim/Jim is Christ. Their 2 minds in BISHOP ARCHER represent the syzygy between me & Christ. Angel Archer is how Christ, who is me, perceives me as she (Angel Archer), the female part of the divine syzygy between me & Christ.

This is 2-3-74. *(1981)*

I started to reread VALIS but this time with conscious knowledge of the Aquarian symbols, & it hits you at once in the opening of Ch. 2: God & clay pot linked. Later, pot will become a pitcher containing a liquid, this linked to xtian immortality & reincarnation, finally to Gnosticism; then to the great scene in the film in which the woman is—

Anyhow, the Aquarian symbols overwhelm the fish symbols; they come first & simply are extensive,

---

[*] This most likely refers to a 1981 letter from Wilson to PKD that praised VALIS highly and compared it, in terms of narrative originality, with ULYSSES.

[**] Published as THE TRANSMIGRATION OF TIMOTHY ARCHER (1982).

[***] Russell Galen, PKD's literary agent.

complex, indomitable, clear & religious *not* astrologi-
cal. What VALIS seems to do—& in fact do primarily!—
is associate the Divine with the Aquarian symbols as
completely as we are accustomed to seeing it linked to
the fish sign, & in a certain real sense I transfer Christ
over from the fish sign, without repudiating it, to the
water pitcher sign (clay pot is pitcher held or filled
with water). *Thus my neo-iconography is exact,* & this,
to me, is indubitable verification; QED. Because *this*
iconography in connection with Christ was not only
totally unknown to me, *it is also totally unknown to
Christianity itself,* & therefore points to Christ & xtianity *outside* Christianity (as does the 5th Savior notion!)

There is a final comment by Kevin[*] about the barefoot woman in the long old-fashioned dress dipping
water from the stream into the pitcher/pot: she is
back in Roman times; thus the Aquarian iconography
carries back to apostolic times, a point that B. Creme[**]
made on the interview program. It *is* in the Gospel.
But obliquely.   *(1982)*

---

[*]   Character in VALIS (1981). See chapter nine of that novel for the
"comment" referenced above.
[**]   Benjamin Creme—a New Age figure who influenced PKD's thinking in
the last months of his life. PKD heard Creme being interviewed on the
radio.

CHAPTER FIVE

PLOT OUTLINES AND EXPLORATIONS FOR WORKS-IN-PROGRESS

Novel plot, the twin-brains/minds: the U.S. fear is that the Soviets are using their research into psychic esp powers for long-distance mind control etc. Like electronic boost of telepathic suggestion via satellite; maybe even specific persons in U.S. affected (or so the U.S. counterin. thinks). Specific individuals reached in their dreams without knowing it, their views and even decisions influenced. This is the theory, anyhow; SOMETHING, ANYHOW, IS HAPPENING. And then it happens to the protag: the Essene reborn inside him; the Parousia is here! That is what's happening! Yep; a superpowerful mind-force was indeed influencing people, causing them to do things they otherwise wouldn't, and yes they are secretive about it, reluctant to talk ... as he himself becomes (since no one would believe him—and he's to help overthrown the tyranny, which adds this to the VALIS-Abendsen[*] plot, of the tyranny overthrow!!!)

This superimposes the two plots: VALISYSTEM A and TO SCARE THE DEAD. Wow!

Plot:

From inside he learns the Albemuth whale's mouth sign and how to fashion the ideograph.

FOMELHAUT

ALBEMUTH

Drawing by PKD (c. 1974) of what he termed the "Albemuth whale's mouth sign." PKD saw a relationship between this ideograph and the Golden Fish necklace, as well as with the homoplasmate which he believed may have bonded with him. PKD further saw a linkage between this sign—when drawn repeatedly, to form a connective chain—and the DNA double helix; DNA and the homoplasmate were, in his view, analogous forms of living information.

A mysterious organization imperils him; he's taken over and subjected to psychological testing to acquire from him the contents of his mind. The psych

[*] Hawthorne Abendsen is the author-character who wrote THE GRASSHOPPER LIES HEAVY, the novel-within-a-novel in THE MAN IN THE HIGH CASTLE (1962). PKD had attempted a sequel to HIGH CASTLE in 1964, and remained fascinated with the possibilities of Abendsen as a character into the mid-1970s, as this reference indicates.

tester of it draws the whale's mouth sign under duress, in a "trance," later finds it and doesn't remember having made it. Protag cannot figure if these are his powers, or Theirs. But they work in his behalf.

He keeps seeing the sign ... like emblem for beer company, used in their ads on billboards; he sees little kids gazing at it, or like emblem for kentucky fried chicken places, where kids always go.

Nobody else can discern it but him (and there must be others like him; this is main plot element; his conviction, his search). They call it "an eye, with a pupil." (The fried chicken designer swears this.) A scientist, when asked to analyze it as a symbol, decides it's the Earth within its magnetic or electrostatic plasma, which is blue. No one but God's Own know it as it is built up, in layers.

Men become what they are not, are transformed; but this doesn't mean into their opposite. What they become can't be predicted (I guess the best bits from each, the ideal pieces, are all retained and used to form the new pattern, plus pieces never used but needed, even if contrary to the person's ego and values as they were.) Like, his friend could be one who has changed who was/is a Nazi; the best parts of that: the remnants in that person to be preserved (micro paradigm of mankind).

One of the most long-lasting and major plot ideas comes when the head of the mysterious organization commissions the building of an observatory like place to screen incoming signals from VALIS; work on The Project begins. It orbits the earth and will be visible to the world, once the parts are joined ... when they are joined, they form the Albemuth sign, although it was impossible to discern this beforehand (he tried to be sure of that: "the sum is greater than the whole of its parts," etc.).

But the signals are interchanged throughout and among everything, even on the "mundane" plane. The Trash of the gutter "conspire" to signal people information. I think reserved for last should be the scene with the little things of the gutter talk [*sic; ing*] to him (to the former or still Antagonist).

Amazing, how like TEARS this is ... the Antagonist must not be desk man, but still, isn't he a cop? Maybe a fanatic of some kind? Maybe never an Interior VP by him, like Buckman was. Always outer, except final scene, when he walks in alley and trash talks to him.

Antag is afraid it'll form a pattern when through, and has as much randomized by computer as possible. Tries to see it himself as world progresses, but can't. Final bit which "makes" Gestalt is dealt in plot outline: why the particular designer of that part came to design it that way ... we follow him as separate plot moving to join other plots, as his part does. He can see that when his part is towed into place it'll make a—that—pattern, but he is motivated: for odd motivations, which we show in detail: the series of motivational events leading up to him consciously deciding to alter away from the design, without in any fashion having any large motive, anything equal to or commensurate with the result. For instance: suppose this minor character is convinced that the Antag is deliberately going to produce the WM [*whale's mouth*] sign, or that "they" will cause it to happen because they control Antag without Antag knowing it; Antag is in their power. Maybe he even has dreams inspiring him to create his segment this way, which he interprets will outwit them; otherwise it will. He is convinced that Antag is deluded—which Antag is; Antag worries that some deluded section chief will cause change without mentioning it—

which minor ch. does. So pattern does emerge: "two
wrongs make a right." Deluded Antag and deluded
section chief at cross purposes, both attempting to
foil pattern, produce pattern.

Better: the shape comes out okay, not the sign, but
like the word which the sign stands for (Albemuth)
appears all over the Project (e.g.: the name Al, for
instance. The initial B. The German word for courage.
Albert or Alfred Muth has his name on all the
papertowel dispensers in the washrooms. The world—
Logos—appears assembled everywhere as it's supposed
to be: albemuth. Made up as an anacryon,[*] by someone to express the idea of Courage to the project, his
own name, Al, be courageous! Or A number one, be
courageous, etc.

Best of all if "Al" is one one item in every washroom, like towel dispenser, and the rest elsewhere.
And then in every washroom the whole name is
assembled from its two parts. "Have or be courageous" could be one part, and then "Al" is A-one," a
stamp indicating # of unit bolted to it. Or poor schizy
guy thinks of Behemuth etc. Takes "Beware Leviathan
and Behemuth come" and so forth from tract, feeds it
into computer; other schizy guy, but this one not
Jesus freak but double domed German sees "be courageous" in it as it's shredded or decyphered, thinks,
"Be courageous," and as it's shredded—the Bible
thing—he punches out the bemuth. To remind himself???? Maybe this sort of method:

Three parts of which "b" is middle. We work it backward, the way mystery stories are written. "B" from
start is their code to destroy, the Adversary organization. "Muth" is German for courage and is name of

---

[*]   This stands as PKD typed it.

mfgr of dispenser. The "Al" is marked on each automatically when it's been installed and read for use. When master machine-computer sees the world "coming along through ortho time" it signals each entity (towel dispenser) destroyed, using B symbol, but symbol must be placed on each entity to mark it, where it remains.

The computer can't mark the dispensers for destruction without using the "B" mark. Which will complete the *Logos*. It knows it. Double-bind.

No, it would be the "A-One Towel Service."

Computer decides not to use "B" stamp; refrains. Then scene of guy who enters washroom. Stands at urinal, and we catch his line of sight; you gotta be there at that spot, at each urinal. First the "A-one" then into a slogan-sign posted (one in each washroom) reading:

> ARE YOUR THOUGHTS YOUR OWN? THE
> ENEMY MAY BE INFLUENCING YOU WITH-
> OUT YOUR REALIZING HE IS!

He catches the ending "be," then finishes pissing, goes to washbasin; already he has seen the "muth" part. In the BG [*background*] the ubiquitous Muzak is playing "I'll see you in Deluth," and to himself he is murmuring. "Deluth ... albemuth" without knowing why. Dries hands. Fade out. Except that the whole orbiting space-station is pointless anyhow because although the info is coming from Albemuth (Fomalhaut) it's everywhere; hence always already here on Earth, so the Project is pointless. Given the pointless duplication of the human Adversary and the computer who check and recheck and monitor each other.

This Group Mind from the stars is their own noösphere, in Earth's ionosphere; the enemy (to the

Adversary) is themselves; they'd have to burn off the ionosphere and stop all radio traffic to abate it.

One of the levels of cover to the drawn symbol (the flux plasma around the Earth) is the or a real meaning.

Duplication of the word; keep the Jesus freak handing out tracts about Leviathan and Behemuth; also in addition keep the German with his "Be Courageous." Computer sees the words in tract shaping up to join the "Be courageous," heads that off; not so the towel biz; it misses that. "Be courageous" gets fed into computer itself because it is thought—i.e., telepath-operated; it notes, rejects; sees how tract will link up with German "muth." No, "German Muth" twice; on towel dispenser and in German's head. How about if guy in washroom gazes briefly into mirror at his teeth to see if they're okay, his whole face. No, just strike these: the name "Muth" on towel dis. and the guy looking in mirror...he sees Al which is A-one, adds the BE from the slogan and *hears* the "Deluth," forms Albemuth in his own head from 2 visual and 1 audio sources. And this: "As he scrutinized his features in the mirror over the wash basin, his hair, then his mouth." So A-one / BE / "Deluth" / mouth. 3 visual, 1 aural. (Sees "five o'clock shadow by mouth (word in text)"[).]

(The plot use of "b" as destruct code: they must eliminate their destruct code finally; also for their German workmen the word "Courage." Sees it shaping up as German word in say slogan, and then the destruct symbol with it; must destruct destruct symbol before it becomes bmuth. or b-muth. Can't order Slogan term al458 "Courage" struck from list; falsely sees this coming up, when any slogan with "Courage" is translated into German.

Nutty Soviet theory: a vast explosion in future, and we are traveling backward in time for limited

period. An explosion so that what we see now as movement toward form is reverse of explosion, or implosion; but we see the universe as expanding . . . why?
Because our perceptions are backward, too. Or maybe
space isn't going backward, but must expand to coun-
terbalance time which is running backward, etc. Anyhow, he announces, (Dr. H.K.)[*] soon we will reach
moment of explosion; he's calculated that, by running
film backward. Soon all the pieces should be in place.
Living in this reverse period, we've learned to adjust
subtemporal events to fit. It's total sweep that's backward, not "subtemporal" adjustments which we insti-
gate due to misperception; he carefully discerns and
divides these from the sweep; these adjustments are
all errors due to our basic perceptual reversal. We
have introduced erroneous views and acts stemming
from them; however, none of these acts have any
effect, we still run away from the explosion ahead in
time (actually are now moving—aw fuck. A see-saw.
Anyhow, there would be a two way time-motion simultaneously[)]:
    The explosion took place. Everything flew apart.
We are in that flying apart (expanding universe) but
see it backward, in that already part of the time flow
has corrected itself and is carrying us in the correct
direction; otherwise we would move away from the
explosion forever. But we are moving, or anyhow
there is the orthogonal flow within the flow going
opposite to the direction we perceive; a mobius strip
with time running both ways at once. This can easily
be represented in terms of gravity, when a boomer-
ang is thrown out . . . at this moment the time-flow is
far greater in one of the two directions, but he has

---

[*] "Dr. HK" is here the proposed name of the fictional protagonist.

picked up the weaker other, and it is the correct one,
the direction we were going in before the Accident.
This one is the rectifying flow (the Holy Spirit: restoring!!!). This retroflow, Dr. HK says, must grow
stronger, will grow stronger, until it balances the
wrong way one (now stronger); overcomes and
reverses our direction so we're heading back toward
the original explosion which took place in the Authentic Future (the Big Bang!!!). We must move back
toward it, finally. Anyhow, Dr. HK detects with his
instruments a growing current of retrotime; this is
why it exists; this was the normal flow-direction until
the Accident. If Dr. Kozyrev[*] is correct, and time is
energy, then reverse time (which throws us "forward"
away from the Big Bang) causes us to lose energy,
which we call movement toward entropy; however, if
we could gather—latch onto—the other time-flow,
which also is energy, we (each of us) could regather
the energy lost in the "forward" time flow toward
entropy! We could get it back because it is gathering
in precisely the sense that our regular time is losing
heat or energy or charge. This gives us our parity, equilibrium equation for time which it now lacks and
should have and shows why first it is absurd to say
"the universe gains energy," as Dr. Kozyrev says—
where does it gain it from? It cannot gain *or* lose.
Entropy is losing energy; energy and matter are the
same; it's losing matter. So: we have an eternal total
double-entry same total of both time—flow energies at
any segment of the universe so extended.

   Look how we run down, wear out, age ... think
what charge, what rebirth, resurrection, new life, the
retrograde time-flow would give us! All that we'd lost,

---

[*]   A Soviet physicist of whose work PKD had read in 1974.

too: and a keen vision of the past-as-alive, the past not *qua* past, but past *qua* future!!!!!!!! Heading for it as surely as we normally head toward say the year 2100 A.D. The future in retro would be 100 A.D. just as surely, but gaining energy and life, through retro time as one moved!

The universe does not go through serial cycles, but moves backward through its own life continually. We are at a point where the thrust backward is vast in comparison to true time, that is, time toward completion of true form before the accident (the universe is in a stall, a doublebind![).] This may be an anomaly; once it reaches either end point, this may be overcome. One can see that; it doesn't repeat itself. We are now in the process of being thrust back incorrectly, away from form-completion; nonetheless, already the other direction time is somewhat strong and its rate of ratio growth is great. Once the direction is reversed and we're again going in the correct way, then we may take a different destiny line (alternate track) and not come to the original explosion; avoid it.

And maybe this isn't even the whole universe; maybe we're part of a subsystem moving in this wrong direction. We do know when the Accident took place: about 6 billion years ago. But we could change directions before that; we don't go back to that; we're not moving away from it, and what you and I should look for is not going back 6 billion years and rectifying that mistake, but wrong-way thrown-back time "slowing" and regular time regaining dominance; we should watch for our cosmos moving the proper direction in time, which would be a reverse from what we are used to—IN THE DIRECTION OF OUR PAST. It is not reaching this explosion 6 billion years ago that is important for us, but slowing our movement away from it and reversing and moving backward into our own past.

Asked when this reversal to proper time direction might be anticipated, Dr. HK said, "By our wrong way time, fairly soon."

"Then we must relive our recent past?"

"Yes, we will move backward into it, but perhaps at quite a different rate; we might move more rapidly than we advanced, I mean, retreated through it."

"People would stop dying?"

"Oh yes—the entropic process, cooling, aging, wearing out, degeneration—all that would cease. Once we picked up time momentum the other way—we might overcome the Accidental-thrust time. Think of a person blown literally from his garage when his hot water heater explodes. In an instant he is in the next field. His rate of return to the scene is much slower. In our universe, the force of Accidental thrust time is weakening; we have no way to ascertain what the 'correct' rate would be going the other way, before this Accident took place. We are presently living within two opposite thrusts, working against each other, like two tides. Think, though, how slowly time moves for a child, esp. a baby. Time is weak now but we might abruptly lock; this accidental wrong may might suddenly stabilize."

"Like the Bible says? Time will suddenly cease?"

"Wrong-direction time—"

"Sounds like the same thing."

"It is possible," Dr. HK said, "that under regular process-conditions there is no time as we know it, lineal time, either way. We may find ourselves back in what we call our past without any interval; there may be no reverse lineal time, because lineal time is solely a result of the Accident, and once overcome—"

"Not backward lineal time, in its place, but time-lessness?"

"I think we will see the damages overcome, when it is stabilized. Either we will lock into timelessness, then begin lineal reversal, which I conceive as natural—"

"Or we may find ourselves jumped back 2000 years."

"Yes." He nodded.

PLOT: It turns out the message which Albemuth is signalling Earth, the secret, is that our planet, solar system, us—we're moving backward in time and it's about to stabilize and change, and the jolt to us will be terrific. Our leaders know this but deny it. Time is about to end (lineal time) as a factor of life; it won't reverse, as in COUNTER-CLOCK WORLD, but our present will dissolve as all the accretions of at least 3500 years will vanish, as if dreamlike. They never took place. Stability, and proper everything, will lock in at 1500 to 2500 BC (is it possible that an explosion, the Cretan civilization, took place then?[)] All events since then are progressively less real, as time runs out of charge ...Jesus was the first messenger from Albemuth come here to tell us that one day time would abruptly cease, to prepare us. Now Earth is full of messengers; they've made many of us so, due to our radio traffic which are [sic] energy; the noösphere, etc. And now is when it's about to lock, but to them at Albemuth, they're outside this kind of lineal time; it just is for them each year realer and realer (what we call Being). But they can penetrate at the point (sic) the place where our noösphere exists, which is circa 1960-1990. Our microwave et al. equipment receive and boost their t-p [telepathic] signals, radio signals. Their help was there but is now artificially boosted for this generation.

"What Dead Men Say." Infringement—FCC regs.

The Albemuth message, though, corrects Dr. HK's theory; there was no explosion, just that Being time slipped into lineal time for this solar system or planet ...hence myth of Garden of Eden days of every race on earth—it ended, we were cast out. The lineal time, which is the only time we recognize, is a slipped onto-logical coordinate of existence; each year should rein-force and totally renew, even add layers to each of us like patina; we should age in that sense, grow until each of us, *qua* entelechy, is perfected. "But what about dinosaur bones and all fossils?" we ask. Answer: Every art work breaks, even though it is complete. A bone China cup doesn't age, but an accident can occur to it. This is what happened to all life; eventually, like all artifacts, each form breaks, but the entelechy escapes the brittle crystallized form and reappears in plastic rebirth. There is also change—this isn't an unmoving, static world. But the processes we know as aging—the entropy of our world, and what we see of the cosmos; (contrast cosmos with universe). Every-thing lost should at the end of each turn be as renewed as at the end of the 24-hour cycle of an elec-tric clock. Something is wrong in our world; we lose. An equilibrium is gone: and we sense it as defeat fail-ure illness age and finally death. Something is out of balance; the two time-forces aren't equal.

"What would we notice as this true (retro) time jumps in ratio? A slowing of our normal lineal time? No, the infusing into our aging world of a bright energy, pouring everywhere, sparkling, vivifying the living things *and* the unliving. We would see a living energy, a sort of shining sap which pours all over, sparkles; and it changes whatever it fluxes itself into like a plasma of n-ions. This is time, true time, plus energy time. It would roll back the accretions which are false, that is, it would roll back the least-Being accretions ... it would add vitality to the Real, and cause the false totally to disappear, as if never there. This is time beginning to reverse itself: a direction. Experienced as energy to Being, as disappearance of the irreal/illusion.

"These slowings and reversings would come in spurts. Not in a lineal fashion; that aspect is of wrong-way time. It would be like childbirth: in surges of energy outward onto the world. At Spring the cyclic life is at its peak; so reverse time would tend to peak with it.

"And we'd have—for those who were influxed directly—the eerie feeling that the clock had been turned back ... hundreds, maybe thousands of years, depending on how much of this energy—and it is energy—infused each of them. Each would vary from the others touched; moved backward—receiving more. It has a quantity (years back) and quality: what one sees qualitatively.

The U.S. Intelligence psychiatric profile on Dr. HK shows that "he was taken over by Dionysus thus lifting him outside time & space," etc., like Nietzsche, but regards the experience as real.

Always, what Zagreus-Dionysus* fears is that they will pen him up, not that they will kill him, after all, he is immortal. He must (one) either display his true strength and escape, or (two) submit and die; either way he is free. He has chosen to submit, in order to conceal his existence; and also they are "civilizing" him, teaching him that he should do that. But he comes to those snared like a small animal: in a trap, and becomes them. Dionysus was member of a visiting expedition. Had qualities of naivety and curiosity, was lured in by

---

* See *Zagreus* in Glossary.

humans to their "game," was gulled and slain. Now he
doesn't know his name (Parsifal, Christ, Siegfried).
They murdered him—in fact they lured him to obtain
what he had with him (whatever). Our ancestors. So
their expedition went on and left him behind, left him
here among us. He wasn't as sophisticated; couldn't
watch detached or disinterestedly as the rest in his
party did. Maybe he was younger than they in the
party: a youth, a child, born on the star-flight...hence
so naive. Human (adults) were more worldlywise than
he. Now he can't be trained by his own race, must be
reborn here in us (they are free of the slaying power of
runaway linear time; this is why he is immortal or eternal; it is how we ought to be and can be again). Their
expedition entered our world from outside the linear
runaway time dysfunction. Dion[*] migrated forward in
lineal time, becoming civilized, "growing up," into
Zagreus and Orpheus and especially Christos. After that
he ceased, (that was the perfection of his entelechy, but
we'll say that no growth took place in Being time on
this world after 100 A.D., as reason). He returns as
Christos; this is why he talked about "sending the Second Helper," but meant himself, secretly. He had been
murdered so often—the prone corpse in fawn garment,
murdered—that he had learned to conceal himself...
and the best way was to forget (*Lethe*) who he was, so he
couldn't by accident blurt it out, as he had done as Jesus.

Fear of imprisonment over all; if arrested, he'd
rather bait the authorities (e.g. Pilate) into "killing"
him, which would free him, rather than languish in
small cage like trapped animal. He has affinity to
small trapped animal because of what was done to
him (in his natural form he is small: an infant, and

---

[*] Possibly a short form of "Dionysus", or an invented name for the god
as avatar.

vulnerable). (So he is the God of the vulnerable and trusting, and especially the snared; those helpless in traps). The fawn, the lamb ... those gulled by curiosity and childishness, wishing to play (with those older and more experienced).

The God of innocence. Now he has forgotten his name, but his nature—and powers—remain. Occasionally anamnesis returns.

He is in many of us (in protag of this novel). But mainly he is the cyclothemic person—oscillating between moods of tenderness and fury. Intoxication and sorrow.

Dion was premey* (v.). He isn't Jesus; he is Elijah and John the Baptist; meets Jesus the Christos who is a later incarnation, a more mature one ... Dionysus is too wild (protag's research had led him to think they're all one, culminating in Jesus; there are at least two of them, and it is Dion who takes him personally over).

(c. 1974-75)

Fat** later developed a theory that the universe is made out of information. He started keeping a journal—had been, in fact, secretly doing so for some time. His encounter with God was all there on the pages in his—Fat's—not God's—handwriting.

The term "journal" is mine, not Fat's. His term was "exegesis," a theological term meaning a piece of writing that explains or interprets a portion of scripture. Fat believed that the information fired at him from time to time was holy in origin & hence a form of scripture.

---

* Possibly short for premature—as in a premature or penultimate avatar (as the paragraph argues).
** Horselover Fat, the alter ego of fictional character Phil Dick in VALIS (1981), for which this is a draft.

One of his paragraphs impressed me enough to copy it out & include it here.

"Summary. (etc—v. tractate)"*

Fat developed a lot of unusual theories to account for his contact with God, & the information derived therefrom. One in particular struck me as thought-provoking. It amounted to a kind of mental capitulation by Fat to what he was undergoing; this theory held that in actuality he wasn't experiencing anything at all. Sites of his brain were being selectively stimulated by tight energy-beams emanating from far off, perhaps millions of miles away. These selective brain site stimulations generated in his head the *impression*—for him—that he was seeing & hearing words, pictures, figures of people, in short God, or as Fat liked to call it, the *Logos*. But, really, he only imagined he experienced these things. They resembled holograms. What struck me was the oddity of a lunatic discounting his hallucinations in this sophisticated manner; Fat had intellectually dealt himself out of the game of madness while still enjoying its sights & sounds. In effect, he no longer claimed that what he experienced was really there. Did this indicate he had begun to sober up? Hardly. Now he held the view that "they" or God or someone owned a long-range very tight information-rich beam of energy focussed on Fat's head. In this I saw no improvement, but it did represent a change. Fat could now honestly discount his hallucinations, which meant he recognized them as such. But, like Gloria, he now had a "they." It seemed to me a

---

*   This line represents a note by PKD to himself to find (in the EXEGESIS) or fashion a suitably meaningful quote as regarded Fat's beliefs. The reference to "v." [*vide*] "tractate" is, apparently, to the "Tractates Cryptica Scriptura" that forms an "Appendix" to VALIS and contains fifty-two numbered entries summarizing key theories and insights discussed at greater length in the EXEGESIS.

pyrrhic victory. Fat's life struck me as a litany of exactly that, as for example the way he had rescued Gloria.

The exegesis Fat labored on month after month struck me as a pyrrhic victory if there ever was one— in this case an attempt by a beleaguered mind to make sense out of the inscrutable. Perhaps this is the key to mental illness: incomprehensible events occur— your life becomes a bin for hoax-like fluctuations of what used to be reality, & not only that—as if that weren't bad enough—you, like Fat, ponder forever over these fluctuations in an effort to order them into a coherency. When in fact the only sense they make is the sense you impose on them, out of the necessity to restore everything into shapes & processes you can recognize. The first thing to depart in mental illness is the familiar.

& what takes its place is bad news because not only can you not understand it, you also cannot communicate it to other people. The madman experiences something. But what it is or where it comes from he does not know.

In the midst of his shattered landscape Fat imagined God had cured him. Once you notice pyrrhic victories they seem to abound.[*]

Either he had seen God too soon, or he had seen him too late. In any case it had done him no good at all in terms of survival. Encountering the living God had not helped to equip him for the tasks of ordinary endurance, which ordinary men, not so favored, handle.[**]

Men & the world are mutually toxic to each other.

---

[*] The preceding paragraphs appear, in slightly different form, in chapter two of VALIS (1981).
[**] This paragraph appears in chapter four of VALIS.

But God—the true God—has penetrated both, penetrated man & penetrated the world, & sobers the landscape. But that God, the God from outside, encounters
fierce opposition. Frauds—the deceptions of madness—
abound, & mask themselves as their mirror opposites:
pose as sanity, the masks, however, wear thin, & the
madness reveals itself. It is an ugly thing.

The remedy is here but so is the malady. As Fat
repeats obsessively, "the Empire never ended." In a startling response to the crisis, the true God mimics the
universe, the very region he has invaded; he takes on
the likeness of sticks & trees & cans in gutters—he pre-
sumes to be trash discarded, debris no longer noticed.
Lurking, the true God literally ambushes reality & us
as well. God, in very truth, attacks & injures us, in his
role as antidote. As Fat can testify to, it is a scary experience to encounter this. Hence we say, the true God is
in the habit of concealing himself. 25 hundred years
have passed since Heraclitus wrote, "Latent form is
the master of obvious form."

Albemuth	Crete	Rome	Calif		x	y
↓	↓	↓	↓		↓	↓

At Y, the entity inc. me, evolves into its ultimate
state (self), the info-firing, quasi-material, quasi-energy
plasmatic nonhumanoid life form I call Zebra—from
perhaps thousands or millions of years in the future.
By then ("Y") it is virtually pure knowing, pure information (& firing it back at/to me). It has died for the
last time & now invades from "the other side" (upper
realm) as well as from the future.

This fits in with the "paranormal crisis discloses
paranormal powers" & the hiding of those powers
overruled by the life-threatening situation; this clearly

states that *I* possess the powers. "I know, too"—i.e., am one of them.

I arranged for my own 2-74 disinhibition.

It's not Jim[*] come back from the other side *but me*; & once I was an Essene. But it is indeed from the other side, no longer humanoid, & it's in me now: I am right now *it*. "We shall see him as he really is & we shall be like him"—not him like *us*. This is a little different from saying "It's *ourselves* in the future"; this says Zebra is specifically *me*.

Fat's obsessive idea these days, as he worries more & more about Sherri, was that the Savior would soon be reborn—or had been already. Somewhere in the world, he walked or would soon walk the earth. Once more.[**]

(1978)

Bishop Timothy Archer.[***]
Mary Ann Domingo. Mother of

Vince Domingo.
Lora Domingo. Vince's wife. S.W.P. [*Socialist Workers Party*].

Vince is chairman of the Save the Marin County Three Committee (3 alleged (Black) terrorists[).] Time: 1970: Place: San Rafael.

Mary Ann works for the Dept. of Labor as an editor of government pamphlets.[****]

Vince wants Bishop Archer to speak at 3-C rally in behalf of civil rights & anti-war. Great hostility

---

[*]   Bishop James A. Pike.
[**] This paragraph appears in slightl;y different form in VALIS.
[***] This character is based on Bishop James A. Pike.
[****]This was a job actually held by PKD's mother, Dorothy Hudner, in the mid-1930s.

between his S.W.P. wife Lora & his mother, but his mother agrees to write the letter to Bishop Archer. Mary Ann is actually working for U.S, G-2.[*] She becomes Bishop Archer's mistress to compromise him (because of his anti-war & pro civil rights stand). Bishop Archer is killed in an auto crash in either San Francisco or in the Golden Gate Bridge or Marin County; she was driving. Later she commits suicide.

The Zadokite Scrolls.[**]

There is a dig in the Dead Sea area by Catholic archaeologists. They've unearthed scrolls predating xtianity of a strictly Jewish sect. Not considered an important find but Bishop Archer has talked to the translator & confides in Vince—who is an atheist—that the scrolls convince Archer that there was no historic Jesus. Archer intends to step down as bishop. He is being tried on charges of heresy, for denying the trinity. Then before he can make his public statement regarding Jesus & the Zadokite document he dies in the auto crash. Few people (1) know what is in the Zadokite document & (2) that Archer was going to step down & what he was going to say—he was going to convert to Judaism.

Sid Herz, orthodox Jewish friend of Vince, based on Avram Davidson.[***] Bishop Archer meets him through Vince.

Part one of the novel: 1970, the anti-war movement. (1970). Bishop Archer.

Part two: After the Vietnam War. Bishop Archer & Mary Ann are dead. 1981, i.e., the present. Vince is no longer politically active (for some reason) finds evi-

---

[*]   A branch of U.S. Army intelligence.
[**] These are a fictional creation by PKD.
[***] Science-fiction writer and friend of PKD.

dence that his mother murdered Bishop Archer. He has nervous breakdown as a result.

Micky Hilliard—his therapist.

Summary: He imagines that he is his dead friend Bishop Archer, who has returned to him from "the other side" (of the grave). Vince "must tell the world that he—Bishop Archer—was murdered by the U.S. government acting through Mary Ann, the Bishop's secret mistress." To verify that he is indeed Bishop Archer, Vince knows (or believes he knows) the contents of the Zadokite Document. Only the Catholic Church, which possesses the still-untranslated document, is in a position to confirm this.

Father Shirm, who translated the scrolls. Friend of Bishop Archer. Will he confirm what Vince says? This will implicate not only Mary Ann (who is dead) but U.S. G-2 as well, & *they* are not dead.

Vince, who may be psychotic, believes that U.S. G-2 assassins now plan to kill him (or "kill him *again*," as it were). Only Lora believes him—at least the political part.

But the real issue (actually) is the Zadokite document & its implications. Vince wants his friend Sid Herz to publish it (or what he claims is it) in a little Zionist rag that Herz puts out. All Vince really cares about is getting the Zadokite material published.

Herz's office is destroyed by "KKK/Nazis" in the L.A. area. Vince suspects the U.S. government.

For this novel to work, it must be the case that what Vince wants Sid to publish is *exactly* what Bishop Archer planned to publish—but was killed in the auto crash before he could publish it. Bishop Archer had access to the media (of course), but Vince does not; viz: Archer was a widely-known figure; Vince is a lunatic & not known to anyone. Vince has no connections whatever.

Only the Catholic Church can confirm what Vince alleges is the articles of the Zadokite Document, known to Bishop Archer.

Resolution: The Church decides that the value of saving an innocent man (Vince) from the condemnation that he is insane & probable murder by U.S. G-2, as Bishop Archer was (murdered) is more important than protecting Jesus' image; & Father Shirm is instructed by the Vatican to release the text of the Zadokite Scrolls.

Ending: Father Shirm says to Vince, "I believe you are Timothy Archer. It is a miracle." U.S. G-2 gives up. Vince is released from the mental institution due to Micky Hilliard.

Herz publishes (the Zadokite document); the Catholic Church confirms it is authentic. They (the Catholic Church) are the only ones in a position to confirm, since it is they who possess the scrolls. This is the essence of xtianity: truth & the life & vindication of one man—even a man who is a heretic—is more important than saving the whole edifice (of the Church); thus the Church proves its right to hold the keys to the Kingdom, &, by extension, validates Jesus & the teachings of Christ himself as the basis of the Church, since he & his teachings are its basis. There is now no point in U.S. G-2 killing or discrediting Vince. (n.: it is hopeless to try to discredit him in the face of an officially authenticated miracle[)]. The Church is pitted against the secular authorities, & the Church wins; & Vince is saved. & the truth—the Zadokite document—is published, Bishop Archer got what he returned for—i.e., wanted. Vince's fear & paranoia become trust, & he splits with Lora who, as a SWP-er, is still hostile & suspicious & an atheist.   *(1981)*

Bishop Tim Archer.

I'm going to assign to him as his major view my *Commedia*[*] 3-coaxial realms view (as expressed in my Metz speech & which were going to be the basis for the 3rd novel in the Valis trilogy). He has been studying the *Commedia* & Sufi teachings, also Quantum mechanics (which he does not understand but nonetheless prattles on about). He is convinced that Dante's 3 realms (*Inferno, Purgatorio* & *Paradiso*) are available in this life; & here he gets into Heidegger & *Dasein* (this makes historical sense, since Heidegger very much influenced Tillich, etc., contemporary Protestant theory).

Now, how does this relate to his later involvement with the Zadokite Document & the *Anokhi* mushroom?[**] The Zadokite sect knew how to get in to the *Paradiso* realm (alternate reality) *in which Christ is here*. (This clearly relates to Allegro's "hallucination" theory;[***] likewise Hoffman's ROAD TO ELEUSIS.)[****] It is quite simply the *restored reality*, & is potentially *always* available. What I want to stress is that none of these ideas is original with Bishop Archer. So I must invent a writer-scholar-philosopher-theoretician who advances this theory about the *Commedia* in his book(s), his published writing—something connected with California outré theorizing.

In other words from the beginning Bishop Archer

---

[*]   The reference here is to the cosmological structure of the DIVINE COMEDY of Dante.

[**]   To PKD, the Hebrew word *anokhi* represented pure consciousness of the divine. The fictional anokhi mushroom would—perhaps—provide such consciousness to one who ingested it.

[***] See John W. Allegro, THE SACRED MUSHROOM AND THE CROSS (1968).

[****]See R. Gordon Wasson, Carl A. P. Ruck, Albert Hoffman, THE ROAD TO ELEUSIS: UNVEILING THE SECRET OF THE MYSTERIES (1978). Co-author Hoffman is the Swiss chemist who in 1943 discovered LSD.

is searching for Christ. The "Dante" formulation initially provides him with a theoretical framework as to
how it can be done (or he *thinks* this is how it can be
done. Now, he drops all this—& the California writer
who is based on Alan Watts, in favor of the Zadokite
scrolls & the *anokhi* mushroom; this is typical of him. *I*
would have built on the first, constructed a synthesis,
but this is not how Jim worked; he rushed from one
thing to the next looking; this California writer is a
Sufi. Edgar Barefoot is his name. This is set in the Bay
Area. Bishop Archer meets Barefoot; they become col-
leagues: an Episcopal Bishop & a Sufi guru living on a
house boat at Pier 5 in Sausalito. The name of all this
is making God (or, as with Archer, Christ)
immediately available to you as a living experience.

There is a certain quality of Jack Isidore[*] in Bishop
Archer: The capacity to believe anything, any pseudo-
science as theosophy. The "fool in Christ," naive &
gullible &—rushing from one fad to another, typical of
California.

The Zadokite Document (scrolls) convinces Bishop
Archer—who had devoted his life to "reaching across
to the living Christ" (which makes sense given the fact
that he is after all a Bishop—that Christ was "irrele-
vant" there is something more important. The exposi-
tor of the 200 BCE Zadokite Sect.

Archer's involvement with Barefoot is "Ecumeni-
cal," but with the Zadokite & Anokhi mushroom stuff
he has ecumenically called himself out of xtianity
entirely. Barefoot is crushed, heartbroken—an example of the casualties Archer leaves along the road
behind him in his speed-rush Faustian quest, always
exceeding itself, surpassing itself (it is really Dionysus

---

[*]   The "fool" protagonist in the PKD novel CONFESSIONS OF A CRAP
ARTIST (1975).

that has hold of him). Barefoot, Calif guru that he is, acts as a rational stable counterpoint to Archer's frenzy. Barefoot is authentically what he seems to be, claims to be: a spiritual person & teacher; he is not a fraud. He is always being demolished in discussions by other more formal thinkers, e.g. those at UC Berkeley, e.g. on KPFA. But—like Watts—he has his followers. He is really quite systematic & rigorous in his thinking. He does not foresee Archer suddenly abandoning him & flying off to Europe vis-à-vis the Zadokite scrolls—he, the Sufi, the non-xtian, is horrified when Archer turns his back on Christ. Archer declares that now he has found the true religion (at last). This very concept ("the true religion") is foreign to Barefoot in fact that is one of his fundamental views: that *all* religions are equally valuable.

Ah. Archer has expropriated Barefoot's views & peddled them as his own. Barefoot does not mind; he just wants the views per se to be promulgated.

What has happened is, Archer has grown weary of Barefoot's "Dante's 3 Realms right here" view, because there is no clear (i.e. easy) way to get to the top realm; Archer has become impatient & restless, &, *before* he learns of the Zadokite find, is discontented, is casting about for a new involvement. Barefoot was dumped *before* Archer latched on to the Zadokite stuff—it just didn't show.

So when we meet Bishop Archer he is already involved in a fusion of Heidegger & Sufism—this means that the book will deal with California grotesques, which is okay. This is how we encounter him, like the grown ups in "The Cherry Orchard."*

Barefoot claims actually to have experienced the 3

---

* Drama by Anton Chekhov.

Realms. I will assign to him my "evasion equals time; *Dasein** equals space" view. Archer can't get the hang of it & wearies of trying; it takes too long. He wants instant solutions. The Anokhi mushroom will do.

This is how the young female protagonist meets Jeff Archer: in one of Barefoot's seminars on his Sausalito houseboat. Maybe I *won't* use flashbacks. (Remember: Jeff is based on me.) (1) (No—he has [*name deleted*] sense of humor: he is like one of the dopers in "Scanner"—funny & wonderful—like [*name deleted*]—Ernie Luckman.) Jeff is there to try to figure out what his father the Bishop is talking about. Has Bishop Archer met his mistress yet?

Her name: Angel Gale. Based on [*name deleted*]. She lives in Berkeley. I've never set a novel in Berkeley. Could she work in a record store & be into music? Based, too, on [*name deleted*]. Calm, rational.

The mistress: Kirsten Lundborg, efficient but sarcastic & bitter.

Jeff has the sort of brilliant hebephrenic humor of [*name deleted*] and [*name deleted*], up until the moment he kills himself. In contrast, Bill Lundborg is melancholy & emotional, filled with *Sturm und Drang*.

Like Angel, Jeff is into music, so they have a lot in common. He has an apartment on Protrero Hill. Has a male roommate who is a fag poet, [...] Sid Fitzpatrick.

Gay bar in S.F.: the Bloody Mary.

Dike friend of his based on [*name deleted*]: Connie Goldstein. She develops a crush on Angel.

Angel supposes that Jeff's problem (he has a problem he won't talk about) is that he is gay or fears he is gay; but in fact she is dead wrong; he is in love with Kirsten, his father's mistress.

---

*   See note on page 108.

The basic story: Zagreus has seized control of Bishop Archer & drives him to his ruin. Whereupon Zagreus leaves the Bishop & enters Bill Lundborg. But in exchange for madness & death—the dues that Zagreus exacts—he confers a vision of Perfect Beauty (Pythagorean *Kosmos*).

So I have the Bay Area gay community, the Bay Area "Alan Watts KPFA" community, poetry & religion (non-xtian) & music & *some* dope. But this is *not* the doper subculture! They are all intellectuals except for Connie.

How about a Trot [*Trotskyite*] too, to bring in radical politics? Angel: former husband Hampton Squires. Has a Russian friend whose real name is Nicholas Kaminsky, but he uses the name of Len Jones. Angel suspects him of being KGB. He owns a restaurant on San Pablo Ave. in Berkeley & is based on [*name deleted*].

& a black guy [*names deleted*], Maury Rivers; he is a painter & bum. Angel is living in the little old house on Dwight Way off Sacramento that she & her husband owned.

(1981)

CHAPTER SIX

POLITICAL AND ECOLOGICAL CONCERNS

Philip K. Dick
1405 Cameo Lane #4
Fullerton
Calif 92631

July 8, 1974: The First Day of the Constitutional Crisis.*

But the state of things is so dreary here in the U.S.—they say the elderly and poor are eating canned dogfood, now, to stay alive, and the McDonald hamburgers are made from cows' eyes. The radio also says that today when Charles Colson, the President's former counsel, went into jail he still wore his Richard M. Nixon tieclasp. "California dreaming is becoming a

---

* This selection does form a part of the EXEGESIS, but due to the letter format in which it was written, it has also been included in THE SELECTED LETTERS OF PHILIP K. DICK—1974, Underwood-Miller, 1991.

reality," is a line from a Mama's & the Papa's song of a few years ago, but what a dreadful surreal reality it is: foglike and dangerous, with the subtle and terrible manifestations of evil rising up like rocks in the gloom. I wish I was somewhere else. Disneyland, maybe? The last sane place here? Forever to take Mr. Toad's Wild Ride and never get off?

The landscape is deformed out of recognition by the Lie. Its gloom is everywhere, and we encounter nothing we recognize, only familiar things without the possibility of accurate identification. There are only shocks, until we grow numb, are paralyzed and die. When I suddenly stopped believing in the Lie I did not begin to think differently—I *saw* differently, as if something was gone from the world or gone from between me and the world which had always been there. Like a scrambling device that had been removed: deliberate scrambling. All, suddenly, was clear language. God seemed to seek me out and expressed things through things and what took place. Everywhere I saw signs along a path, marking His presence.

Any lying language creates at once in a single stroke a pseudo-reality, contaminating reality, until the Lie is undone. As soon as one lies one becomes separated from reality. One has introduced the falsification oneself. There is one thing no one can force you to do: to lie. One only lies for one's advantage. It is based on an inner decision invisible to the world. No one ever says to you, "Lie to me." The enemy says, You will do and believe certain things. It is your own decision to falsify, in the face of his coercion. I am not sure this is what the enemy wants or anyone [*sic; anyhow?*] the usual enemy. Only a Greater Enemy, so to speak, would want that, one with greater objectives, and a clearer idea of what the ultimate purpose of all motion is.

Sometime in the past, about three months ago, I must have become aware for the first time in my life that the cause of misery was the Lie and that the enemy, the real enemy, was a liar. I remember somewhere along the line saying loudly, "He is a liar; he is a liar," and feeling it to be very important, that discovery. I forget—or rather I guess it does not matter—what specific lie by which person made it all change. There was a person, there was a lie. A week after I realized that with no possibility of evading it everything altered radically for me, and the world began to talk, in a true language of signs: silently. The Lie had slipped away. The Lie deals with talk, written or spoken. Now it's gone. Something else shines forth at last. I see the cat watching it at night, for hours. He has seen it all his life; it is the only language he knows.

I think a lot about my early childhood and remember events in it vividly, which I guess is a sure sign of senility. Also events that took place within the past ten years seem dim and not really a part of me. Their sadness is gone: used up. I encounter new fresh sadnesses in my remote past, like stars that burst into life when I notice them. When I pass on, they again are forgotten. Usually, however, senility is a gradual process; mine came on abruptly when I noticed the cat trying to discern what was causing me pain (I had stomach flu) and then what he could do to help me. He finally got up on my abdomen transversely and purred. It helped, but then when he jumped down the pain returned, whereupon the cat got up again. He lay on me for hours, purring, and finally the disturbed rhythm of my stomach began to match the pace of his purrs, which made me feel much better. Also the sight of his jowly face gazing down at me with concern, his keen interest in me his friend—that changed me, to suddenly open my eyes (I had been lying for an hour on the couch) and see his concerned large furry face, his attention silently fixed on me. It was not an illusion. Or, put another way, his field of energy, his strength, was at that moment greater than mine, small as he was, since mine had dimmed from the flu and his was as always. Perhaps his soul was at that unusual moment, that critical moment, stronger than mine. It is not usual for a small animal's soul to be larger than a man's. He warmed me and I recovered, and he went his way. But I changed. It is an odd senility, to be comforted and healed by a small animal who then goes on as always, leaving you different. I think of senility as a loss of contact, a drop in perception, of the actual reality around one. But this was true and in the present. Not a memory.

The Constitutional guarantees of our country have been suspended for some time now, and an assault has begun on the checks and balances structure of the government. The Republic is in peril; the Republic has been in peril for several years and is now cut away almost to a shadow of itself, barely functioning. I think they are carving it up in their minds, deciding who sits there forever and ever, now. In the face of this no one notices that virtually everything we believed in is dead. This is because the people who would have pointed this out are dead: mysteriously killed. It's best not to talk about this. I've tried to list the safe things to talk about, but so far I can't find any. I'm trying to learn what the Lie is or what the Lies are, but I can't even discern that any more. Perhaps I sense the Lie gone from the world because evil is so strong now that it can step forth as it is without deception. The masks are off.

But nevertheless something shines in the dark ahead that is alive and makes no sound. We saw it once before, but that was a long time ago, or maybe our first ancestors did. Or we did as small children. It spoke to us and directed and educated us then; now perhaps it does so again. It sought us out, in the climax of peril. There was no way we could find it; we had to wait for it to come to us.

Its sense of timing is perfect. But most important it knows everything. It can make no mistakes. It must be back for a reason. *(8 July 1974)*

I can suppose no explanation but the Gnostic one. Creation is not only irrational, it is only semi-real or even only seeming; "rational," then, signifies real; "irrational" signifies, irreal. Here lies the ontological value of Gnostic knowing—Gnosis itself. "Knowing" signifies "knowing that the irreal is irreal" & being able, then, to counter-distinguish the truly real (these categories relate to Pan-Indian doctrines of *Maya* = The Grand Illusion both inner & outer). What must be realized is that, like hallucination, the merely seeming can exert decisive power over you, & it is precisely this deplorable state (of ignorance & hence enslavement) that is reversed by Gnosis.

Now about Tagore.* He is Lord Krishna. His presence here signifies *two* things, one good (rescue, extrication) the other bad (terrible danger; the on-going destruction of the ecosphere). This is, time of need; Tagore alerts us to our peril, warns us of the consequences to us & to him—Holy Wisdom; we will kill him & cause him to depart thus we have a clear

---

* On 17 September 1981, PKD experienced a hypnagogic vision of a world savior named Tagore who was living in Sri Lanka. In a 23 September 1981 letter (which was ultimately published in the fanzine *Niekas*) PKD described Tagore as "burned and crippled" and "dying voluntarily: Tagore has taken upon himself mankind's sins against the ecosphere."

choice. This has a non-oriental Zoroastrian quality. We choose good or evil, &, in choosing, choose life & God or death & God; forsaking us; Jesus: This is like the O.T.! YHWH often speaks thus to Israel through the prophets!

Ach; this perforce makes me a Biblical prophet: "Cease your evil ways or good will abandon you (i.e. the world); & you will destroy yourselves." & the N.T. comes into it as well in that our evil actions injure God—we again "crucify" him—&, in true N.T. fashion, he has taken on our sins (in the form of passion & death) *voluntarily*, this incarnation leading to his suffering & death is not forced on him, he is here for this reason as a protest, to awaken us to what we are doing; vis: if we understand that in wounding the eco-system we wound God, we may—should thereby—know to cease.

Hence, I see Judo-xtian themes here, quite beyond Pan-Indian, & I continue to identify Tagore with Christ (yet still he is Lord Krishna, paradoxically).

My perception of this in terms of Teilhard [*de Chardin*]: point omega & the noösphere correlates my total exegesis, my 2-3-74 experience & VALIS with Tagore & his mission as *vox* [*voice*] & anima of the ecosphere.

But the final ultimate purpose of VALIS & DI is not to analyze or report but to predict, as John the Baptist (Elijah) did 2000 years ago: the imminent coming—i.e., return—of the Savior. This is clear from the internal evidence of the two novels. What this makes me think is: remember how when Tom Disch visited me in 1974 I strongly suspected that it was Elijah whose spirit had taken me over (being then also the Baptist)?[*] I very soon

---

[*]   PKD footnote: "i.e., 'Thomas' who so feared the Romans—well, they killed the Baptist, garroted Thomas, which is to say, decapitated him there in his little jail cell! *Dio*! & it all happened to me at Passover!"

pondered the utterance derived from Scripture. Elijah
will return shortly before Christ returns, preparing the
way. Well, hence Elijah shows up in DIVINE INVASION &
his ability repeatedly to incarnate himself is discussed!

    & ever since the eleventh grade I have heard the
still small (low, murmuring) voice.*

    Let me say this: *if* you start with Tagore as the
premise & work backwards, 2-3-74—2-75 et al.
becomes logical: Elijah came, before the second
advent to prepare the way—no; not Elijah; the *spirit*
of Elijah! Now, if this be the case re 2-74—2-75, was it
futile? Well, I wrote the [*VALIS*] trilogy** about it, &
have already gotten the first two into reasonably
good circulation, one [*VALIS*] a low-priced mass-distri-
bution paperback, the other [*THE DIVINE INVASION*] an
expensive hardback library edition, each read solo,
tells of the Savior coming.

    It was not up to the Baptist to teach the xtian
kerygma but, rather, to announce the imminent coming of the long-awaited messiah. There *is* (in VALIS) a
vague *kerygma* but it is only guesswork (what Sophia
says, & she dies anyhow): the Savior is still yet to
come, at the end of VALIS, explicitly, as if she, too, like
the Baptist, only prepares the way "for one Creator."
("Who is yet to come.") Both novels are essentially
anticipatory! Even DI! Since in DI YHWH has come but
not disclosed to the world his presence (yet).   *(1981)*

    I must ask what God wants of me: to promulgate
Tagore's *kerygma*? or to sacrifice myself? As of today I
see only the latter as lying within my power; I do not
have the strength left for the former, so he cannot

---

*   See note on page 62 herein.
**   PKD termed VALIS (1981), THE DIVINE INVASION (1981), and THE
TRANSMIGRATION OF TIMOTHY ARCHER (1982) the "VALIS trilogy."

want the former. I must emulate Tagore. The vision of Tagore both is a *kerygma* & *contains* a *kerygma*. My receiving it changes everything. It is no longer, "The Savior is coming" but (& this is much more complex & is new): "The Savior is here as the ecosphere; we are crucifying him by wounding the ecosphere & if we do not stop, he will depart this world & abandon us to our doom." Thus the ecosphere is viewed as holy, sentient, unitary, & its psyche is Christ himself.   *(1981)*

CHAPTER SEVEN

TWO SELF-EXAMINATIONS

Listening to the Platt tape[*] I construe by the logic presented that Valis (the other Mind) which came *at* me from outside & which overpowered me from inside was indeed the contents of my collective unconscious, & so technically a psychosis, since this is how you define psychosis (it certainly would explain the animism outside, & the interior dissociated activity) but—well, okay; it would account for the AI voice, the 3 eyed sibyl, & the extreme archaicism of the contents. & seeing Rome CAD[**] 45 would simply be psychotic delusion—I did not know where or when I really was.

Q: What about the resemblance to my writing?

---

[*]   In May 1979, Charles Platt interviewed PKD; the interview is included in Platt's book DREAM MAKERS: THE UNCOMMON PEOPLE WHO WRITE SCIENCE FICTION (1980). PKD made his own tape of the interview and listened to it afterwards. As this selection indicates, listening to the tape spurred him to intensive self-examination.
[**]   Circa A.D.

A: The content was originally in my unconscious, e.g., TEARS and UBIK.

Q: What about external events? The girl? The letters?

A: Coincidence.

Q: & the written material? Huge books held open?

A: Verbal memory.

Q: Why would I believe that my senses were enhanced, i.e., I could see for the first time?

A: Psychotomimetic drugs indicate this happens in psychosis.

Q: & *Kosmos*? Everything fitting together?

A: "Spread of meaning," typical of psychosis.

Q: Foreign words & terms I don't know?

A: Long-term memory banks open. Disgorging their contents into consciousness.

Q: Problem solving—i.e., the xerox missive.

A: There *was* no problem; it was harmless.

Q: Why the sense of time dysfunction?

A: Disorientation.

Q: Why the sense that the mind which had taken me over was wiser than me & more capable?

A: Release of psychic energy.

Q: Why was that mind & the whole experience syntonic to me? If it was syntonic to my ego, why had it been repressed?

A: My ego was destroyed, so "syntonic" has no meaning here. Syntonic to what?

Q: From a practical standpoint I functioned better. How could this be?

A: It only subjectively *felt* better. No anxiety.

Q: Why would I seek the experience again if it was repressed contents breaking through? Could I not let them through again, or never have excluded them following 3-74? The contents & the other mind leaked away; I tried to hold onto them but in vain.

A: I was occluded to my own best interests. I *liked* being high.

Q: Oh? "high"? Does psychosis equal high?

A: Mania. I am manic depressive.

Q: & schizophrenic? One is extraverted & one is introverted. Please clarify.

A: Mixed or "borderline" psychosis.

Q: No, it was florid schizophrenia with religious coloration. Not satisfactory.

A: Catatonic excitement, then.

Q: So the OCMH[*] diagnosis was incorrect? Not manic depressive?

A: That is so. Incorrect.

Q: Why, then, was the onset one in which thought came faster & faster? That is mania.

A: The lithium would have blocked mania. I was lithium toxic.

Q: Then it wasn't schizophrenia; it was chemical toxicity.

A: Perhaps. A combination. Plus the orthomolecular ws[**] vitamins.

Q: But the orthomolecular ws vitamins are *anti*-schizophrenic.

A: That is only speculation.

Q: If 2-3-74 was psychosis, then what was the ego state which it obliterated?

A: Neurotic. Or mildly Schizophrenia [sic]. Under stress the weak ego disintegrates.

Q: Then how could the phobias associated with my anxiety neurosis remain? e.g., agoraphobia?

A: It does not compute. Something is wrong. They

---

* Orange County Mental Health—an intake unit facility not far from his Santa Ana, California apartment at which PKD intermittently sought psychotherapy.
** ws = water-soluble

should have gone away or become totally overwhelming. The impaired ego must have still been intact.

Q: Was my "dissociated" behavior bizarre?

A: No, they were problem-solving. It does not compute.

A: Perhaps there were no real problems.

A: Not so. It was tax time.[*]

Q: What we are talking about then is inhibition bypass behavior oriented toward crisis problem solving.

A: Yes.

Q: This is 180° opposed to *any* meaningful definition of psychosis. We can reason overwhelming by unconscious material but there is no way to account for it being more capable in terms of problem solving. *Skills* were involved: adaptation to reality & not fugue from. Fugue & adaptation are mutually opposed. One cannot run from & solve simultaneously; these are diametrically contrary movements, one away from, one toward. We have to attribute the mutually exclusive postures of retreat from pressing crisis problems & motion toward problems & the expert solving thereof. Please explain how an organism can simultaneously flee & stand & fight.

A: The organism is compound, not simple. One part fled & another part replaced it & problem-solved.

Q: Did the part that problem-solved do so successfully?

A: Yes.

Q: Could the part which fled have done a better job if it had stayed in control?

A: No.

---

[*]   PKD had, since the late 1960s, harbored fear of the IRS. In large measure, this fear stemmed from his signing of the *Ramparts Petition*. See Glossary. PKD did not file tax returns until the Vietnam War ended. Also, in 1969, due to past tax liabilities, the IRS seized his car.

Q: Then a part which had never had to deal with reality proved more adaptive & effective.

A: It was adequate.

Q: On what basis did it act? Experience? Trial & error?

A: On instinct. It *knew* what to do.

Q: Then it was ideally suited to the problem-solving required.

A: Yes, it matched it perfectly.

Q: This is not psychosis. This is *reserve* psyche kept in readiness for a unique crisis problem.

A: Yes.

Q: Q.E.D. You are talking about meta- or paranormal functioning, not psychosis, which by definition is incapable of adapting, problem-solving, reality-testing. Did it test reality? Or did it withdraw?

A: It tested.

Q: This is null-psychosis. You have contradicted yourself. This is a latent higher brain center. A psychotic episode *creates* problems; it does not solve them. It *is* a problem, as well as the collapse of rational efforts at problem-solving. Were its decisions & actions rational?

A: Although religious in coloration—

Q: That is not the issue. Were the problems solved?

A: Yes. But by a psychotic self.

Q: That is an oxymoron. A "psychotic self took over & problem solved." This is where the inquiry has led. The ego could not face or solve the crisis problem because of its severity, fled, & in its place another self solved the problem successfully. This leads us to a new frontier which is not mapped.

A: Then the enigma remains.

Q: We have learned nothing.

A: Nothing.

Q: After finishing listening to the tape do you

have any intuition or guess as to who & what the Valis mind is? (Later)

A: Yes. It is female. It is on the other side—the *post mortem* world. It has been with me all my life. It is my twin sister Jane. This was referred to in one dream, & that is enough. "Specifically, fairies are the dead." Two clues. This would explain why no one else has had my experience. The other psyche I carry inside me is that of my dead sister—v. DR. BLOODMONEY when the situation is reversed, v. SCANNER."

1) It's another psyche in me. In my right hemisphere. 2) It's female. 3) It's on the other side (after death). 4) It's my tutelary spirit. What does this point to? To my sister.   *(1979)*

Q: Does someone (Divine) speak to me?
A: Yes.
Q: Do I remember (my true identity)?
A: Yes.
∴ : this is Gnosticism. The voice that speaks is the call. My true forgotten identity is primal man or a spark thereof. & it is myself awakening myself.
Q: Did I see the many become the one?
A: Yes. I called it Valis.
∴ : this is Gnostic restoration.
Q: Did I remember past lives?
A: Yes.
Q: & see infinite space?
A: Yes.
∴ : I experience vast time & vast space. This is Gnosticism.
Q: Did I see a prison around us?
A: Yes.
∴ : This is Gnosticism.
After I wrote this (4 a.m.) I went to bed thinking,

"It is Gnosticism for sure." The explanation almost fits—*almost*, & yet—it occurred to me then that a much simpler & much more convincing explanation would be that *it was Christ*, the real presence of the actual Christ & an expression of the power of Christ to bind & to loosen, to save, Christ as pantocrator & eschatological judge. (Hence the Good Friday & Easter overtones; hence the role of my moral act vis-a-vis Covenant House).*

(c. 1981)

---

*   PKD contributed funds to Covenant House, a New York-based shelter for runaway and homeless children.

CHAPTER EIGHT

THREE CLOSING PARABLES

For God did not make death & takes no pleasure in
the destruction of any living thing: he created all
things that they might have being. The creative forces
of the world make for life; there are no deadly poisons
in them. Death is not King on Earth, for Justice is
immortal.

But the good man, even if he dies an untimely
death, will be at rest. For it is not length of life & number of years which bring the honor due to age; if men
have understanding, they have gray hairs enough, &
an unspotted life is the true ripeness of age. There was
once a man who pleased God, & God accepted him &
took him while still living from among sinful men. He
was snatched away before his mind could be per-
verted by witchcraft or his soul deceived by falsehood
... in a short time he came to the perfection of a full
span of years. His soul was pleasing to the Lord, who
removed him from a wicked world. The mass of men
see this & give it no thought; they do not lay to heart

this truth, that those whom God has chosen enjoy his grace & mercy, & that He comes to the help of his holy people. Even after his death the just man grown old in sin. Men see the wise man's end, without understanding: the Lord has purposed for him & why he took him into safe keeping ... then the just man shall take his stand, full of assurance, to confront those who oppressed him & made light of his sufferings. At the sight of him there will be terror & confusion, & they will be beside themselves to see him unexpectedly safe home.   (1975)

This is not an evil world, as Mani supposed. There is a good world under the evil. The evil is somehow superimposed over it (Maya), and when stripped away, pristine glowing creation is visible.

Did our ancestors go insane and cease to be able to see what is there? The layers of veils of evil must be stripped or washed away (waking up, the washing away by the blood of the Lamb, baptism etc). To awaken is to awaken to truth, also to beauty: to unity. Delusion means to see lies, to see evil. Evil equals lies equals evil equals delusion equals the unreal. God is good, the world is good, we are like him, but somehow we got estranged. Equally from world (!) as from God. God equals world as seen properly (clearly). Who deludes us? Vide Zimmer:* We ourselves weave the webs of illusion; the unreal frightening masks are projections of our unaccepted portions of ourselves. They are inside, projected out to become evil. When withdrawn back into us, we see a lovely world.

We've got ugly and evil confused, frightening (to us) and evil confused. Maybe all we mean by "evil" is

---

*   Heinrich Zimmer. See note on page 101.

ugly and frightening plus strange, beyond our understanding (which is limited). Evil is (are you ready?)
unnatural.

One day the contents of my mind moved faster
and faster until they ceased being concepts and
became percepts. I did not have concepts about the
world but perceived it without preconception or even
intellectual comprehension. It then resembled the
world of UBIK. As if all the contents of one's mind, if
fused, became suddenly alive, a living entity, which
took off within one's head, on its own, saw in its own
superior way, without regard to what you had ever
learned or seen or known. The principle of emer-
gence, as when nonliving matter becomes living. As if
information (thought concepts) when pushed to their
limit became metamorphosed into something alive.
Perhaps then in the outer world all the energy or information when pushed far enough will do the same.
Fuse into something everywhere (the force Ubik) that
is sentient and alive. Then inner-outer, then-now,
cause-effect, all the antinomies will fade out. We will
see only a living entity at its ceaseless building: at
work. Creating. (Has continual creation almost
reached completion?) (Such dichotomies as big-small
me-not me will be transcended.)   *(1975)*

Here is an example of hierarchical ranking. A new
ambulance is filled with gas and parked. The next day
it is examined. The finding is that its fuel is virtually
gone and its moving parts are slightly worn. This
appears to be an instance of entropy, of loss of energy
and form. However, if one understands that the ambulance was used to take a dying person to a hospital
where his life was saved (thus consuming fuel and
somewhat wearing the moving parts of the ambu-

lance) then one can see that through hierarchical out-
ranking there was not only no loss but in fact a net
gain. The net gain, however, can only be measured
outside the closed system of the new ambulance. Each
victory by God as intelligence and will is obtained by
this escalation of levels of subsumation, and in no
other way.   *(1979)*

I UNDERSTAND PHILIP K. DICK

True stories have no beginnings and neither does the tale of PKD's encounters with the Overmind. But we writers understand narrative economy, and for purposes of narrative economy his story seemed to him to begin with the mysterious break in and riffling of his papers that was made notorious by an article in Rolling Stone, which brought Phil long-delayed and much-deserved fame. The break-in date was 11/17/71. It was a date and a style of referring to time that Phil used frequently.

I turned twenty-five the day before. It was no casual birthday either. I met my natal day by sitting down and sincerely preparing myself for an Apocatastasis, the final Apocalyptic ingression of novelty, the implosion really, of the entire multidimensional continuum of space and time. I imagined the megamacrocosmos was going to go down the drain like water out of a bathtub as the hyperspatial vacuum fluctuation of paired particles that is our universe collided with its own ghost image after billions of years of separation. The Logos assured me that parity would be conserved, all sub-atomic particles except photons would cancel each other, and our entire universe would quietly disappear. The only particles that would remain, according to my fantastic expectation, would be photons, the universe of light would be exposed at last, set free from the iron prison of matter, freed from the awful physics that adhered to less unitary states of being. All mankind would march into the promised garden.

I felt I was well situated for the event as I, quite consciously and deliberately, and to the concern of my friends, had placed myself in the teeming, hallucinogen saturated center of the largest garden I could find, the trackless rain forest of the Upper Amazon Basin of Colombia. My confidence in my vision was unshakable. Had not the Logos itself lead me to this vision, not only by revelation but by painstaking explanation? I had no radio, no way to contact the outside world at all. Who needed that? I knew with perfect clarity that the world of time, the illusion of history was ending. Divine Parousia was entering the world, and the just, the meek and the humble were leaving their fields and factories, pushing back their chairs from their office desks and workbenches and walking out into the light of a living sun that would never set for there could be no setting for the eternal radiance of the Logos. Tears of joy streaming down their cheeks, the illumined billions were turning their eyes at last to the sky and finding there a consolation that they had never dared hope for.

However, Nixon's weary world ignored the eschatological opportunity I thought my brother's inspired fiddling with hyperspace had afforded. The world continued grinding forward in its usual less than merry way. There was only one small incident that might subsequently be construed, even within the framework of the schizoid logic that was my bread and butter then, to support my position. Unknown to me, a struggling, overweight SF writer, an idol of mine since my teens, discovered the next day that his house have been broken into, his privacy violated by the Other. How peculiar that on the first day of the new dispensation in my private reformist calendar, he had been burglarized by extrater- restrials, the CIA or his own deranged self in an altered state. The torch had been passed, in a weird way the most intense phase of my episode of illumination/delusion ended right where Phil's began.

This raises some questions:

Can we refer to a delusional system as a *folie à deux*, if the *deux* participants have never met and are practically speaking, unaware of each others' existence?

Does the delusion of one visionary ecstatic validate the delusion of another? How many deluded, or illuminated ecstatics does it take to make a reality? PKD proved that it only takes one. But two is better.

When my brother looked over the edge in the Amazon and felt the dizziness of things unsaid in March of 1971, he came back with two words bursting from his lips, "May Day! May Day!"—the pilot's call of extreme emergency.

May Day found me in Berkeley sheltered by friends so concerned about my state of mind that they considered committing me. I was only a few miles from Phil, who was rapidly going nuts too, as his psych admission of 3 May '71 attests. It was always like that with PKD and me. We never met but we lived around each other for years. In Berkeley, we both lived on Francisco St. within five blocks and a few years of each other.* We both had roots in Sonoma County, in Orange County. How many times were we a table or two away from each other in the Cafe Med? How many times did I hurry past him on the Ave on some stoned errand? Later his homeopathic doctor was my doctor. There is a garbled mention of me (or my brother) on pg. 74 of this book.

Yah, yawn, the world is fuckin' strange, right bro?

Wrong. Or rather, of course, sure. But that is not the point, the point is that I understand Philip K. Dick. I know that sounds like *hubris* and if I am wrong I am sorry (as

---

*   PKD lived at 1126, then a few years later and for six months I lived at 1624.

Phil says somewhere.) But part of the delusional system in which I live contains and adumbrates the notion that I know what happened to the poor dude. We shared an affliction, a mania, sort of like Queequeg and Ishmael. And like one of those whale chasing sailors "I alone escaped to tell thee of it".

Phil wasn't nuts. Phil was a vortex victim.[*] Schizophrenia is not a psychological disorder peculiar to human beings. Schizophrenia is not a disease at all but rather a localized traveling discontinuity of the space time matrix itself. It is like a travelling whirl-wind of radical understanding that haunts time. It haunts time in the same way that Alfred North Whitehead said that the color dove grey "haunts time like a ghost."

There is an idea that wants to be born, it has wanted to be born for a very long time.[**] And sometimes that longing to be born settles on a person. For no damn good reason. Then you're "it," you become the cheese, and the cheese stands alone. You are illuminated and maddened and lifted up by something great beyond all telling. It wants to be told. It's just that this idea is so damn big that it can't be told, or rather the whole of history is the telling of this idea, the stuttering rambling effort of the sons and daughters of poor old Noah to tell this blinding, reality-shattering, bowel-loosening truth. And Phil had a piece of the action, a major piece of the action.

But I anticipate myself. Those who grasp a piece of the action end up with two things on their plate; the experience and their own idiosyncratic explanation of the experience based on what they have read, seen and been told.

---

[*]   "ZEBRA (VALIS): 'a vortex of intelligence extending as a supra-temporal field, involving humans but not limited to them, drawing objects & processes into a coherency which it arranges into information. A FLUX of purposeful arrangement of living information, both human & extra-human, tending to grow & incorporate its environment as a unitary complex of subsumations.' "
(pg. 72)
[**]   "Okay, fertilization is what takes place: it isn't a seed such as a plant has, but an egg such as a human woman ovulates, and cosmic spermatika fertilizes it; a zygote is produced." (pg. 22.)

The experience is private, personal, the best part, and ultimately unspeakable. The more you know the quieter you get. The explanation is another matter and can be attempted. In fact it must be told, for the Logos speaks and we are its tools and its voice. Phil says a lot of things in the Exegesis, he is aware that he says too much, so he keeps trying to boil it down to ten points or twelve parts or whatever. I have my own experience, equally unspeakable, and my explanation, equally prolix. Phil (sometimes) thought he was Christ,* I (sometimes) thought I was an extraterrestrial invader disguised as a meadow mushroom. What matters is the system that eventually emerges, not the fantasies concerning the source of the system. When I compare Phil's system to mine, my hair stands on end. We were both contacted by the same unspeakable something. Two madmen dancing, not together, but the same dance anyhow.

Truth or madness, you be the judge. What is trying to be expressed is this: The world is not real. Reality is not stranger than you suppose, it is stranger than you *can* suppose. Time is not what you think it is.** Reality is a hologram.*** Being is a solid state matrix and psychosis is the redemptive process *ne plus ultra*.**** The real truth is splintered and spread throughout time. Appearances are

---

* "I am a homoplasmate: Zebra acting in syzygy with a human." (pg. 79 but also: "Did I *do* something? Absolutely. But I don't know what I did, so I don't know who (so to speak) I am in the drama." (pg. 42.)
** "If the *Logos* is outside time, imprinting, then the Holy Spirit stands at the right or far or completed end of time, toward which the field-flow moves (the time flow). It receives time: the negative terminal, so to speak." (pg. 64.) See also "If there is to be immortality, there must be another kind of time: one in which past events (i.e., the past in its entirety) can be retrieved—i.e., brought back. I did experience such a time." (pg. 79.)
*** "It (reality) is a hologram. 1) My augmented sense of space proves it. And 2) the information element; consisting of *two* parts: set and ground.
"All this points to: hologram. Based on two information-rich signals." (pp. 98-99.)
**** "The Gospels, then, depict a sacred mythic rite outside of time, rather than a historical event.
"Note: This whole process can be regarded as a psychological transformation, that of a redemptive psychosis." (pg. 95.)

a vast and interlocking lie.[*] To finally know the Logos truly, if that means anything, is to know it as for, as what Phil called a "unified abstract structure." In a way this was where PKD went wrong. It wasn't his fault. He saw that the world of 1975 was a fiction and behind that fiction was the world of AD 45. But he lacked an essential concept, lacked it because it really hadn't been invented yet. Anyhow the man was a SF writer and a scholar of classical philosophy, he could not be expected to stay in touch with arcane discoveries beginning to take place on the frontiers of research mathematics. But he got very close, his intuition was red hot when he reached the conclusion that a unified abstract structure lay behind the shifting always tricky casuistry of appearances. The concept he needed was that of fractals and fractal mathematics. The infinite regress of form built out of forms of itself built out of forms of itself ... unto infinity. The principle of self similarity. Phil was right, time is not a linear river. He was right, the Empire never ended. Parallel universes is too simple a concept to encompass what is really going on. The megamacrocosmos is a system of resonances, of levels, of endlessly adumbrated fun-house reflections. PKD really was Thomas and Elijah and all the other precursive concrescences that came together to make the cat-loving fat man who compacted trash into gold. The logic of being that he sought, and largely found, was not an either-or logic but a both-and and and-and kind of logic.

PKD was never more right than when he wrote:

---

[*]   "Probably the wisest view is to say: the truth—like the Self—is splintered up over thousands of mile and years; bits are found here and there, then and now, and must be recollected; bits appear in the Greek naturalists, in Pythagoras, in Plato, Parmenides, in Heraclitus, Neo-Platonism, Zoroastrianism, Gnosticism, Taoism, Mani, orthodox Christianity, Judaism, Brahmanism, Buddhism, Orphism, the other mystery religions. Each religion or philosophy or philosopher contains one or more bits, but the total system interweaves it into falsity, so each as a total system must be rejected, and none is to be accepted at the expense of all the others. . ." (pp. 111-112)

I actually had to develop a love of the disordered & puzzling, viewing reality as a vast riddle to be joyfully tackled, not in fear but with
tireless fascination. What has been most
needed is reality testing, & a willingness to face
the possibility of self-negating experiences: i.e.,
real contradictions, with something being both
true & not true.

The enigma is alive, aware of us, & changing. It is partly created by our own minds: we
alter it by perceiving it, since we are not outside it. As our views shift, it shifts. In a sense it
is not there at all (acosmism). In another sense
it is a vast intelligence: in another sense it is
total *harmonia* and structure (how logically can
it be all three? Well, it is).*

One cannot learn these things. One can only be told
these things. And it is the Logos that does the telling. The
key is in the *I Ching*, which Phil loved and used but which
occupies a disappointingly small fraction of his rumina-
tions in the Exegesis.** Almost as if the counter flow, the
occluding intelligence, kept Phil's eyes diverted from the
key element necessary to the universal decipherment
that he was attempting. Time is a fractal, or has a fractal
structure. All times, moments, months and millennia,
have a pattern; the same pattern. This pattern is the
structure within which, upon which, events "undergo
the formality of actually occurring," as Whitehead used
to say. The pattern recurs on every level. A love affair, the
fall of an empire, the death agony of a protozoan, all
occur within the context of this always the same but ever
different pattern. All events are resonances of other
events, in other parts of time, and at other scales of
time.*** The mathematical nature of this pattern can be

---

*   (pg. 91.)
**   "MITHC seems to be a subtle, even delicate questioning of, what is
real? As if only the 2 books in it, GRASSHOPPER & the I CHING are really
the only actual reality. Strange." (pg. 181.)
***   "Through anamnesis and restoration to the Form realm you have
access to several space-time continua based on your universals." (pg. 102.)

known.* It can be written as an equation, just like the equations of Schrodinger or Einstein.

The raw material, the Ur text, out of which this mathematical pattern can be drawn is the King Wen sequence of the I Ching. That is where the secret lies. In the world's oldest book. Of course. Once possessed the pattern can then be discerned everywhere. Of course. It is ubiquitous. One of Phil's favorite words. I know this because the Logos taught me the pattern and I escaped the black iron prison of the world to tell thee of it. I have published it, I have lectured it and have had it written into software. My books are on the way, some with Phil's old publisher Bantam. I would bet dollars to donuts that if Phil had lived to see, to feel, and to understand what this PKD-inspired servant of the Logos has managed to drag home from the beach, he would embrace it. This cannot be said without sounding like a madman or a jackass. I am sorry about that. As Phil Dick said, "What's got to be gotten over is the false idea that hallucination is a *private* matter."**

What is important is that the birth of this idea is now very near, has in fact already happened, and PKD showed the way. The answer is found. And this incredible genius,

---

*   "The agent of creation (*Logos* or Forms, whatever called) is at the same time the abstract *structure* of creation. Although normally unavailable to our cognition and perception, this structure—and hence the agent of creation can be known..." (pg. 125) Also, "...this insubstantial abstract structure *is* reality properly conceived. But it is not God. Here, multiplicity gives way to unity, to what perhaps can be called a field. The field is self-perturbing; *it initiates its own causes internally; it is not acted on from outside*". (pg. 127). Also, "'The agent of creation is its own structure'. This structure must not be confused with the multiplicity of physical objects in space and time governed by causation; the two are entirely different. (The structure is insubstantial, abstract, unitary and initiates its own causes internally, it is not physical and cannot be perceived by the human percept-system sensibly; it is known intelligibly, by what Plato called *Noesis*, which involves a certain ultimate high-order meta-abstracting.)" (pg. 128). And finally: "I ... posit ontological primacy to the insubstantial abstract structure, and, moreover, I believe that it fully controls the physical spatiotemporal universe as its basis and cause." (pg. 129)

**   pg. 177

this gentle, long-suffering, beauty-worshipping man showed the way. When it counted he was right. All hail Philip K. Dick.

Terence McKenna
Occidental, California
June 1991

Terence McKenna, with his brother Dennis McKenna, wrote *The Invisible Landscape*, 1975, which is scheduled to be reprinted by Harper San Francisco in 1992. He is also the author of *The Archaic Revival: Essays and Conversations by Terence McKenna*, Harper San Francisco, 1991. His laboratory for exploring the unified abstract structure of time was written into MS-DOS software as *Timewave Zero* Version 4.0, from Dolphin Software, 48 Shattuck Sq. #147, Berkeley, CA 94704.

Novels

SOLAR LOTTERY (1955)

EYE IN THE SKY (1956)

THE MAN WHO JAPED (1956)

THE COSMIC PUPPETS (1957)

TIME OUT OF JOINT (1959)

THE MAN IN THE HIGH CASTLE (1962)

THE GAME PLAYERS OF TITAN (1963)

THE PENULTIMATE TRUTH (1964)

MARTIAN TIME-SLIP (1964)

CLANS OF THE ALPHANE MOON (1964)

THE THREE STIGMATA OF PALMER ELDRITCH (1965)

DR. BLOODMONEY (1965)

THE UNTELEPORTED MAN (1966)

NOW WAIT FOR LAST YEAR (1966)

COUNTER-CLOCK WORLD (1967)

DO ANDROIDS DREAM OF ELECTRIC SHEEP? (1968)

GALACTIC POT-HEALER (1969)

UBIK (1969)

A MAZE OF DEATH (1970)

OUR FRIENDS FROM FROLIX 8 (1970)

WE CAN BUILD YOU (1972)
FLOW MY TEARS, THE POLICEMAN SAID (1974)
CONFESSIONS OF A CRAP ARTIST (1975)
DEUS IRAE (1976) (Collaboration with Roger Zelazny)
A SCANNER DARKLY (1977)
VALIS (1981)
THE DIVINE INVASION (1981)
THE TRANSMIGRATION OF TIMOTHY ARCHER (1982)
RADIO FREE ALBEMUTH (1985)

Stories

"Impostor" (1962)
"Second Variety" (1953)
"Human Is" (1955)
"Precious Artifact" (1964)
"Retreat Syndrome" (1965)
"We Can Remember It For You Wholesale" (1966)
"Faith of Our Fathers" (1967)
"The Electric Ant" (1969)
THE PRESERVING MACHINE (story collection) (1969)
THE BEST OF PHILIP K. DICK (story collection) (1977)
"Frozen Journey" (1980) (later retitled "I Hope I Shall Arrive Soon")

Nonfiction

THE DARK-HAIRED GIRL (1988) (letter and essay collection with special focus on early 1970s)

GLOSSARY

SELECTED SIGNIFICANT TERMS

The *Exegesis* roams through all of western and eastern philosophy and religion. To thoroughly elucidate all concepts discussed within it, a glossary would have to expand to the size of a separate volume. The present Glossary limits itself to the most vital terms utilized by PKD in the *Exegesis* excerpts presented in this volume. In addition, personal and otherwise inscrutable references by PKD are clarified. For general subjects, such as Brahmanism, Buddhism, Christianity, Gnosticism, Judaism, Platonic and Neoplatonic thought, Sufism, Zoroastrianism and the like, the reader must turn to the numerous competent reference works that are already available.

Those readers interested in studying reference works that were of particular value to PKD may wish to begin by perusing the philosophical and religious entries in the BRITANNICA 3, which was PKD's most frequently utilized reference source. Another favored reference work was the four-volume ENCYCLOPEDIA OF PHILOSOPHY published by Prentice-Hall. They should also seek out the works referenced in the editorial footnotes that accompany the *Exegesis* selections in this volume.

Acosmism: A belief which denies the genuine existence of a universe apart and distinct from God. PKD wrestled with this belief but seldom embraced it, often positing instead a complex separate universe in need of divine restoration. See *Two-Source Cosmology.*

Acts: The *Book of Acts* in the New Testament. PKD often believed that there was a significant overlap of spiritual content between *Acts* and his own novel, FLOW MY TEARS, THE POLICEMAN SAID (1974). According to PKD, this overlap was completely unconscious, as he had not read *Acts* at the time of writing TEARS (1970-73). Thus, PKD would often analyze TEARS in the *Exegesis* as a precursive confirmation of the spiritual validity of his 2-3-74 experiences.

AI Voice: Artificial Intelligence Voice. Terms coined by PKD to name the hypnagogic voice that he heard often in 1974-75 and intermittently in the years thereafter until his death. It is a misleading term in that PKD did not consistently hold that the voice was AI in nature. Most often, he described it as "female," and his theoretical attributions for it included the Gnostic goddess Sophia (see *Sophia*) and PKD's own sister Jane.

Anamnesis (Greek): Recollection; abrogation of amnesia. It is one of the key concepts of Platonic philosophy. For Plato, anamnesis—recollection of the ultimate World of Ideas in which the soul dwelled before incarnating in human form—explained the human capacity for understanding abstract, universal truths, such as the geometric theorems of Euclid. For PKD, anamnesis served as one term by which to describe his encounter, in 2-3-74, with what he regarded as a higher wisdom.

Ananke (Greek): The blindness that follows *hubris* (overweening pride or self-absorption).

Black Iron Prison (BIP): PKD's term for the unredeemed (spiritually) and spurious (ontologically) world of everyday consciousness. The reality that enchains us. See *Orthogonal Time.*

Crypte morphosis (Greek): Latent shape or form. In 1974, PKD found himself thinking in Greek phrases (including this one) during a hypnagogic state. He later related the concept of latent shape to Fragment 51 (the Bow and the Lyre) of Heraclitus.

Dokos (Greek): Deception, lack of true perception. PKD employed this term as a Greek cognate for the Sanskrit *maya*.

Eidos (Greek): Ultimate Form or Idea. A fundamental term in Platonic Philosophy, in which the Idea of the Good is the unifying principle of the World of Ideas, which in turn is the source of all being.

Enantiodromia: Sudden transformation into an opposite form or tendency. The term was used by Heraclitus, but PKD first became familiar with it through his reading of C.G. Jung. Jung employs it to describe the tendency for the psyche to overcome deep-seated psychic resistance by shifting (seemingly suddenly) to the opposite pole of attitude, belief, and emotion. For PKD, enantiodromia was one term by which to describe the force and extent of his inner transformation in 2-3-74.

Entelechy: Actualized being or process that has fully realized its potential.

Firebright: Name coined by PKD for ultimate, living wisdom. See *Plasmate*.

Golden Fish: On February 20, 1974, a young woman working for a local pharmacy delivered a bottle of prescription Darvon tablets to the Fullerton, California apartment of PKD. She was wearing a necklace with a golden fish emblem. According to PKD, the sight of that emblem triggered the events of 2-3-74. PKD regarded the golden fish as both a Christian symbol and as a spur to anamnesis of the eternal truths of all philosophies and religions.

Heimarmene (Greek): The deluding, entrapping power of the spurious, unredeemed world of everyday reality.

Homoplasmate: A human being who has been transformed through crossbonding with living knowledge bestowed or transmitted by a higher source of wisdom. See *Plasmate*.

James-James: The name given by PKD to a mad god of whom he dreamed in 1974 or 1975. His nature was that of an evil magician. He corresponds closely to the Gnostic demiurge *Yaldabaoth*.

Macrometasomakosmos: PKD's own term for ultimate, genuine reality; a cognate term to the Platonic World of Ideas. See *Eidos*. Literally, this term breaks down into Great–Ultimate–Body–of–the–Cosmos.

MITHC: PKD novel THE MAN IN THE HIGH CASTLE (1962).

Moira (Greek): Justice.

Morphological Realm: As used by PKD, this phrase refers to the realm of ultimate, genuine reality. As such, it is analogous to the Realm of Ideas of Plato (see *Eidos*) and the *Palm Tree Garden*.

Negentropic: A force or influence which counters or reverses the process of entropy.

Noesis (Greek): The experience of direct perception of the Realm of Ideas posited by Plato. See *Eidos*.

Noös (Greek); *Nous* (Latin): Ultimate Reason.

Orthogonal Time: Time in its genuine mode, moving perpendicularly to spurious linear time. In a 1975 essay, "Man, Android and Machine," PKD described orthogonal time as containing within "a simultaneous plane or extension everything which was, just as grooves on an LP contain that part of the music which has already been played; they don't disappear after the stylus tracks them." Orthogonal time was one theory by which PKD attempted to explain the sense bestowed upon him by the experiences of 2-3-74 that "The Empire Never Ended," i.e. that Imperial Rome and modern day America were simultaneous or superimposed aspects of the enduring *Black Iron Prison*.

Palm Tree Garden (PTG): The redeemed (spiritually) and genuine (ontologically) world, revealed to PKD in January-February 1975, when the southern California world around him seemed to transform into the Levant, and goodness seemed to pervade the whole. In chapter 18 of the PKD-Roger Zelazny collaborative novel DEUS IRAE (1976), the vision of Dr. Abernathy—which was written by PKD alone—is that of the Palm Tree Garden.

Pigspurt: See *Plasmate*.

Plasmate: Literally, *living* knowledge. PKD often felt that he had bonded with it in 2-3-74, and that, as a result, there dwelled within his psyche what seemed to be a *second*, entirely other self. See *Homoplasmate*. At times, PKD believed that the identity of this second self was the late James A. Pike, with whom PKD had been friends in the mid-1960s. At other times, he posited an early Christian named Thomas (who lived circa 45-70 A.D., in the time of the *Book of Acts*) as this second self. Yet another identity posed by PKD was Pigspurt, a malevolent force that had filled him with fear and a craven attitude toward governmental authority; but it should be noted that Pigspurt was seldom mentioned—PKD rarely regarded this second self as malevolent. As for the plasmate itself, he most often regarded it as the living transmission of the Gnostic goddess Saint Sophia, Holy Wisdom. Another name coined by PKD for this Holy Wisdom was Firebright. With respect to PKD's use of the term "plasmate" to describe living information that pervades the universe, it should be noted that a similar information metaphor is now being employed by certain quantum physics theorists.

Ramparts Petition: PKD was a signatory to a "Writers and Editors War Tax Protest" petition that appeared in the February 1968 issue of "Ramparts," a new left magazine that opposed the Vietnam War. In subsequent years, PKD came to fear that he had thus earned the enduring wrath (and surveillance attention) of the U.S. government and its military intelligence branches.

RET: Acronym for Real Elapsed Time.

Rhipidos (Greek): Fan or fan-like shape. PKD associated *rhipidos* (one of the Greek words that came to him in his hypnogogic visions) with the fins of the fish, which is a symbol of Christ as well as of the benign deity of the Dogon people. The Rhipidon Society in VALIS takes as its motto: "fish cannot carry guns."

Set and Ground: Terms used by PKD (apparently borrowed from gestalt perception theory) to both distinguish between genuine reality (set) and spurious reality (ground), and to describe their seeming admixture in the everyday world. See Two-Source Cosmology.

Sophia: Gnostic goddess of wisdom. See *AI Voice* and *Plasmate*.

Spaciotemporal Realm: As used by PKD, this phrase refers to the spurious world of accepted, everyday reality, which is bounded by static, linear concepts of time and space. See *Morphological Realm*.

Tagore: On the night of September 17, 1981, Phil was falling asleep and then was suddenly startled awake by a hypnagogic vision of Tagore, a world savior who was living in Ceylon. On September 23, PKD sent a letter to the science-fiction fanzine "Niekas" (and to some eighty-five other individuals, friends and distant contacts) describing Tagore as dark-skinned, Hindu or Buddhist, and working in the countryside with a veterinary group.

TDHG: Narrative sequence of letters by PKD, THE DARK-HAIRED GIRL, written in 1972 and published posthumously in 1988.

To Scare the Dead: Proposed title for PKD novel—the principle subject of which would be the events of 2-3-74—as to which PKD made notes in 1974-75. The novel was never written. The title was intended to refer to the reawakening of seemingly dead personages (such as the early Christian *Thomas*) as a result of the same forces that were at work in PKD's 2-3-74 experiences. See *Valisystem A*.

Thomas: Early Christian personage who, according to one line of speculation of PKD, had crossbonded with PKD during the events of 2-3-74. Thomas was the embodiment of the living knowledge of early Christianity. See *Homoplasmate* and *Plasmate*.

Two-Source Cosmology: Phrase employed by PKD to describe one of his most persistent theoretical viewpoints in the Exegesis: that the universe (and, in particular, our own world) was a dualist admixture of genuine and spurious reality. This dualistic viewpoint was intertwined with PKD's own tragic experience as a surviving twin—his sister Jane died at age five weeks. See chapter one of my DIVINE INVASIONS: A LIFE OF PHILIP K. DICK (1989) for an extensive discussion of this episode and its reverberations in PKD's thought. On a more formal level, PKD drew from the dualisms of Gnosticism, the Presocratic philosophers Heraclitus and Parmenides, Taoism, and Zoroastrianism in fashioning (and ceaselessly refashioning) his various theories on the nature of the two-source cosmology.

Valis: Acronym coined by PKD; its meaning is "Vast Active Living Intelligence System." PKD utilized Valis in the *Exegesis* in a variety of contexts to express his sense of the nature of ultimate reality. See definition set forth by PKD as the opening epigram to his novel VALIS (1981).

Valisystem A: PKD novel as to which he made notes in 1974-76 (sometimes in conjunction with notes on TO SCARE THE DEAD). The novel was finally written in 1976; it was posthumously published in 1985 as RADIO FREE ALBEMUTH.

Xerox Letter or Xerox Missive: See the "Editor's Preface" to this volume at page xiii.

Yaldabaoth: Blind, deranged Gnostic demiurge who created the spurious world—the *Black Iron Prison* that ensnares consciousness. See *James-James*.

Zagreus (Greek): A name of the Greek god Dionysus, which means literally "torn to pieces." The name reflects the Orphic myth that Dionysus (god of vegetation and of the spring renewal) was, as a child, torn to pieces by the Titans, only to come back to life through the agency of his father Zeus, who restored his son to life by eating the heart of his sundered corpse. Zagreus was regarded by PKD as an alternate divine form of Christ.

Zebra: Term coined by PKD to describe how ultimate reality conceals itself in the spurious world through mimicry of the everyday banal "trash" that surrounds us. The analogy, of course, is to the concealing mimicry afforded by the stripes of a zebra. Zebra is a cognate term for *Valis*.

Lawrence Sutin

INDEX OF PERSONS AND WRITINGS